Automating DevOps with GitLab CI/CD Pipelines

Build efficient CI/CD pipelines to verify, secure, and deploy your code using real-life examples

Christopher Cowell

Nicholas Lotz

Chris Timberlake

BIRMINGHAM—MUMBAI

Automating DevOps with GitLab CI/CD Pipelines

Copyright © 2023 Packt Publishing

All rights reserved. No part of this book may be reproduced, stored in a retrieval system, or transmitted in any form or by any means, without the prior written permission of the publisher, except in the case of brief quotations embedded in critical articles or reviews.

Every effort has been made in the preparation of this book to ensure the accuracy of the information presented. However, the information contained in this book is sold without warranty, either express or implied. Neither the authors, nor Packt Publishing or its dealers and distributors, will be held liable for any damages caused or alleged to have been caused directly or indirectly by this book.

Packt Publishing has endeavored to provide trademark information about all of the companies and products mentioned in this book by the appropriate use of capitals. However, Packt Publishing cannot guarantee the accuracy of this information.

Group Product Manager: Mohd Riyan
Publishing Product Manager: Surbhi Suman
Senior Editors: Divya Vijayan and Athikho Sapuni Rishana
Technical Editor: Nithik Cheruvakodan
Copy Editor: Safis Editing
Project Coordinator: Ashwin Kharwa
Proofreader: Safis Editing
Indexer: Rekha Nair
Production Designer: Shankar Kalbhor
Marketing Coordinator: Ankita Bhonsle
Senior Marketing Coordinator: Marylou De Mello

First published: February 2023

Production reference: 1310123

Published by Packt Publishing Ltd.
Livery Place
35 Livery Street
Birmingham
B3 2PB, UK.

ISBN 978-1-80323-300-0

www.packt.com

To Marya DeVoto, for reminding me that words actually mean things.

– Christopher Cowell

To my parents, Tom and Deborah, for encouraging me to never stop asking "why?"

– Nicholas Lotz

Contributors

About the authors

Christopher Cowell was formerly a technical trainer at GitLab, and now builds educational content at Instabase. He also worked for 2 decades as a research scientist, consultant, and QA engineer at big and small software companies, including Accenture, Oracle, and Puppet. He thinks the software industry undervalues code quality and thoughtful design and overvalues delivering mediocre code quickly. Slow down, simplify, and get it right!

He dreams of being able to play every Beatles song on guitar, but would settle for knowing just one really well. He holds a Ph.D. in philosophy from Berkeley and a B.A. in computer science from Harvard. He lives in Portland, Oregon, with his wife, his four kids, and the two best cats.

Thank you to my family, for their unending patience whenever I disappeared into the basement to work on this book, which I did a lot. I especially hope I can repay my wife, Marya DeVoto, by being just as accommodating when she launches into writing her Space Rabbi *series of novels. Soren, I owe you a ski trip. Kirin, consider yourself to have a lifetime pass for playing* Ticket to Ride *whenever you want. Thanks also to my wonderful parents, Nick and Priscilla, for giving me whatever minor skills or talent I may have at explaining things.*

Nicholas Lotz is a technical trainer at GitLab, where he teaches organizations how to use GitLab to build and ship better software. He previously worked as a systems engineer, trainer, and consultant in the software infrastructure space. He is passionate about open source and its capacity to help teams innovate. Nicholas holds a B.S. in chemical engineering from the University of Pittsburgh. He lives in Nashville, Tennessee, with his Labrador Retriever.

Chris Timberlake is a senior solutions architect at GitLab, where he works closely with the product, services, and sales teams. Previously, he worked at Red Hat as a senior consultant and owned and managed a digital marketing firm, and he has a background in security and law enforcement. Chris loves technical engineering problems and does whatever possible to ensure successful customer outcomes. Chris is passionate about open source software, collaborative development, and education. He lives in Chattanooga, Tennessee, with his family.

About the reviewers

Jean-Philippe Baconnais has been a developer for more than 15 years. Initially focused on Java, he later learned new languages such as Go, as well as about frontend frameworks such as Vue.js and Angular. Curious by nature, he enjoys learning about and trying out new technologies, applying them, and sharing them, whether in his own company, Zenika, in communities as a speaker at conferences, or at local events in his home city of Nantes, France. As an open source developer, he has had the pleasure of participating in two open source communities and has been given the recognition of GitLab Hero and GitPod Community Hero.

Philippe Charrière is a customer success engineer at GitLab (having worked there for the last 5 years). He started working in computer science in 1995 and has held positions as a developer, architect, project manager, manager, bid manager, customer success manager, solution engineer, strategic account leader, and customer success engineer. Today, his favorite subject is WebAssembly, particularly with Go, TinyGo, and Rust.

Table of Contents

Preface · xv

Part 1 Getting Started with DevOps, Git, and GitLab

1

Understanding Life Before DevOps · 3

Introducing the Hats for Cats web app · 4	Manual security testing summary · 15
Building and verifying code manually · 4	Packaging and deploying code manually · 16
Building code manually · 4	
Verifying code manually · 5	License compliance scanning · 17
More challenges of verifying code · 11	Deploying software · 17
Security-testing code manually · 12	Problems with manual software development life cycle practices · 18
Static code analysis · 12	Solving problems with DevOps · 21
Secret detection · 13	How GitLab implements DevOps · 22
Dynamic analysis · 14	
Dependency scanning · 14	Summary · 23
Container scanning · 15	

2

Practicing Basic Git Commands · 25

Technical requirements · 26	Why Git is popular · 30
Why use Git? · 27	Drawbacks of Git · 32
What is a version control system? · 27	Committing code to keep it safe · 33
What problems does a VCS solve? · 28	Excluding files from a repository · 37

Tagging commits to identify versions of code	39	The "golden" repository	47
		Configuring remote repositories	48
Branching code for developing in an isolated space	40	Pushing	51
		Fetching	51
Git commands for managing branches	43	Pulling	52
Handling merge conflicts	44	Additional resources for learning Git	53
Syncing local and remote copies of repositories	47	Summary	54

3

Understanding GitLab Components 55

Technical requirements	56	Labels	67
Emphasizing the "why" over the "how"	56	Issue workflows	68
		Editing files safely with commits, branches, and merge requests	69
Introducing the GitLab platform	57		
What is GitLab?	57	Commit history	73
What problem does GitLab solve?	57	Merging one Git branch into another	74
The verify, secure, and release stages	59	The three amigos – issues, branches, and merge requests	78
Organizing work into projects and groups	60	When two amigos are enough	79
Example – organizing your Hats for Cats work	63	How are issues and merge requests different?	79
Tracking work with issues	64	Enabling DevOps practices with GitLab flow	80
The structure of a GitLab issue	65		
The kinds of tasks that issues can represent	67	Summary	82

4

Understanding GitLab's CI/CD Pipeline Structure 85

Technical requirements	86	Viewing a list of pipelines	87
Defining the terms pipeline, CI, and CD	86	CI – finding out if your code is good	89
		CD – finding out where your code should go (and putting it there)	90
Understanding what a pipeline is	86		
Defining one pipeline per project	87	GitLab Runners	93
Understanding different uses of the term "pipeline"	87	Parts of a pipeline – stages, jobs, and commands	94

Stages	94	Other types of pipelines	100
Jobs	96	Skipping pipelines	101
Commands	97	Reading GitLab CI/CD pipeline statuses	102
Fitting the pipeline pieces together	98	Configuring GitLab CI/CD pipelines	103
Running GitLab CI/CD pipelines	98	Summary	107
Branch pipelines	98		
Git tag pipelines	100		

Part 2 Automating DevOps Stages with GitLab CI/CD Pipelines

5

Installing and Configuring GitLab Runners — 111

Technical requirements	112	Each runner has a defined executor	118
Defining GitLab runners and their relationship to CI/CD	112	Runner tags restrict which runners can pick up which jobs	122
GitLab Runner is an open source application written in Go	112	Installing the Runner agent	122
GitLab Runner runs CI/CD jobs specified in .gitlab-ci.yml	112	Installing GitLab Runner	123
		Registering a runner with GitLab	123
The runner architecture and supported platforms	113	Considerations regarding the various runner types and executors	129
GitLab Runner is supported on most platforms and architectures	114	Performance considerations	129
Runners can be specific, group, or shared	115	Security considerations	131
		Monitoring considerations	132
		Summary	135

6

Verifying Your Code — 137

Technical requirements	138	Compiling Java with Maven	141
Building code in a CI/CD pipeline	138	Compiling C with Gnu Compiler Collection (GCC)	143
Compiling Java with javac	138	Storing built code as artifacts	145

Checking code quality in a CI/CD pipeline	**146**	Extra considerations when fuzz testing	159
		Fuzz testing with a corpus	159
Enabling Code Quality	146	**Checking accessibility in a CI/CD pipeline**	**160**
Viewing Code Quality results	147		
Running automated functional tests in a CI/CD pipeline	**149**	Enabling accessibility testing	161
		Viewing accessibility testing results	161
Enabling automated functional tests	149	**Additional ways to verify your code**	**163**
Viewing automated functional test results	150	Code coverage	163
Fuzz testing in a CI/CD pipeline	**153**	Browser performance testing	163
The architecture and workflow of fuzz testing	153	Load performance testing	163
A fuzz testing workflow	157	**Summary**	**164**
Viewing the results of fuzz testing	158		

7

Securing Your Code   165

Technical requirements	**166**	Enabling and configuring Secret Detection	177
Understanding GitLab's security scanning strategy	**166**	Viewing Secret Detection's findings	178
		Using DAST to find vulnerabilities in web applications	**179**
GitLab uses open-source scanners	167		
Scanners are packaged as Docker images	167	Understanding DAST	179
Some scanners use different analyzers for different languages	168	Enabling and configuring DAST	180
		Viewing DAST's findings	182
Vulnerabilities don't stop the pipeline	169	**Using Dependency Scanning to find vulnerabilities in dependencies**	**182**
Findings appear in three different reports	170		
Pipelines can use non-GitLab-provided scanners	170	Understanding Dependency Scanning	183
		Enabling and configuring Dependency Scanning	184
Using SAST to scan your source code for vulnerabilities	**170**	Viewing Dependency Scanning's findings	184
Understanding SAST	170	**Using Container Scanning to find vulnerabilities in Docker images**	**185**
Enabling SAST	171		
Configuring SAST	173	Understanding Container Scanning	185
Viewing SAST's findings	175	Enabling and configuring Container Scanning	186
Using Secret Detection to find private information in your repository	**175**	Viewing Container Scanning's findings	187
		Using License Compliance to manage licenses of dependencies	**188**
Understanding Secret Detection	176		

Understanding License Compliance	188	Viewing IaC Scanning's findings	194
Enabling and configuring License Compliance	192	Understanding the different types of security reports	195
Viewing License Compliance's findings	192	Managing security vulnerabilities	196
Using IaC Scanning to find problems in infrastructure configuration files	**193**	Integrating outside security scanners	198
Understanding IaC Scanning	193	Summary	199
Enabling and configuring IaC scanning	193		

8

Packaging and Deploying Code 201

Technical requirements	202	Using images from the container registry	217
Storing code in GitLab's package registry for later re-use	**202**	Using packages from the package registry	218
Locating GitLab's container and package registries	202	**Deploying to different environments using GitLab Flow**	**220**
Getting started with the package registry	205	Deploying to a review app for testing	221
Supported package formats	206	Deploying to real-world production environments	223
Authenticating to the registry	206	Deploying to a Kubernetes cluster	225
Building and pushing packages to the package registry	210	The CI/CD workflow	225
Building and pushing packages to the container registry	212	A GitOps workflow	226
Storing code in GitLab's container and package registries for later deployment	**217**	Summary	227

Part 3 Next Steps for Improving Your Applications with GitLab

9

Enhancing the Speed and Maintainability of CI/CD Pipelines 231

Accelerating pipelines with directed acyclic graphs and parent-child architecture	231	How to create a DAG in GitLab CI	232
		Building code for multiple architectures	233

When and how to leverage caching or artifacts	234	Improving maintainability by combining multiple pipelines and leveraging parent-child pipelines	244
Caching characteristics	235	Leveraging includes for maintainability	244
Artifact characteristics	236	Leveraging includes for reusability	246
Using caching	236	Includes from remote areas	247
Using artifacts	237	Leveraging parent-child pipelines	247
Leveraging artifacts as job dependencies	238		
Reducing repeated configuration code with anchors and extensions	**239**	**Securing and accelerating jobs with purpose-built containers**	**248**
Anchors	240	A purpose-built container example	250
The extends: keyword	241	**Summary**	**251**
Reference tags	243		

10

Extending the Reach of CI/CD Pipelines — 253

Using CI/CD pipelines to spot performance problems	253	Automating our container's build	261
		Container scanning	262
How to integrate browser performance testing	254	Invoking the third-party tool	262
How to integrate load performance testing with k6	255	**Using CI/CD pipelines for developing mobile apps**	**262**
Using feature flags to allow business-driven release decisions	256	Requirements	263
		Fastlane	263
How to configure your application for feature flags	258	Fastlane – deployment	264
		Fastlane – automated testing	265
Integrating third-party tools into your CI/CD pipelines	**259**	**Summary**	**266**
Creating our tool container's Dockerfile	260		

11

End-to-End Example — 267

Technical requirements	267	Setting up a local Git repository	271
Setting up your environment	267	**Writing code**	**271**
Making a GitLab project	268	Creating a Git branch to work on	271
Planning work with GitLab issues	269	Creating an MR	272

Committing and pushing code — 272

Establishing the pipeline infrastructure — 273
Creating a pipeline — 273
Creating a runner — 274

Verifying your code — 277
Adding functional tests to the pipeline — 277
Adding Code Quality scanning to the pipeline — 280
Adding a fuzz test to the pipeline — 281

Securing your code — 284
Adding SAST to the pipeline — 284
Adding Secret Detection to the pipeline — 285
Adding Dependency Scanning to the pipeline — 287
Adding License Compliance to the pipeline — 288
Integrating a third-party security scanner into the pipeline — 289

Improving your pipeline — 290
Using a DAG to speed up the pipeline — 290
Breaking the pipeline into several files — 292

Delivering your code to the right environment — 293
Deploying the code — 293

Summary — 295

12

Troubleshooting and the Road Ahead with GitLab — 297

Technical requirements — 298

Troubleshooting and best practices for common pipeline problems — 298
Troubleshooting CI/CD syntax and logic — 298
Troubleshooting pipeline operation and runner assignment — 304

Managing your operational infrastructure using GitOps — 306
Using Terraform to deploy and update infrastructure state — 307
Using Ansible to manage resource configurations — 308

Future industry trends — 309
Automation will create more software at a larger scale — 309
Abstraction will lead to everything-as-code business models — 310
Reduced cycle time will help teams release better software faster — 311

Conclusion and next steps — 311

Index — 313

Other Books You May Enjoy — 324

Preface

Organizations in recent years have recognized the benefits of more collaborative and iterative approaches to software development. The traditional model, where development and operations teams worked in silos, made it difficult for companies to quickly and reliably deliver new features. The adoption of DevOps has addressed these challenges by promoting integration and communication between development and operations. The additional proliferation of tooling and automated workflows have helped improve software quality and stability.

A key element of DevOps is continuous integration and continuous delivery (or deployment) (**CI/CD**). CI/CD is the practice of regularly integrating developer contributions into a shared repository, and then automatically building, testing, and releasing the application. The goal is to minimize the cycle time required to deploy software updates, as well as reduce human error during the process.

This book presents and teaches GitLab as a unified DevOps platform for managing the stages of the software development life cycle. The content will focus primarily on concepts and examples, without locking you into feature capabilities and UI workflows that will likely change over time. After completing this book, you will be equipped to use GitLab to manage almost any software project, while also learning about the best practices that can be applied across other DevOps workflows and CI/CD tools.

Who this book is for

This book is intended for anyone involved in the software development life cycle with software projects of any size. If that sounds broad, that's because it is! GitLab has something to offer people in a huge variety of roles. Traditional GitLab users include developers, QA, security testers, performance testers, product owners, project managers, UX designers, technical writers, release engineers, and the broad range of roles that fall under the amorphous terms of "DevOps" and "DevSecOps." So if you find yourself involved with planning, writing, testing, securing, building, packaging, or deploying software, or managing any of those tasks, and you're wondering how to automate any of the slow, error-prone tasks that you currently perform manually, this book will almost certainly give you ideas about how to improve your life using GitLab and its automated CI/CD pipelines.

This book assumes no prior knowledge other than some familiarity with one or more of the major stages of the software development life cycle. We expect every reader will be involved with different parts of the life cycle, so will focus on the parts of the book that are most relevant to them. That's a perfectly good way to approach this book, although we recommend everyone read the four chapters that make up the first section since they explain background concepts and terminology that are required knowledge for all GitLab users.

What this book covers

Chapter 1, Understanding Life Before DevOps, offers a short review of the major software development life cycle stages, and how they can be problematic when done manually.

Chapter 2, Practicing Basic Git Commands, provides an introduction to Git, the powerful version control system that GitLab is built around.

Chapter 3, Understanding GitLab Components, presents a survey of the major components of GitLab that every GitLab user needs to be familiar with.

Chapter 4, Understanding the GitLab CI/CD Pipeline Structure, explains the purpose and structure of GitLab CI/CD pipelines: how they work, how to configure them, and how to view their results.

Chapter 5, Installing and Configuring GitLab Runners, explores the critical support tool that powers GitLab CI/CD pipelines.

Chapter 6, Verifying Your Code, presents the GitLab CI/CD pipeline features dedicated to ensuring that your code is of high-quality and functionally correct.

Chapter 7, Securing Your Code, discusses the GitLab CI/CD pipeline scanners that identify security vulnerabilities in your code.

Chapter 8, Packaging and Deploying Your Code, explains how to use GitLab CI/CD pipelines to automate the usage of common build and package tools to get your code into a deployable form.

Chapter 9, Enhancing the Speed and Maintainability of CI/CD Pipelines, surveys some techniques for speeding up GitLab CI/CD pipelines and making them easy to read and maintain.

Chapter 10, Extending the Reach of CI/CD Pipelines, explains how to use GitLab CI/CD pipelines to spot performance problems in your code, how to enable or disable product features from the GitLab dashboard, and how to use GitLab to develop mobile applications.

Chapter 11, End-to-End Example, demonstrates an end-to-end example that combines many of the GitLab techniques you've learned into a single, realistic software development workflow.

Chapter 12, Troubleshooting and the Road Ahead with GitLab, provides a collection of tips for troubleshooting problematic GitLab CI/CD pipelines, along with some thoughts on using GitOps to manage your infrastructure and possible future directions for GitLab.

To get the most out of this book

You will get the most out of this book if you have an account on a GitLab instance, whether on `gitlab.com` (that is, a software-as-a-service instance) or on a self-hosted instance. It will also be useful to have access to a Linux, macOS, or Windows terminal with Git installed. Some familiarity with the major stages of the software development life cycle will be helpful as well. No programming knowledge is assumed, but some experience with YML or other structured data formats will make many parts of the book easier to follow.

The code examples in this book were tested with GitLab version 15.x. They should work with future versions as well. All screenshots are also taken from GitLab version 15.x. Future versions are likely to introduce some drift in the GUI, but the fundamental concepts and operations should remain the same.

Software/hardware covered in the book	Operating system requirements
GitLab 15+	Linux, macOS, or Windows
Git	Linux, macOS, or Windows

Conventions used

There are a number of text conventions used throughout this book.

`Code in text`: Indicates code words in text, database table names, folder names, filenames, file extensions, pathnames, dummy URLs, user input, and Twitter handles. Here is an example: "Mount the downloaded `WebStorm-10*.dmg` disk image file as another disk in your system."

A block of code is set as follows:

```
employee_name = get_user_input()
sql = "SELECT salary FROM employee_records WHERE employee_name
= $employee_name" ENTERcall_database(sql)
```

When we wish to draw your attention to a particular part of a code block, the relevant lines or items are set in bold:

```
deploy-to-staging:
stage: staging
script: ./deploy-staging.sh
tags:
- windows
- staging
```

Any command-line input or output is written as follows:

```
$ git --version
git version 2.25.1
```

Bold: Indicates a new term, an important word, or words that you see onscreen. For instance, words in menus or dialog boxes appear in **bold**. Here is an example: "Select **System info** from the **Administration** panel."

> **Tips or important notes**
> Appear like this.

Get in touch

Feedback from our readers is always welcome.

General feedback: If you have questions about any aspect of this book, email us at `customercare@packtpub.com` and mention the book title in the subject of your message.

Errata: Although we have taken every care to ensure the accuracy of our content, mistakes do happen. If you have found a mistake in this book, we would be grateful if you would report this to us. Please visit `www.packtpub.com/support/errata` and fill in the form.

Piracy: If you come across any illegal copies of our works in any form on the internet, we would be grateful if you would provide us with the location address or website name. Please contact us at `copyright@packt.com` with a link to the material.

If you are interested in becoming an author: If there is a topic that you have expertise in and you are interested in either writing or contributing to a book, please visit `authors.packtpub.com`.

Share Your Thoughts

Once you've read *Automating DevOps with GitLab CI/CD Pipelines*, we'd love to hear your thoughts! Scan the QR code below to go straight to the Amazon review page for this book and share your feedback.

`https://packt.link/r/1803233001`

Your review is important to us and the tech community and will help us make sure we're delivering excellent quality content.

Download a free PDF copy of this book

Thanks for purchasing this book!

Do you like to read on the go but are unable to carry your print books everywhere? Is your eBook purchase not compatible with the device of your choice?

Don't worry, now with every Packt book you get a DRM-free PDF version of that book at no cost.

Read anywhere, any place, on any device. Search, copy, and paste code from your favorite technical books directly into your application.

The perks don't stop there, you can get exclusive access to discounts, newsletters, and great free content in your inbox daily

Follow these simple steps to get the benefits:

1. Scan the QR code or visit the link below

```
https://packt.link/free-ebook/9781803233000
```

2. Submit your proof of purchase
3. That's it! We'll send your free PDF and other benefits to your email directly

Part 1
Getting Started with DevOps, Git, and GitLab

In this part of the book, you will learn why the software development life cycle was slow and error-prone before GitLab came along, which will help you understand the problems GitLab solves. You will also learn about the basics of the Git version control system and be introduced to the fundamental concepts and components of GitLab. Finally, you will get your first look at GitLab CI/CD pipelines, which will form the focus of most of the rest of the book.

This section comprises the following chapters:

- *Chapter 1, Understanding Life Before DevOps*
- *Chapter 2, Practicing Basic Git Commands*
- *Chapter 3, Understanding GitLab Components*
- *Chapter 4, Understanding the GitLab CI/CD Pipeline Structure*

1
Understanding Life Before DevOps

To appreciate the power of **GitLab CI/CD pipelines** and the **DevOps** method of software development, we must understand how software was built before tools like GitLab appeared. Although you won't learn anything practical in this chapter, you'll learn about the world that GitLab CI/CD pipelines grew out of and get a clear picture of what problems GitLab CI/CD pipelines solve. Having a grasp of these things will set you up to understand why GitLab CI/CD pipelines operate the way they do and will open your eyes to the amazing power that they bring to the software development life cycle. In short, the best way to understand how things are now is to understand how bad they used to be!

This chapter will introduce you to a fictional but realistic web app called **Hats for Cats+**, which sells – you guessed it – head coverings for felines. You'll get a quick overview of what's involved with turning Hats for Cats from an idea into a well-written, tested, and deployed web app. You'll see how these tasks would have to be done in a world where GitLab CI/CD pipelines don't exist so that the benefits of GitLab will be even more obvious when you learn about them in later chapters.

In this chapter, we're going to cover the following main topics:

- Introducing the Hats for Cats web app
- Building and verifying code manually
- Security-testing code manually
- Packaging and deploying code manually
- Problems with manual software development life cycle practices
- Solving problems with DevOps

Introducing the Hats for Cats web app

Hats for Cats is a pretend web app for selling baseball caps, cowboy hats, and bowlers for your favorite furry friends. Imagine that it's a standard online store like hundreds or thousands of others that you've used. It lets people browse through the catalog of hats, put items in a shopping cart, and enter billing and shipping information.

The user experience or graphic design of Hats for Cats doesn't matter for this book. The web app framework that it's based on doesn't matter. Even the computer language that it's written in doesn't matter. I'll say that again because it's an important but possibly surprising point: *this book is language-agnostic*. It will include examples in several computer languages, to increase the chances that at least some of the examples are in a language that you're familiar with. But whether your apps – or the Hats for Cats web app – are written in Java, JavaScript, Python, Ruby, or any other language doesn't matter. The general GitLab CI/CD principles described in this book apply regardless.

What *does* matter are the general steps that you need to take to make sure the code is of high quality, behaves as expected, is secure, has adequate performance, is packaged sensibly, and is deployed to the right environments at the right times. This book focuses on how GitLab CI/CD pipelines can make various steps in the **software development life cycle** (**SDLC**) easier, faster, and more reliable. It won't show you how to write the Hats for Cats web app. It will be assumed that all the coding happens behind the scenes, after which you'll be shown how to build, verify, secure, package, and release that code.

With that in mind, let's walk through the high-level steps that you'd need to follow to get your code ready for users, in a world before GitLab existed. These are all the manual equivalents of what GitLab CI/CD pipelines can do for you automatically. But understanding the limitations of the manual processes, and the pain and tedium involved with following them, will help you understand the real power of GitLab.

Building and verifying code manually

Before GitLab CI/CD pipelines appeared, you needed to build and verify your code manually. This was often a terrible, soul-crushing experience, for reasons we'll discuss here.

Building code manually

Building code depends on what language you use. If you use an interpreted language such as Python or Ruby, then building might not be necessary at all. But if you're writing in a compiled language, you'd need to build your app by compiling its source code.

Imagine that you're using Java. The following are just some of the different ways to compile Java source code into executable Java classes:

- You could use the `javac` Java compiler that ships with the Java Development Kit
- You could use the Maven build tool
- You could use the Gradle build tool

There are lots of reasons that this manual build process is a tedious, annoying chore that most developers would happily leave behind:

- It's subject to user error: how many times have you forgotten whether you need to point `javac` at the top-level package that your classes are in, or at the individual class files?
- It's slow, taking anywhere from a few seconds to several minutes, depending on how big your application is. That can add up to a lot of downtime.
- It's easy to forget, causing confusion when you accidentally execute old code that doesn't behave like you thought it would.
- Badly written code can fail to compile, causing everyone to waste time as the build engineer sends the code back to the developers for fixes, and waits for those fixes to arrive.

Verifying code manually

Once you've built your code, you need to verify that it's working correctly. Testing takes countless shapes and forms, and there are more kinds of tests than we could describe in this book. But here are some of the most common forms that you may want to subject your code to:

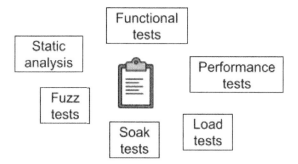

Figure 1.1 – Tests for verifying code

Functional tests

Does your program do what it's supposed to? That's the question that **functional tests** answer. Most programming projects begin with a specification that describes how the software should behave: given a certain input, what output should it provide? The developers are only done with their jobs when the code they write conforms to those specs. How do they know that their code conforms? That's where functional tests come in.

Just like there are many forms of testing in general, there are many sub-categories of testing that, together, make up functional tests.

Happy path testing makes sure that the program works as expected when it's fed common, valid input. For example, if you feed 2 + 2 into a calculator, it had better return 4! Happy path tests seem like the most important kind of tests because they check behavior that users are most likely to run into when they use your software. But in fact, you can usually cover the most common use cases with just a few happy path tests. The tests that cover unusual or unexpected cases tend to be far more numerous.

Speaking of unusual cases, that's where **edge-case testing** enters the scene. If you imagine a spectrum of input values, most values that users will input will fall in the middle of that spectrum. For example, calculator users are more likely to enter something such as 56 ÷ 209 (where these values are in the middle of the range of values the calculator will accept) than they are to enter 0 + 0 or 999,999 - 999,999 (since those values are at the edges of the range). Edge-case testing makes sure that input values at the far edges of the acceptable spectrum don't break your software. Can you create a username that consists of a single letter? Can you order 9,999 copies of a book? Can you deposit 1 cent into a bank account? If the specifications say that your software should be able to handle these edge cases, you'd better make sure it really can!

If edge-case testing ensures that your software can handle an input value that's right up against the edge of acceptable values, **corner-case testing** confirms that your software can handle two or more simultaneous edge cases. Think of it as turbocharged edge-case testing that challenges your software by placing it in even more uncomfortable (but still valid) situations. For example, does your banking app allow you to schedule a withdrawal for the smallest valid amount of currency at the farthest valid date in the future? There's no need to limit corner-case testing to two input values: if your software accepts three or ten or 100 input values at a time, you'll need to make sure it works when *every* input is pushed all the way to the extreme end of the range of values valid according to the specifications.

That handles cases where the software is given valid values. But do you also need to make sure it behaves correctly when it receives *invalid* values? Of course you do! This form of testing is sometimes called **unhappy path testing** and is usually a lot more fun for testers to perform since it's more likely to reveal bugs. All software must gracefully handle unexpected, invalid, or malformed data, and you need tests to prove that it does so. To return to our earlier examples, you'll need to make sure your calculator doesn't crash when you ask it to divide a number by zero. You have to check that the banking app doesn't accidentally give you a deposit when you ask to withdraw negative-6 dollars. And your currency conversion software should give a sensible error message when you ask about an exchange rate on February 31, 2020.

Since there are usually more ways to enter bad data than good data into an application, developers often concentrate on correctly processing *expected* data but fail to think through the types of unexpected, malformed, or out-of-range data that their users might enter. Programs need to anticipate and gracefully handle *all* sorts of data – both good and bad. Writing complete sets of both happy path and unhappy path tests is the best way to make sure that the developer has written code that behaves well no matter what data a user throws at it.

Those are some of the *kinds of behavior* that involve both valid and invalid data that tests can check for. But there's another dimension that you can use to categorize tests: the *size of the code chunk* that a test targets.

In most cases, the smallest piece of code that a test can check is a single method or function. For example, you may want to test a function called **alphabetize** that takes any number of strings as input and returns those same strings, but now in alphabetical order. To test this function, you would probably use a kind of test called a **unit test**. It tests a single *unit* of code, where a unit in this case is a single function. You could have a collection of several unit tests that all cover that function, albeit in different ways:

- Some might cover happy paths. For example, they could pass the `dog`, `cat`, and `mouse` strings as input.
- Some might cover edge or corner cases. For example, they could pass the function a single empty string, strings that consist only of digits, or strings that are already alphabetized.
- Some might cover unhappy paths. For example, they could pass the function an unexpected data type, such as booleans, instead of the expected data type of strings.

To verify the behavior of bigger pieces of code, you can use **integration tests**. These don't look at single functions, but instead at how groups of functions interact with each other. For example, imagine that your currency conversion application has four functions:

- `get_input`, which takes input from the user in the form of a source currency, a source amount, and a target currency.
- `convert`, which converts that amount of source currency into the correct amount of the target currency.
- `print_output`, which tells the user how much target currency the conversion produces.
- `main`, which is the main entry point to your app. This is the function that is called when your app is used. It calls the three other functions and passes the output of each function as input to the next.

To make sure these functions play nicely together – that is, to check if they *integrate* well – you need integration tests that call `main`, as opposed to unit tests that call `get_input`, `convert`, and `print_output`. This lets you test at a higher level of abstraction, which is to say a level that gets closer to how a real user would use your application. After all, a user isn't going to call `get_input` in isolation. Instead, they will call `main`, which, in turn, will call the other three functions and coordinate passing values between them. It's easy to write a function that works as expected on its own, but it's harder to make a collection of functions cooperate to build a larger piece of logic. Integration tests spot this type of problem in a way that pure unit tests can't.

Testers often think of various sorts of tests as forming a pyramid. According to this model, unit tests occupy the wide, low base of the pyramid: they are low-level in the sense that they test fundamental pieces of code, and there are many of them. Integration tests occupy the middle of the pyramid: they operate at a higher level of abstraction than unit tests, and there are fewer of them. At the top of the pyramid is a third category of tests, which we'll talk about next – **user tests**:

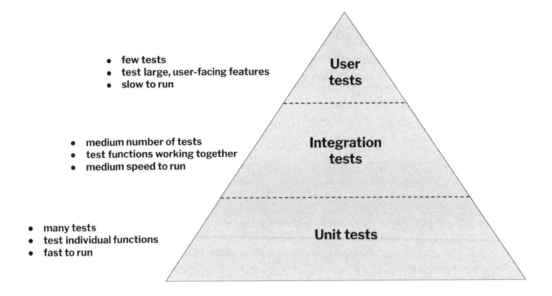

Figure 1.2 – The test pyramid

The final type of test, user tests, simulate a user's behavior and exercise the software the same way a user would. For example, if users interact with a foreign exchange app by entering a source currency, an amount of that source currency, and a target currency, and then expect to see the output in the form of an amount of the target currency, then that's exactly what a user test will do. This might mean that it uses the app's GUI by clicking on buttons and entering values in fields. Or it might mean that it calls the app's REST API endpoints, passing in input values and inspecting the result for the output value. However, it interacts with the application and does so in a fashion that's as similar to a real user as possible. As with unit and integration tests, user tests can include happy path tests, edge- and corner-case tests, and unhappy path tests to cover all the scenarios that the software's specifications describe, as well as any other scenarios that the test designer can concoct.

So far, we've explained the different purposes of unit, integration, and user tests, but we haven't described another fundamental difference. Unit and integration tests are almost always automated. That is, they are computer programs that test other computer programs. While user tests are automated whenever possible, there are enough difficulties with writing reliable, reproducible tests that interact with an application's GUI that many user tests must be run manually instead. Web applications are notoriously hard to test because of unpredictable behavior around load times, incomplete page rendering, missing or incompletely loaded CSS files, and network congestion. This means that while software development teams often attempt to automate user tests of web applications, more often than not, they end up with a hybrid of automated and manual user tests. As you may have guessed, manual user tests are extraordinarily expensive to run, both in terms of time and tester morale.

Performance tests

After that high-level tour of functional testing, you may be thinking that we've covered all the testing bases. But we're just getting started. Another aspect of your application that should probably be tested is its performance: does it do what it's supposed to do quickly enough to keep users from getting frustrated? Does it meet performance specifications the developers may have been given before they started coding? Is its performance significantly better or worse than the performance of its competitors? These are some of the questions that performance tests are designed to answer.

Performance testing is notoriously difficult to design and carry out. There are so many variables to consider when gauging how quickly your application runs:

- What environment should it be running in during the tests? Creating an environment identical to the production environment is often prohibitively expensive, but what corners can you cut in the test environment that won't skew the results of performance tests too badly?
- What input values should your performance tests use? Depending on the application, some input values may take significantly longer to process than others.
- If your application is configurable, what configuration settings should you use? This is especially important if there is no standard configuration that most users settle on.

Even if you can figure out how to design useful performance tests, they often take a long time to run and, in some cases, produce inconsistent results. This leads teams to rerun performance tests frequently, which causes them to take even more time. So, performance tests are among the most critical, and also more expensive, of all the test types.

Load tests

Performance tests have a close cousin called **load tests**. Whereas performance tests determine how quickly your software can perform one operation (a single currency conversion, a single bank deposit, or a single arithmetic problem, for example), load tests determine how well your application handles many users interacting with it at the same time. Load tests suffer from many of the same design difficulties as performance tests and can produce similarly inconsistent results. They can be even more expensive to set up since they need a way to simulate hundreds or thousands of users.

Soak tests

As your application runs for hours or days, does it allocate memory that it never reclaims? Does it consume huge amounts of disk space with overzealous logging? Does it launch background processes that it never shuts down? If it suffers from any of these resource "leaks," it could lose performance or even crash as it runs low on memory, disk space, or dedicated CPU cycles. These problems can be found with **soak tests**, which simply exercise your software over an extended period while monitoring its stability and performance. It's probably obvious that soak tests are extraordinarily expensive in terms of time and hardware resources to run and monitor.

Fuzz tests

An underutilized but powerful form of testing is called **fuzz testing**. This approach sends valid but strange input data into your software to expose bugs that traditional functional tests may have missed. Think of it as happy path testing while drunk. So, instead of trying to create an account with the username "Sam," try a username that consists of 1,000 letters. Or try to create a username that is entirely spaces. Or include Klingon alphabet Unicode characters in a shipping address.

Fuzz testing introduces a strong element of randomness: the input values it sends to your software are either completely randomly generated or are random permutations of input values that are known to be unproblematic for your code. For example, if your code translates PDF files into HTML files, a fuzz test may start by sending slightly tweaked versions of valid, easily handled PDF files, and then progress to asking your software to convert purely random strings that bear no resemblance to PDF files at all. Because fuzz testing can send many thousands of random input values before it stumbles on an input value that causes a crash or other bug, fuzz tests must be automated. They are simply too cumbersome to run manually.

Static code analysis

Another strictly automated form of testing is **static code analysis**. Whereas the other tests we've discussed try to find problems in your code as it runs, static code analysis inspects your source code without executing it. It can look for a variety of different problems, but in general, it checks to make sure you're conforming to recognized coding best practices and language idioms. These could be established by your team, by the developers of the language itself, or by other programming authorities.

For example, static code analysis could notice that you declare a variable without ever assigning a value to it. Or it could point out that you've assigned a value to a variable but then never refer to that variable. It can identify unreachable code, code that uses coding patterns known to be slower than alternative but functionally equivalent patterns, or code that uses whitespace in unorthodox ways. These are all practices that may not cause your code to break exactly but could keep your code from being as readable, maintainable, or speedy as it could have been.

More challenges of verifying code

So far, we've described just some of the ways that you may want to verify the behavior, performance, and quality of your code. But once you've finished running all these different types of tests, you face the potentially difficult question of how to parse, process, and report the results. If you're lucky, your test tools will generate reports in a standard format that you can integrate into an automatically updated dashboard. But you'll likely find yourself using at least one test tool or framework that can't be shoehorned into your normal reporting structure, and which needs to be manually scanned, cleaned, and massaged into a format that's easy to read and disseminate.

We've already mentioned how performance tests in particular often need to be run repeatedly. But in fact, *all* of these types of tests need to be run repeatedly to catch regressions or smooth out so-called "flickering" tests, which are tests that sometimes pass and sometimes fail, depending on network conditions, server loads, or countless other unpredictable factors. This means that the burden of either manually running tests, or managing and triggering automated tests, is far greater than it appears at first. If you're going to run tests repeatedly, you need to figure out when and how often to do so, you need to make sure the right hardware or test environments are available at the right times, and you need to be flexible enough to change your testing cadence when conditions change, or management asks for more up-to-date results. The point is that testing is tough, time-consuming, and error-prone, and all these difficulties are exaggerated every time humans need to get involved with making sure the tests happen in the right way at the right time.

Even though we've just said that tests *should* typically be run and then repeatedly rerun, there's another countervailing force at play. Because executing tests is expensive and difficult, there's a tendency to want to run them as *infrequently* as possible. This tendency is encouraged by a common development model that has developers building a feature (or sometimes an entire product) and then *throwing the code over the wall* to the **Quality Assurance (QA)** team for validation. This strict division between building the code and testing the code means that on many teams, tests are only run at the end of the development cycle – whether that's at the end of a two-week sprint, the end of a year-long project, or somewhere in-between.

The practice of infrequent or delayed testing leads to an enormous problem: when the developers turn over a huge batch of code for testing – thousands or tens of thousands of lines of code that had been developed by different people using different coding styles and idioms over weeks or months – it can be extremely hard to diagnose the root cause of any bugs that the tests unearth. This, in turn, means that it's hard to fix those bugs. Just like big haystacks hide needles more effectively than small haystacks, large batches of code make it hard to find, understand, and correct any bugs that they contain. The longer a development team waits before passing code on to the QA team, the bigger this problem becomes.

This concludes our lightning-fast survey of functional tests, load tests, soak tests, fuzz tests, and static code analysis. In addition, we explained some of the hidden difficulties involved with running all of these different sorts of tests. You might be wondering why we've discussed testing at all. The reason is that understanding the challenges of testing – getting a feel for how many ways there are to verify your code, how important the different forms of tests are, how time-consuming it is to set up test environments, how much of a hassle it is to manually run non-automatable user tests, how tricky it can be to process and report the results, and how tough it can be to find and fix bugs that are lurking within a huge bundle of code – is a huge part of understanding how difficult software development was before the advent of DevOps. Later in this book, when you see how GitLab CI/CD pipelines simplify the process of running different kinds of tests and viewing their results, and when you understand how tests that run early and often make problems easier to detect and cheaper to fix, you can look back at these cumbersome test procedures and feel sympathy for the poor developers who had to wade through this part of the SDLC before GitLab existed. Life is much better in the GitLab era!

Security-testing code manually

We mentioned that functional testing is just one form of testing. Another important form is **security testing**. It's so important and so difficult to get right that it's typically performed by specialized teams that are separate from traditional QA departments. There are many ways approaches to security testing, but most boil down to one of three categories:

- Inspect source code
- Interact with running code
- Inspect the third-party dependencies used by your project

Also, there are different kinds of problems that security tests can look for. At first glance, some of these problems may not look like they fall under the umbrella of security, but they all contribute to potential data loss or manipulation of your software by malicious actors:

- Non-standard coding practices
- Unsafe coding practices
- Source code dependencies that contain known vulnerabilities

Let's look at some specific varieties of security testing and see how they use different techniques to look for different sorts of problems.

Static code analysis

You can often find unsafe coding practices simply by asking a security expert to review your source code. For example, if you ask for user input and then use that input to query a database, a wily user might be able to launch a so-called *SQL injection attack* by including database commands in their input. Competent code reviewers will spot this sort of problem immediately and can often propose easy-to-implement solutions.

For example, the following pseudocode accepts input from the user but doesn't validate the input before using it in a SQL statement. A clever user could enter a malicious value such as `Smith OR (0 = 0)` and cause more information to be revealed than the developer intended:

```
employee_name = get_user_input()
sql = "SELECT salary FROM employee_records WHERE employee_name = $employee_name" ENTERcall_database(sql)
```

Code reviews can also identify code that might not be obviously unsafe, but that uses non-standard idioms, unusual formatting, or awkward program structure that make code harder for other team members (or even the original author) to read and maintain. This can indirectly make the code more susceptible to security problems in the future, or at the very least make future security problems harder for code reviewers to find.

For example, the following Python function accepts an unusually large number of parameters and then ignores most of them. Both these traits are considered to be poor programming practices, even if neither threatens the behavior or security of the code:

```
def sum(i, j, k, l, m, n, o, p, q, r):
    return i + j
```

Static code analysis can sometimes happen automatically. Many IDEs offer static code analysis as a built-in feature: they draw red warning lines under any non-standard or unsafe code they detect. This can be a great help but is best thought of as a complement to manual code reviews rather than a full substitute.

Secret detection

You can think of **secret detection** as a special form of static code analysis. There are many types of sensitive data that you want to keep out of your software's source code. It's not hard to think of examples:

- Passwords
- Deploy keys
- Public SSH or GPG keys
- US Social Security numbers
- Unique personal identification numbers that are used by other countries

Just as static code analysis scans source code to search for programming or security problems, secret detection scans source code to find secrets that should be removed and stored in a more secure location. For example, the following Java code contains a Social Security number that can be seen by anyone with read access to the code:

```java
String bethSSN = "555-12-1212";
if (customerSSN.equals(bethSSN))) {
     System.out.println("Welcome, Beth!");
}
```

Dynamic analysis

Looking at source code is useful, but there are many categories of software defects that are more easily found by interacting with executing code. This interaction could take the form of using an application's GUI just like a human would, sending requests to a REST API endpoint, or hitting various URLs of a web app with different values in the requests' query strings.

For example, your web server might be configured in such a way as to include its version number in the headers of every response. This might seem like harmless information, but it can provide clues to malicious actors about which web server-targeted exploits are likely to work against your site, and which exploits your web server is probably immune to.

To take another example, complicated logic in your code might obscure the fact that you can trigger an unhandled divide-by-zero error by entering a particular set of input values. As discussed earlier, problems like this may not initially feel like security risks, but a clever hacker can often find ways to exploit simple bugs in ways that expose data, cause data loss, or result in denial-of-service attacks.

For example, the following Ruby code could produce a `ZeroDivisionError` instance when it runs, which, in turn, could cause the program to crash:

```ruby
puts 'how many hats do you have?'
num_hats = gets.to_i
puts 'how many cats do you have?'
num_cats = gets.to_i
puts "you have #{num_hats / num_cats} hats per cat"
```

Dependency scanning

Dependency scanning is the practice of comparing the names and version numbers of each of your product's dependencies against a database of known vulnerabilities and identifying which of those dependencies should be upgraded to a later version or removed entirely to improve your software's security. Virtually every non-trivial piece of software written these days relies on tens, hundreds, or thousands of third-party, open source libraries. The source code of the most popular libraries is pored over by Black Hat hackers looking for possible exploits. These exploits are often quickly fixed by the library's maintainers, but if your project is using old, unpatched versions of those libraries, dependency scanning will let you know that your code might be vulnerable to those known exploits.

A perfect example of the need for this type of security scanning is in the news at the time of writing. Many Java projects rely on an open source Java library called Log4j, which provides a convenient way to log informational, warning, or error messages. A vulnerability was recently discovered that allows hackers to remotely run commands or install malware on any computer Log4j is running on. That's a huge problem! Fortunately, it's exactly the kind of problem that dependency scanning can spot. Any up-to-date dependency scanner will let you know if your software has a dependency – either directly or via other dependencies – on an unpatched version of Log4j, and will advise you what version of Log4j you should upgrade to.

Container scanning

These days, many software products are delivered as **Docker** images. The simplest possible description of a Docker image is that it is a Linux distribution that has your application installed on it and is then packaged in an *image* format that can be executed by Docker or similar tools. If you build a Docker image that includes an out-of-date version of a Linux distribution that contains security vulnerabilities, your application will not be as secure as it could be.

Container scanning looks at the base Linux image that your *Dockerized* application is installed on and checks a database of known security vulnerabilities to see if your packaged application might be susceptible to exploits. For example, because CentOS 6 stopped being maintained in 2020, the libraries that it includes have many severe security vulnerabilities. Container scanning would alert you to this problem and suggest that you consider upgrading your application's Docker image to use CentOS 7 or later as a base image.

Manual security testing summary

With that, we've looked at a variety of tests designed to detect security vulnerabilities or security-adjacent problems, such as failing to adhere to coding best practices. While it may seem like a lot of different steps to go through before you can put a simple web app into production, there has never been more ways to steal information or shut down a service, and there's no reason to think that trend will turn around any time soon. So, like it or not, responsible developers need to think about – and probably implement – all these different security tests:

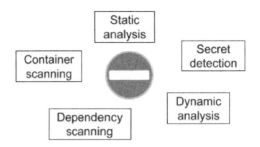

Figure 1.3 – Some of the many types of security testing

Some of these tests must be performed manually. Others have automated tools to help. But automated tests are still burdensome: you still have to install security testing tools or frameworks, configure testing tools, update test frameworks and dependencies, set up and maintain test environments, massage reports, and display reports in some integrated fashion. If you try to simplify matters by outsourcing some of these tasks to outside companies or **Software-as-a-Service** (**SaaS**) tools, you'll need to learn separate GUIs for each tool, maintain different user accounts for each service, manage multiple licenses, and do a host of other tasks to keep your tests working smoothly.

This section has shown you more ways that life before GitLab was difficult for development teams. As you'll learn in an upcoming chapter, GitLab's CI/CD pipelines replace the awkward, multi-step security testing processes described previously with fast, automated security scanners that you configure once and then benefit from for as long as you continue to develop your software project. We'll revisit this topic in much more detail later.

Packaging and deploying code manually

Now that your software has been built, verified, and is secure, it's time to think about packaging and deploying it. Just like the other steps we've discussed, this process can be an annoying burden when done manually. How you package an application into a deployable state depends not only on the computer language it's written in but also on the build management tool you're using. For example, if you're using the Maven tool to manage a Java product, you'll need to run a different set of commands than if you're using the Gradle tool. Packaging Ruby code into a Ruby gem requires another, completely different, process. Packaging often involves collecting tens, hundreds, or thousands of files, bundling them with a language-appropriate tool, double-checking that documentation and license files are complete and in the right place, and possibly cryptographically signing the packaged code to show that it's coming from a trusted source.

We've already mentioned the task of specifying which license your code is being released under. This leads to another kind of testing that needs to be done before you can deploy your code to production: **license compliance scanning**.

License compliance scanning

Most open source, third-party libraries are released under a particular software license. There are countless licenses that developers can choose from, but the bulk of open source libraries use just a handful of them, including the MIT License, GNU **General Public License** (**GPL**), and the Apache License. It's critical to know which licenses your dependencies use because you are not legally allowed to use dependencies that use licenses that are incompatible with your project's overall license.

What would make two licenses incompatible? Some licenses, such as the Peaceful Open Source License, explicitly prohibit the use of the software by the military. Another, more common cause of license clashes is between so-called *Copyleft* licenses and proprietary licenses. Copyleft licenses such as the GPL stipulate that any software that uses libraries covered by the GPL must themselves use the GPL license. Copyleft licenses are sometimes called *viral licenses* because they pass their license restrictions on to any software that uses dependencies that are covered by those types of licenses.

Since you're legally required to make sure that your main license is compatible with the licenses of any third-party libraries you use, you need to add a license scanning step to your packaging and deployment workflow. Whether this is done manually or with an automated tool, you must identify and replace any dependencies that you're not allowed to use.

Deploying software

Once your software has been packaged and you've double-checked the licenses of your dependencies, you face the hurdle of deploying the code to the right place at the right time.

Most development teams have several environments they deploy code to. Every organization sets these up differently, but a typical (albeit minimal) environment structure might look like this:

- One or more **test environments**.
- A **staging environment** or **pre-production** environment that's configured as similarly to the production environment as possible, but usually much smaller in scale.
- A **production environment**.

We'll talk about the use of these different environments in more detail later, but for now, you just need to understand how each of these environments is used as part of the basic deployment workflow. As code is being developed, it is normally deployed to the test environment so that the QA team or *release engineers* can make sure it does what it's supposed to do, and integrates with the existing code without causing any problems. As the new code is declared to be ready to add to the production code base, it is traditionally deployed to the staging environment so that a final round of tests can be made to make sure there are no incompatibilities between the new code and the environment in which it will ultimately run. If those tests go well, the code is finally deployed to the production environment, where real users can benefit from whatever feature, bug fix, or other improvements the new code introduced.

As you might imagine, making sure that the right code gets deployed to the right environment at the right time is a tricky but critically important job. And deploying is just half the battle! The other half is making sure the various environments are available and healthy. They must be running on the right types and scale of hardware, they must be provisioned with the right user accounts, they must have network and security policies configured correctly, and they must have the correct versions of operating systems, tools, and other infrastructure software installed. Of course, there are maintenance tasks, upgrades, and other system reconfiguration jobs that must be planned, carried out, and fixed when they go awry. The mind-boggling scope and complexity of these tasks are why big organizations have whole teams of release engineers making sure everything works smoothly and frantically troubleshooting when it doesn't.

This completes our tour through the most common SDLC tasks that happen after you've checked in the new code:

1. Build the code.
2. Verify the code's functionality, performance, resource usage, and more with a variety of tests.
3. Make sure the code doesn't have security vulnerabilities by using even more tests.
4. Package the code into a deployable format.
5. Look for and remediate any problems with incompatible licenses.
6. Deploy the code to the appropriate environment.

By now, you should be sensing a theme: life before GitLab was complicated, error-prone, and slow. These adjectives certainly apply to the package, license scan, and release tasks that occur near the end of the SDLC. But as you'll learn in more detail in a later chapter, GitLab CI/CD pipelines take care of the most burdensome aspects of these jobs for you. By letting the pipeline handle the boring and repetitive stuff, you can concentrate on the more creative and satisfying parts of writing software.

Problems with manual software development life cycle practices

Now that you have the general picture of what happens to software between the time that developers have finished writing it and the time that users can get their hands on it, you can start to understand how tough this process can be. Many tasks need to happen along this path of delivering secure, working code to users:

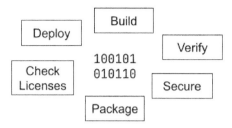

Figure 1.4 – Major tasks in the SDLC

Some of these tasks are normally done manually, while others can be automated either partially or fully. But both approaches have problems associated with them, which turn each task into a potential pain point.

What are the difficulties of manually performing these tasks? Let's take a look:

- **They take time**. They often take significantly more time than you budget for them, even after you've had experience manually performing them in the past. There are countless ways things can go wrong when performing any of these tasks, all of which require time-consuming troubleshooting and remediation. Even when everything goes right, there is simply a lot of work involved with each of these tasks. And remember the 1979 law proposed by physicist Douglas Hofstadter: *It always takes longer than you expect, even when you take into account Hofstadter's Law.*

- **They are error-prone**. Because you're relying on humans to perform them – humans who might be tired, bored, or distracted – they're all susceptible to misconfigurations, data entry mistakes, or steps that have been forgotten or applied in the wrong order, to name just a few ways human error can lead to things going wrong.

- **They are tough on employee morale**. Nobody likes doing routine, repetitive work, especially when the stakes are high and you must get it right. The prospect of running through a standard 2-hour set of manual tests for the 20th time in 2 weeks has caused many a QA engineer to wonder if maybe software wasn't the smartest career choice for them after all.

- **They have a high potential for miscommunication or misreporting**. When a manual tester has finished running their stultifying 2-hour test suite, do they have enough brain cells left to accurately record what worked and what didn't? All that testing is pointless if we can't rely on the results being recorded accurately, but anyone who has executed a difficult manual test plan knows how many ambiguities there can be in the results, how many unexpected conditions there can be to potentially skew the tests, and how hard it can be to know how to explain these factors to the people who rely on that reporting. And that's not even factoring in the very large possibility of simply recording results incorrectly, even when they're unambiguous.

For all these reasons, you can see how expensive – in terms of time, money, and employee goodwill – manual tasks are likely to be.

But if some of the tasks we've described can be automated, would that eliminate the problems that we face with manual tasks? Well, it would solve some problems. But adding a series of automation tools to the SDLC would introduce a whole new set of problems. Consider all the extra effort and expense involved with doing so and all the tasks that building custom toolchains entail:

- Researching and selecting tools for each automatable task.
- Buying and renewing licenses for each tool
- Choosing a hosting solution for each tool
- Provisioning users for each tool
- Learning different GUIs for each tool
- Managing databases and other infrastructure for each tool
- Integrating each tool with other tools in the SDLC
- Figuring out how to display the status and results of each tool in a central location if that's even possible
- Deal with tools that are buggy, that become deprecated, or that become less compelling as better alternatives appear on the market

Even after all the problems of manual or automated tasks are handled, there's one big problem that's unavoidable for teams that use this model: *it's a sequential workflow*. Steps happen one after another. One team writes the software, then *throws the code over the wall* to another team that builds the software. That team, in turn, tosses the code to a third team that's responsible for validating the software. When they're done, they generally send it to yet another group of engineers who do security testing. Finally, a release team gets ahold of it so that they can deploy the code to the right place. There are plenty of ways this process can deviate from this basic description, but the fundamental concept of doing one step at a time, passing the code to the next step only after the earlier steps are complete, is a trait that many, many software development teams' workflows shared.

So far, it might not be obvious why sequential workflows pose a problem, so let's spell it out. Because of the difficulty of executing these steps manually, or the hassles of keeping automated steps running smoothly and reliably across multiple tools, this workflow typically happens only sporadically. How often the code gets run through these steps varies from team to team, but the time and expense involved means that code changes typically stack up over days, weeks, or sometimes even months before they get built, validated, secured, and deployed properly. And that, in turn, means that *problems detected during this process are expensive to fix*. If a functional test fails, a security test detects a vulnerability, or an integration test reveals that the code doesn't play well together once it's all deployed to the same environment, identifying what code is causing the problem is like finding a needle in a very large haystack. If 5,000 lines of code across 25 classes have changed, 16 dependencies have been upgraded to more recent versions, the Java version has changed from version 16 to version 17, and the test environment is running on a different version of Ubuntu, those are a whole lot of variables to investigate when you're tracking down the source of the problem and figuring out how to fix it.

At this point, you know enough about traditional, pre-DevOps software development that we can summarize the biggest problem it faces in one sentence: *sequential workflows that involve manual tasks or automated tasks performed by different tools cause development to be slow, releases to be infrequent, and the resulting software to be of less high quality than it could be.*

But there's good news: DevOps was invented to solve these problems. And GitLab CI/CD pipelines were invented to make DevOps easier to use. We'll look at both of those things next.

Solving problems with DevOps

What do we mean by **DevOps**? Despite the term being used by the software community for at least 10 years (the first session of **devopsdays**, which is now the biggest DevOps-focused conference, was held in 2009), today, there is no single, standard definition that everyone agrees on.

When GitLab talks about DevOps, it's referring to a new way of thinking about the SDLC, which focuses on four things:

- Automation
- Collaboration
- Fast feedback
- Iterative improvement

Let's look at each of these in more detail.

The primary focus of DevOps is to **automate** as many software development tasks as possible. This removes the challenges associated with manually building, testing, securing, and releasing. But this is of limited usefulness if it exchanges those challenges for the hassles and expense associated with assembling a collection of manual tools. We'll see how GitLab solves that problem later, but for now, just understand that a proper DevOps workflow is fully automated.

By fostering **collaboration** among all the teams involved with writing software, and among all the members of each team, DevOps helps dissolve the points of friction and potential trouble that happen every time the code is transferred from one team to another. If there's no "wall" to throw the code over – if every step in the process is transparent to everyone involved with writing and delivering the software – everyone feels committed to the overall quality of the code and feels like they're playing for the same team. Different people still have primary responsibility for specific tasks, but the overall culture moves toward joint ownership of the code and commonly shared goals.

Fast feedback might be the most crucial and revolutionary element of DevOps. It can be thought of as the result of two other concepts we talked about previously: concurrent workflows and shifting left. When you stop to think about it, those two terms boil down to the same thing: do all the building, verifying, and securing tasks as soon as possible for each batch of code that developers check in. Do them all concurrently instead of sequentially, to ensure that they happen at the far left of the software development timeline. And run all these tasks immediately for every chunk of new code that's contributed, no matter how small. By running these tasks early and often, you minimize the size of the code changes that are tested, which makes it cheaper and easier to troubleshoot any software bugs, configuration issues, or security vulnerabilities found by the tests.

If you're finding and fixing problems quickly, you'll be able to release your software to customers more often. By getting new features and bug fixes to them sooner, you're helping them benefit from the **iterative improvement** of your product. By releasing smaller code changes at shorter intervals with a lower risk of breaking things and needing to roll back, you're living up to the catchphrase of *making your releases boring*. In this case, boring is a good thing: most customers would rather have frequent, small upgrades that pose little risk than infrequent, massive changes that have a greater chance of wreaking havoc and needing to be reverted.

By taking advantage of automation, collaboration, fast feedback, and iterative improvement, DevOps practices produce code that's higher quality, cheaper to develop, and delivered more frequently to users.

How GitLab implements DevOps

GitLab is a tool that enables all the software development tasks we've discussed, using the DevOps principles we've just outlined. The most important trait of GitLab is that it's a *single* tool that unifies all the steps in the SDLC under one umbrella.

Remember how shifting from manual processes to automated processes solved some problems but raised a host of new problems associated with automation? GitLab's single-tool approach solves those problems as well. Consider the benefits of having the following single, unified toolchain approach:

- One license to buy (unless your team uses the free, feature-limited version of GitLab, in which case there are no licenses to buy)
- One application to maintain and upgrade
- One set of user accounts to provision
- One database to manage
- One GUI to learn
- One place to look – one radar screen, so to speak – to see the reports and statuses of *all* your build, validation, security, packaging, and deploy steps

So, GitLab being a single tool solves the problems you get from using disparate automation tools. Even better, the fact that it uses a single set of components and entities, all of which are aware of and communicate well with each other, enables and encourages the collaboration, concurrency, transparency, and shared ownership that are such critical aspects of DevOps. Once you have concurrent tasks, you get fast feedback. And that, in turn, allows for iterative improvement via *boring* releases.

The bulk of the rest of this book deals with the technique that GitLab uses to put those DevOps principles into practice: **CI/CD pipelines**. We won't define what that term means quite yet, but you'll learn all about it in future chapters. For now, you just need to know that CI/CD pipelines are where the GitLab rubber meets the DevOps road: they are how GitLab's single-tool model performs all the building, verification, securing, packaging, and deploying that your code has to go through.

We'd be remiss not to mention that a large part of GitLab is dedicated to helping you plan, assign, and manage work. But that's separate from the CI/CD pipelines, and therefore is beyond the scope of this book. We will touch on ancillary topics from time to time, simply because everything in GitLab is so interrelated that there's no way to stay entirely within the boundaries of CI/CD pipelines. But most of the rest of this book will explain what GitLab pipelines can do, and how to use them.

Summary

People who don't work for software companies might not realize there's more to writing software than just... *writing software*. After it's checked in, a long and complicated series of steps must be followed to build, verify, secure, package, and deploy code before users can get their hands on it. All these steps can be done manually, or some of them – under certain conditions – can be automated. But both manual and automated approaches to preparing software pose problems.

DevOps is a relatively new approach to accomplishing these steps. It combines automation, collaboration, fast feedback, and iterative improvement in a way that lets teams make software better, faster, and more cheaply.

GitLab is a DevOps tool that collects all these tasks under one umbrella, allowing a software development team to accomplish everything with a single tool, using a single GUI, with all the test results and deployment status displayed in a single place. Its focus on automation addresses the problems raised by manual processes. Its single-tool model addresses the problems raised by automated processes. GitLab puts all the DevOps principles into practice through the use of CI/CD pipelines, which will be the main focus of the rest of this book.

But before we deal with CI/CD pipelines, we need to take a quick, one-chapter detour into Git, the tool around which GitLab is built. Without a solid grounding in the basics of Git, you'll likely find many of GitLab's concepts and terminology confusing. So, batten down the hatches, grab a big mug of your favorite caffeinated beverage, and let's jump into Git.

2
Practicing Basic Git Commands

The **GitLab** product is built around a separate tool called **Git**. GitLab makes Git easier to use and gives you a central place to store all the files that Git is looking after, in addition to providing many other non-Git-related features. We like to think of GitLab as a *wrapper* around Git, making it more pleasant to use and more powerful.

Although GitLab and Git are different tools, GitLab borrows many concepts from Git. This means that to understand GitLab, you need to understand Git. Fortunately, you only need to get to grips with the very basics of Git. We say "fortunately" because Git is an enormous and complicated tool and learning all of its nooks and crannies would take a huge effort. But trust us: if you understand the first 10% of Git, you can use GitLab effectively. That 10% is exactly what we're going to introduce you to in this chapter.

First, we'll show you why version control systems such as Git are such a useful part of software development. Then, we'll explain how you can store your code in Git, including any edits that you or your team members make to that code. We'll also show you how to develop your code in a safe place called a branch, which is isolated from other team members. This ensures that you don't step on other people's toes and overwrite their code. You'll learn how to mark a particular version of your code so that you can easily refer to it later or release it to customers. Finally, you'll learn about storing code in remote locations. You'll learn how to sync local and remote copies of files, and you'll understand how this architecture enables an entire team to work on a single code base at the same time.

In this chapter, we're going to cover the following main topics:

- Why use Git?
- Committing code to keep it safe
- Tagging commits to identify versions of code
- Branching code for developing in an isolated space
- Syncing local and remote copies of repositories
- Additional resources for learning Git

Technical requirements

For this chapter, you need to have Git installed on your local computer. Git works on Linux, macOS, and Windows, as well as many Unix variants. There are easy-to-follow instructions for installing Git on any of these operating systems at https://git-scm.com/downloads. If you're asked to set configuration options during installation, it's safe to accept all the default values.

To type the Git commands that you'll see in this chapter, use your favorite terminal application on Linux or macOS. If you're a Windows user, you can type them in Command Shell, PowerShell, or Git Bash. The default configuration options while installing Git on Windows should make Git available on any of these types of Windows terminals, and they should all produce identical results when you run Git commands in them.

The Git examples you'll see in this book are operating system-agnostic: *Git works the same no matter where you run it.*

To see if it's already installed, or to verify that you installed it correctly, open the appropriate terminal for your operating system and run the following command. If the output shows a version number instead of an error, Git has been installed properly on your computer:

```
$ git --version
git version 2.25.1
```

Don't worry about seeing a particular version number; virtually any version of Git will perform identically for the simple commands we use in this book.

Before using Git, you must tell it your name and email address. This information is added to every edit you store in Git so that other team members know which edits you are responsible for.

First, check if Git is already configured with this information:

```
$ git config --list
```

If the output includes entries for user.email and user.name, you're all set and can skip the following two commands. Otherwise, let Git know who you are by running these two one-time commands, replacing the email address and name with your information:

```
$ git config --global user.email "george.spelvin@example.com"
$ git config --global user.name "George Spelvin"
```

An optional but recommended step is to configure Git to use `main` instead of `master` as the name of the default branch in new projects. We haven't discussed what branches are yet, so this may not make much sense. For now, it's enough for you to know that many software companies are shifting to `main` as the name for the place where a project's stable code base lives. You'll see both terms in use in the wild (and even in this book), but if you'd like to configure your computer so that new projects use `main`, run the following command once:

```
$ git config --global init.defaultBranch main
```

With all the technical requirements done and dusted, let us begin!

Why use Git?

Just like it was helpful to understand how we built software before automation tools such as GitLab CI/CD pipelines came along (as discussed in *Chapter 1*), it's helpful to know how teams coordinated the complicated process of making edits to the same files before Git or similar tools came along.

These tools are designed to solve many problems that developers face, but let's look at just one. Imagine that you and your teammate Elizabeth are working on the same code base and both of you want to edit some of the same files. Furthermore, imagine that this is a time before the advent of Git or any other **version control system** (**VCS**). The only way to write software in this pre-Git era is for you to edit a file and then email it, put it on a shared network drive, or copy it to a portable disk. Then, you must let Elizabeth know that she's free to edit it. She *checks it out* in some sense (maybe by adding an entry to a spreadsheet saying that she's got control of the file, or maybe through some other mechanism), and she retains control of the file for as long as she needs it. If you have new ideas and want to edit the file again, you need to ask her to stop editing it and transfer it back to you. When she does, you need to scan through the whole file to see what changes she's made, in the hope that they don't conflict with the changes you want to make. Then, you repeat this process for each file the two of you are working on, every time either of you wants to edit any of those files. You can imagine how slow and cumbersome this process is, and how many chances there are to mess something up during all the transfers of ownership!

With this understanding of how things worked in the bad old days, we can look at what a VCS is, how it solves this problem, and in what other ways it makes developers' lives easier.

What is a version control system?

A VCS is a tool designed to make it easier for one or more developers to work with a set of files. It does this by making snapshots of all the files in your project at a particular time and letting you view, compare, and restore files in different snapshots.

Each VCS has slightly different functionality, but here are some features that most offer:

- Provides backups of files in case current versions are lost or accidentally overwritten.
- Shows how a file's contents have changed over time.
- Shows who made which changes to which files, and when.
- Labels certain file snapshots for future reference.
- Provides a human-readable description of each set of changes so that team members can understand why changes were made.
- Allows developers to edit files in a way that's compatible with other developers editing the same files at the same time.

There have been many competing VCSs over the years, both open source and proprietary. Some of the best-known examples are Microsoft Visual SourceSafe, CVS, Apache Subversion, and now Git. For reasons we'll explain shortly, Git has largely taken over the VCS space and now serves as the default VCS for any team that doesn't have a company mandate to use one of Git's competitors. In other words, Git has *won* the VCS competition, to the extent that such a victory is possible.

VCSs work with any computer language. For example, you could use the same VCS to manage files in separate Java, Python, and Ruby projects. And although we typically think of a VCS as helping you work with source code files in a computer language, they can be used with *any* file in a software project, including (but not limited to) the following:

- Documentation, such as Markdown or PDF files
- Configuration, such as JSON or YAML files
- Test code and data
- Metadata or configuration information for your **integrated development environment** (IDE)
- Other project assets, such as pictures, video, or sound files

There's no need to limit VCSs to just software projects! You could use Git or any VCS to manage the poems in an anthology, recipes in a cookbook, or chapters in a novel. VCSs are useful for literally any project that involves files on a computer.

What problems does a VCS solve?

Now that you understand what kinds of features a VCS such as Git offers, your mind is probably spinning with all the possible ways a VCS could solve everyday problems faced by software developers. Here are just some scenarios, but you can no doubt think up more.

Why was this code changed?

You may open some source code in your text editor one morning only to discover that a method that you're familiar with now uses an entirely different algorithm. Why was it changed? Was the old algorithm broken? Is the new algorithm faster? Is the code that implements it shorter or easier to read? By looking at the *commit message* of your VCS, you can read a description of why the change was made. Some of these messages are more complete than others, depending on how conscientious the developer who made the commit was, but you can usually get the general picture of what motivated the change.

When was this code changed?

Imagine that you revisit a Java class that you haven't looked at in a few months, and notice that it has had some features added and others removed. When did these changes take place? More importantly, did they take place before or after the last deployment to production? Your VCS's commit log will tell you each time that class was touched, and even what lines were modified each time it was edited. That will let you pinpoint which changes were made when so that you know which version of the class is being used by customers today.

Who added this buggy code?

Git has a feature called *blame* that tells you which developer edited which lines of a file. This is helpful when you discover that some newly added code is buggy or slow because you know exactly whom to ask to fix it! But it also has a positive use case: if you spot an especially clever piece of code, your VCS can let you know whom you should praise and, hopefully, learn from. So, the *blame* feature provides a great way to improve professional relationships between developers and strengthen team morale.

I need to restore my copy of Foo.java

I'm sure *you've* never accidentally deleted a file after working on it all day, but we sure have. And I'm sure *you* are scrupulous about making backups for exactly that sort of event, but we sure aren't. But since we always use a VCS, restoring a lost file is easy: every VCS gives you a simple way to view and restore the last version of any file that it manages.

I want to revert to this morning's version of all the files in the test directory

You're not limited to restoring just the last version of a file; you can restore *any* version of a file, no matter how old it might be, so long as you added a snapshot that includes that version. For example, imagine that you spent hours rewriting automated tests to make them run faster, only to discover that your new tests are either slower or don't work at all. Your VCS will let you replace just one file, all the files in a directory, or all the files in a project, with any old version of those files. Go ahead and edit whatever files you want, as often as you want. If you're careful to regularly check your changes into your VCS, you can quit worrying about losing work or reverting to old code if the new code doesn't work out.

A colleague and I want to edit Foo.java at the same time

Probably the most frequently used feature of VCSs is their ability to safely partition the edits you're making in a file so that they don't overwrite work that other people are doing in the same file. Each developer has a *branch* of the code, where they can edit whatever files they want, even if other people are editing the same files on their branches. As each developer finishes their work, they *merge* their branch into the project's stable code base. In this way, multiple developers can all edit the same file at the same time without anyone losing any work or having to coordinate ownership of the file.

I need to deploy last Friday's version of the code to the production environment

VCSs let you *tag* specific versions of your files so that it's easy to view or restore those versions. For example, you may tag your entire code base before undertaking a major refactoring project so that it will be easy to revert to a known-good state if the refactoring doesn't work out. More commonly, development teams often tag a specific version of the code so that they know exactly which code was deployed with a particular release. For example, you may apply a `version-6-1-0` tag to code that you deployed as version 6.1.0 of your product. When someone reports a bug in that version of your product, you know which version of your product's files to troubleshoot.

I want all my coworkers to have access to my edited code

When you edit a file, your team members must know that you've edited it and be able to see your edits. VCSs make it easy for you to *push up* your edits to a centralized location. Then other team members can *pull down* those changes onto their local computers, keeping the entire team in sync.

Why Git is popular

We've already mentioned that Git has become the dominant VCS. Why is that? Different Git users would give different explanations for its rise to the top, but here are some characteristics that probably helped.

Pedigree

Git was invented by Linus Torvalds as a tool for storing and managing the source code for the Linux kernel. The fact that Git was originally used to store high-profile, successful, and widely adopted code such as the Linux kernel no doubt gave it instant credibility and cachet: if it's robust and reliable enough for Linus and Linux, it's good enough for you.

As an aside, it's amazing that one programmer is responsible for launching two major software projects: Linux and Git. It's as if Shakespeare invented the pencil just to make his plays easier to write.

Simple branch management

As you'll learn shortly, branches are one of the most important components of any VCS. Git was designed from the beginning to make it simple to create, use, and merge branches. The ease with which developers can work with branches encourages them to use lots of branches, which promotes safe and rapid development workflows.

Speed

Git is fast. Adding new files, checking in changes, reverting to old code, and syncing files to incorporate coworkers' edits – these operations all happen in just a few seconds, even with large projects. In particular, creating, using, and merging branches are all lightning-fast operations, and that's one of the key reasons why developers love working with Git so much.

Reliability

You may think that reliability would be basic table stakes for any VCS: if the VCS loses your files or edits, it's useless at its role. But a surprising number of VCSs over the years have been less than 100% reliable. A hundred-person development team that one of us worked on in the early 2000s used the dominant proprietary VCS of the time, and even though it was thought of as the best-in-breed of that sort of tool, it frequently lost or scrambled our edits.

Git is famously reliable. It's a complex tool, and if you don't understand exactly how to use its commands, you could inadvertently lose data through human error. But it's virtually unheard of for Git to suffer from technical glitches that result in data loss. It's trusted by countless teams of skeptical software engineers around the world, and that trust is well-earned.

Distributed architecture

Before Git, many VCSs used a *centralized* architecture. That means that to work on a file, you needed to fetch its latest version from a central server, make edits, and then resubmit that file to the central server so that other team members could access it.

There are a few problems with a centralized architecture. First, some (but not all) centralized VCSs *lock* any files that you've checked out, so no one else can make changes to those files while you're editing them. This results in a lot of "*Hey, are you done with* `Foo.java` *yet?*" conversations in the workplace, which creates an awkward, inconvenient, and annoying workflow.

The second problem with using a VCS with a centralized architecture is that it requires you to be connected to that central server whenever you need to check out a file or check in edits. You can't work effectively without internet connectivity. This is less of a problem than it used to be, but there are still times when you're between hot spots and still want to get work done.

Centralized architectures also create a single point of failure. If the server goes down, all the developers are dead in the water. If it loses data or is physically destroyed, it could be days before the data is restored or the hardware is rebuilt.

Finally, centralized architectures don't always scale well as development teams grow. Rapidly growing teams that rely on an underpowered VCS server can find their work blocked as they queue to access that server.

Fortunately, the distributed architecture that Git is built around solves all these problems. These problems vanish when you have many copies of the project's files on different computers. When using a distributed VCS, each developer has a copy of the entire project on their local computer. This includes all the files, edit history, tags, commit messages, and other metadata needed to let them work on the files without any connection to a central server.

How does this strategy help with the problems faced by centralized VCSs? First, if every developer has a local copy of all the files in the project, there's no concept of *locking* a file that you're editing: anyone can edit their local copy of any files at any time. Second, there's no need to contact a central server to check out files, and there's no need to contact a server to check in your edits. You can work locally for as long as you want. It's true that, eventually, you'll need to sync your edits to a server so that your coworkers can see your edits (and you can see theirs), but you can do that as often or as infrequently as makes sense for your team. Third, since there's a copy of the entire project's files on every developer's machine, there's no longer a single point of failure. If the central server that you use to sync changes goes down, you can designate any developer's machine as a temporary central server while you rebuild the original server. Finally, because developers who use a distributed VCS sync their code with the central server far less often than developers who use a centralized VCS to check files in and out of that server, distributed VCSs scale much better than their centralized competitors. Most teams who use Git experience no VCS-related scaling problems as they add new team members.

Drawbacks of Git

Remember how we mentioned that Git gained credibility by being invented by Linus Torvalds? Unfortunately, there's a downside to this: it was designed to fit Linus's mind, not yours. This means that its commands can be inconsistent, confusing, and counterintuitive. To give just one example, let's look at how one command uses three different ways to modify its behavior:

- `git branch` lists all available branches.
- `git branch foo` makes a new branch called *foo*.
- `git branch --delete foo` deletes a branch called *foo*.

You might expect these commands to be the following instead:

- `git branch --list` (this does work but isn't necessary and no one uses it)
- `git branch --create foo`
- `git branch --delete foo`

But that's not the case; you must remember the different option syntaxes instead. And that's just for one command.

The other big problem with Git is that it's so big. It has so many features and options and configurable settings that it can seem overwhelming. The official reference documentation, a book called *Pro Git*, is 511 pages long! When you're getting started with the tool, it's easy to get the sense that you'll never know enough about Git's concepts and commands to be able to use it productively, and you may wonder how anyone is ever able to get to grips with something so complicated.

Fortunately, you don't need to know all the ins and outs of Git's inconsistencies and syntactical complexities, and you don't need to know all the features that Git provides. You just need to know a handful of common commands and their variants to perform 95% of the Git-related tasks you need. Most Git users learn 20 or so common operations, commit those to memory over time, and look up the details of other Git operations only as needed. *So, don't panic, and don't try to learn and memorize all of Git.* If you feel comfortable with the simple commands and concepts described in this chapter, you're equipped to do real work with Git. It may turn out to be all you'll ever need from the tool.

That's enough of an introduction to Git. Now, it's time to look at some actual commands.

Committing code to keep it safe

To benefit from all the advantages described previously, you need to know how to add files to Git. How do you do that?

First, let's discuss the concept of a **repository**, which is often shortened to **repo** A repository is a place where Git stores a project's files and a history of all the changes made to those files. It's the bank vault where it puts files to keep them safe.

There are two main ways to create a repository. The first way is to convert an ordinary directory on your Linux, macOS, or Windows filesystem into a Git repository. This is easy: use the `git init` command from inside the directory, and voilà – it turns into a Git repository. Then, you can use the `git status` command to prove that it's a repo.

Let's use those commands to create a new repository for our Hats for Cats project. First, make a new directory that will become a repository, and move into that directory (the example in this chapter is using a Linux Terminal, so the prompt and output may look slightly different if you use another terminal or OS, but the concepts will be the same):

```
$ mkdir hats-for-cats
$ cd hats-for-cats
```

Prove that it's not a Git repo yet:

```
$ git status
fatal: not a git repository (or any of the parent directories):
.git
```

Turn the directory into a Git repo with the `git init` command:

```
$ git init
```

Now, watch how `git status` doesn't explicitly tell us that we're in a repo, but it does provide information that only makes sense if the directory has been turned into a repository. It tells us that we're on the `main` branch, that Git is not tracking any files in the repository, and that we haven't edited any files in this directory that we may want to ask Git to manage:

```
$ git status
On branch main
Your branch is up to date with 'origin/main'.
nothing to commit, working tree clean
```

The second, and probably more common, way to create a repository is to copy an existing repository from another computer using the `git clone` command. Earlier in this chapter, we talked about how Git's distributed architecture means that each team member has a full copy of their project's Git repository on their computer. Cloning is how you download a new copy of that repo from someone else's computer to your computer. We'll talk about this process in detail later when we discuss remote repositories. For now, just understand that if you're working as a member of a software development team, most of the time, you'll be cloning a repository from another computer instead of creating a new repository just on your computer.

Now that we have a repository, let's add a file to it. For this example, let's add a to-do list. First, use the `touch` command or a text editor to create a file called `todo.txt` in the `hats-for-cats/` directory. Fill the file with whatever content you want or leave it empty. Git can manage empty files just fine:

```
$ touch todo.txt
```

Your directory contains a file, but Git is not tracking that file yet, since you haven't officially added it to the repository. Doing so is a two-step process:

1. Move one or more files into something called the *staging area*.
2. *Commit* all the files in the staging area.

It's important to understand that a file is not stored in Git, meaning that Git will not manage the versions of that file until *you stage it and then commit it*.

Remember how we talked about VCSs making "snapshots" of the state of your files at a particular time? This stage-and-commit process is how you make a new snapshot with Git. This means you are in complete control of when to make snapshots, and also of what files are included in each snapshot. If you're editing `foo.py` and `bar.py` but only want to snapshot `foo.py` right now, just add that file to your staging area and commit it. When it's time to make a snapshot with edits to `bar.py`, add that file to the staging area, optionally add `foo.py` as well if you want to snapshot any edits you made to it since the last time you snapshotted it, and then commit the file(s) that is in the staging area.

You may have noticed that we've talked about staging and committing both new files and edits to existing files. That's because you use the same stage-and-commit process for both cases. You may find it easiest to think of staging and committing as something you do to capture *any changes to files*, where changes can take four different forms:

- Creating a new file
- Editing the content of an existing file
- Renaming or moving a file (as far as the filesystem is concerned, these are the same operation)
- Deleting a file

No matter which of these operations you perform, when you add one or more files to the staging area and then commit, you're making a new Git snapshot of the state of whatever files were in the staging area.

You might be wondering why the stage-and-commit dance contains two separate steps. Couldn't Git just provide a single command to make a new snapshot of a file? The reason for this extra complication is to allow you to include *multiple files in a single commit*. For example, you may edit a source code file, edit some associated test code that lives in a different file, and finally edit a documentation file, all as part of one bug fix. You'd want to include all three of these files in a single commit since the edits to all the files logically belong together.

First, let's stage your new `todo.txt` file using the `git add` command. This doesn't move or copy the file anywhere. Rather, it adds an invisible label to the file saying that it is in the staging area:

```
$ git add todo.txt
```

If you run `git status` again, you'll see that `todo.txt` is now included in a list of *changes to be committed*, which means that it's been added to the staging area but hasn't been committed yet:

```
$ git status
On branch main
Your branch is up to date with 'origin/main'.
Changes to be committed:
  (use "git restore --staged <file>..." to unstage)
        new file:   todo.txt
```

Now, you can commit it with the `git commit` command. But first, a word about commit messages. An important part of every commit is the human-readable commit message that the committer must provide. The easiest way to add this message is as a parameter to `git commit`, using the `--message` option:

```
$ git commit --message "add list of tasks to do"
```

If you run `git status` again, you'll see that no files are waiting to be committed, which means your to-do list has been safely stashed in the repository, and all future edits to it will be tracked by Git. Congratulations, you've just performed your first work with Git!

Let's pause for a minute and talk about what Git includes with every commit. You've already learned that a commit contains the contents of any file(s) included in that commit and a message that describes the purpose of the commit, but there are a few other pieces of information it includes as well. Here's the complete list:

- Any changes made to the file's contents (or the filename or location in the filesystem).
- A 40-character string of hexadecimal digits that's called a **Secure Hash Algorithm** (**SHA**), which is the code that generates this string based on the contents of the committed files. A commit's SHA uniquely identifies that commit; think of it as a unique *name* for that commit. SHAs are not sequential: each SHA is completely different from the SHA of the previous commit.
- The name and email of the person who made the commit.
- A timestamp of when they made the commit.
- A human-readable message describing why they made the commit.
- A pointer to the previous commit (or parent commit) on the branch. We'll introduce the concept of branches in the next section and talk about this pointer more then.

The `git log` command shows you all this information for all the commits on your current branch (again, we'll explain branches in more detail later). Let's imagine that you've made two commits: one to create an empty to-do list and another to add an item to that list. Running `git log` gives an output similar to the following:

```
$ git log
commit 7d4c98438ade780531e1baa283b3239c21943171 (HEAD -> master)
Author: George Spelvin <george.spelvin@example.com>
Date:   Tue Jan 4 09:57:37 2022 -0800

    add first item to list

commit 63ea581d1bc693dac159c146fa10d1cbfa4e6366
```

```
Author: George Spelvin <george.spelvin@example.com>
Date:   Sun Jan 2 12:31:27 2022 -0800
    add list of tasks to do
```

This output includes information for your two commits, with the most recent commit at the top. Can you spot the SHA, author information, timestamps, and commit message for each commit? If you're running these commands on your computer, you'll see different details for each commit, but the format of the output will be the same.

In this example, all the commit information is for commits that you've made. But that's simply because you're the only person who has added commits to this branch. If other people had made commits to the same branch, you would see information for their commits in this output as well.

Excluding files from a repository

At this point, you might be thinking that it would be wise to stage and commit *all* the files in a project. But there are a few types of files that you usually do not want to store in Git or any other VCS. These include, but are not limited to, the following:

- Files that are generated from other files
- Extremely big files
- Files that contain secrets

The first category includes files such as executables that are compiled from source code, or PDFs that are generated from the source text that's stored in Markdown. Since you can always regenerate these files from their sources, there's no need to store them in Git. Also, putting them in Git introduces the possibility of *drift*, where the source files and the generated files are out of sync with each other. For example, the source file may contain code from last week, while the compiled executable may contain code from last month. This can cause all sorts of unexpected problems.

Big files pose a different sort of problem. If you add a 5 GB ISO file or a 10 GB dataset, then anyone who copies your project's repository to their local machine will be forced to download that file. We mentioned earlier that Git is fast, but there's nothing it can do about congested or slow networks. Since copying repositories is a fairly common operation among Git users, including enormous files in your repository is something you'd generally like to avoid. It often makes more sense to put these files outside of Git, on a shared drive or some other accessible data storage system. Removing a large file after you've added it won't solve the problem. Because Git keeps a record of the entire edit history of every file ever added to the repository, that large file will stick around in your repository forever, annoying you and your coworkers every time someone copies the repo to their local computer.

Finally, secrets such as deploy keys, SSH private keys, or passwords usually should not be stored in Git. As explained in the previous paragraph, any secrets that you commit to a repository will be there forever. Unless your IT and Git administrators are extremely careful about limiting permissions to repositories, this means they can be viewed by anyone with access to your repository. So, these sorts of things are normally stored not in Git, but in a specially designed system that's dedicated to keeping sensitive data safe.

This is an important topic, so let's investigate it further by looking at a concrete example. Imagine that your `hats-for-cats/` directory contains a file called `personal-notes.txt` and a directory called `.ide-config/`. The former is where you store ideas for project features as they occur to you, while the latter holds several files that your IDE uses to configure the project on your local machine. You may not want to share either of these with the other members of your development team since the ideas are meant just for your eyes and the configuration files will only work with your computer setup.

You can keep this file and directory private simply by never using the `git add` command to add them to your project's Git repository. That works, but there's a problem with this approach. Whenever you run `git status` to find out if there are any edited files that you should add and commit, Git will always point out that `personal-notes.txt` and `.ide-config/` are not in the repository:

```
$ git status
On branch main
Untracked files:
  (use "git add <file>..." to include in what will be committed)
        .ide-config/
        personal-notes.txt
```

There's a simple solution to this problem: create a new file called `.gitignore` in the root of your project's directory. For the content of this file, add the names of any files or directories that you'd like Git to ignore. You can add explanatory comments by starting a line with a hash character. The following code in `.gitignore` instructs Git to exclude the files we've been talking about:

```
# notes to myself that are not for public consumption
personal-notes.txt

# configuration files for my IDE
.ide-config/
```

You need to add this `.gitignore` file to the repository, just like any other file you want Git to track:

```
$ git add .gitignore
$ git commit --message "exclude notes file and IDE config directory"
```

Thanks to `.gitignore`, Git no longer warns you about uncommitted files and directories when you run `git status`:

```
$ git status
On branch main
nothing to commit, working tree clean
```

It's not unusual for large projects to end up with tens or even hundreds of entries in `.gitignore`, and we encourage you to use this feature to keep your Git repository clean and your `git status` output uncluttered.

Let's review the commands and concepts you've learned about in this section for keeping code safe by committing it to a Git repository:

- Use `git init` or `git clone` to create a Git repository on your computer.
- Use `git add` to add one or more files to Git's staging area.
- Use `git commit --message "<MESSAGE>"` to make a new Git commit (or snapshot) that includes any files that were in the staging area.
- Use `git status` to see if you have edited files waiting to be moved to the staging area, or staged files waiting to be committed.
- Use `git log` to see information about all the commits that have been made to your current branch.
- Use a `.gitignore` file to exclude certain files or directories from the repository.

Now, let's learn how to *tag* a particular version of the files that you so carefully committed to Git so that you can easily view or revert to that version in the future.

Tagging commits to identify versions of code

Now that you understand how and why developers commit code to Git, we can explain tagging. Tagging is simple: it's a way to add a permanent label to a commit. There are many reasons to tag, but the two most common are to mark the exact version of code that is released to customers and to have a convenient way to return to a particular version of the code if you need to revert a large batch of changes. Let's look at an example of each.

Imagine that Hats for Cats is ready to release version **0.1-beta** to users. Tagging a particular commit with that version number lets you know exactly what features have been deployed into production and are available to your users, which tells you which version of the code to fix as you triage bug reports. Adding this sort of identification via a tag is easy in Git. First, make sure that you have committed all the edits to all the files you want to include in your release. Then, use the `git tag` command to add a tag representing the version number to the latest commit on your branch:

```
$ git tag version-1-0-beta
```

If you run `git log`, you'll see that Git has applied the tag to your latest commit.

As a separate example, imagine that you decide to undertake a major refactoring to change your classes to use a more complicated class inheritance structure. You know how easy it is to mess up this kind of large-scale change, and you want an easy way to return to today's version of pre-refactored code in case everything goes sideways. Tagging is just the solution:

```
$ git tag before-class-reorganization
```

Tagging has many options, but two of the most useful are `--delete` and `--list`, both of which do exactly what you would expect. Try them and see:

```
$ git tag --list
$ git tag --delete version-1-0-beta
```

That's tagging in a nutshell. As with most Git commands, there's much more you can do with tagging, but this covers the basics. Fortunately, you now know as much about tagging as most Git users, so don't worry about exploring `git tag` further unless you need more flexibility or features when it comes to marking versions of your files.

You've now mastered the fundamentals of storing your files in Git for safekeeping, excluding files that you don't want to store in Git, and labeling certain commits for easy future reference. Now, it's time to learn how to edit, store, and label files in a way that doesn't step on the toes of other developers who might be working on the same files. It's time to look at Git branches!

Branching code for developing in an isolated space

After commits, **branches** are probably the most important concept in Git. Strictly speaking, you don't need to know anything about branches and branching to use Git. This is especially true if you're a solo developer. But any non-trivial software development effort that involves more than one person will generally make heavy use of branches. Let's figure out what they are and why we need them.

A branch is just a series of ordered commits. Remember when we said that each commit includes a backward pointer to the previous commit? If you follow those backward pointers from the latest commit back to the first commit ever made to the repository, you've just described the branch that your commit is on. *Again, a branch is just a series of commits, assembled in a particular order, linked by backward-pointing arrows.*

Whenever you're working on files within a Git repository, you're *on* exactly one branch. This means that you can only see the versions of files that are on that branch, and any commits you make will only be added to that branch. Or, more technically, any commits you make while on that branch will include a backward-pointing arrow that links the commit to the previous commit on that same branch.

You can think of being on a branch as analogous to driving down a street. Imagine a town with only two streets. Main Street runs south to north. First Street forks off Main Street, runs parallel to it for a few blocks, and then eventually merges back into Main Street. Your car must be on exactly one of these two streets at any time. To stretch the analogy a little, imagine there's a helicopter with a huge magnet that can pick your car up and move it between Main Street and First Street whenever you want. To make the analogy even stranger, pretend there's a child in the back seat of your car who throws marbles out of the open window onto the street every block or so. In this analogy, the streets represent *branches*, the car represents *a developer*, the marbles represent *commits* that the developer adds to whatever branch they're on, and the helicopter represents a *Git command* (which we'll learn about soon) that lets the developer switch to any branch they want, whenever they want:

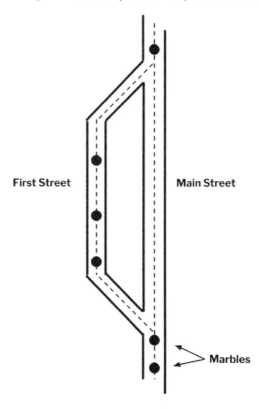

Figure 2.1 – Streets and marbles, representing branches and commits

Every repository has at least one branch, informally referred to as the **default branch**. Branches have formal names, and the default branch is almost always formally named **main** or **master**, with the former now generally preferred.

For reasons explained earlier, drawings of branches usually include arrows from each commit to the previous commit on the branch. In other words, the arrows point backward in time, from later branches to earlier branches. So, if your repository has one branch called **main** with three commits on it (called **A**, **B**, and **C**), and another branch called **branch-a** with two commits on it (called **D** and **E**), and **branch-a** branched off from **main**, you could draw your repository's state like this:

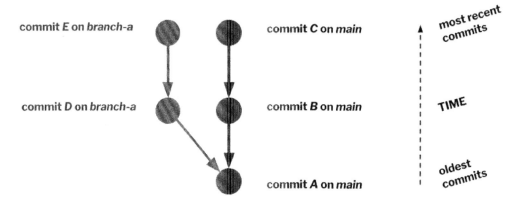

Figure 2.2 – Branches and commits

Why do you need branches? *They let you develop code that is safely isolated from the stable code base until it's ready to be added to that code base.* Here's a typical workflow to demonstrate how this happens:

1. Your product code lives in a Git repository. The stable version of that code lives in a branch within that repo called **main**.
2. You are assigned to write a feature for your product that lets users log in.
3. You create a branch called **login-feature**.
4. You switch to the **login-feature** branch.
5. You edit files and add one or more commits to that branch.
6. Other team members review the edits in those commits and give you feedback.
7. You add another commit that incorporates the feedback.
8. Your team lead approves your work, declaring that the login feature has been implemented properly. Your QA team may also sign off on your work.

9. You *merge* the **login-feature** branch into the **main** branch. This means that all the commits you made to the **login-feature** branch are now part of the **main** branch as well. Your login feature is now part of the product's main code base.

10. Since the **login-feature** branch has been merged and no longer serves any purpose, you can safely delete it.

The important thing to notice in this workflow is that while you were developing the login feature, your partially complete code was *not* available in the main code base (that is, in the **main** branch). Your incomplete code was safely separated from your product's stable code so that your code couldn't destabilize it. The login feature wasn't added to the main code base until it was formally reviewed, approved, and was passing all its tests. That's what we mean by saying that branches let you develop your code in an isolated environment, away from other developers' work and away from the stable code base.

This example involved just one developer, but typically, several developers will work on separate branches at the same time. For example, two developers might be working on branches to add new features (each on their own branches), and two other developers might be working on separate branches to fix bugs (each on their own branches). One particular developer may switch back and forth between multiple branches in a single day, as the focus of their work shifts from one task to another. The point is that branches are all separate from each other – when you're on one branch, you can't see or change code on the other branches until they are all eventually merged into the **main** branch.

Git commands for managing branches

Let's learn the Git commands that you need to follow the workflow described previously.

Here's how to create a new branch called `login-feature`:

```
$ git branch login-feature
```

This command shows a list of all the branches that exist in this repository, with an asterisk next to the branch that you're currently on:

```
$ git branch
```

There are two different commands you can use to switch to a different branch. They do the same thing, and you'll see both in use. In this case, they switch you to the `login-feature` branch:

```
$ git checkout login-feature
$ git switch login-feature
```

It takes two commands to merge one branch (called the *source branch*) into another branch (called the *target branch*) so that all the commits on the source branch become part of the target branch. To merge all the commits that are in `login-feature` into `main`, first, make sure you are on the *target* branch:

```
$ git checkout main
```

Then, perform the merge while specifying the *source* branch:

```
$ git merge login-feature
```

Some organizations like to keep all branches around forever as a matter of historical record, but most organizations ask you to delete a branch once you've merged it into `main`. Here's how to delete the `login-feature` branch:

```
$ git branch --delete -login-feature
```

If you haven't merged a branch before you try to delete it, Git will warn you and will *not* delete that branch. You can force the branch to be deleted (for example, if you've created an experimental branch and want to delete it without merging), like this:

```
$ git branch --delete --force experimental-branch
```

Handling merge conflicts

When you try to merge one branch into another, you will sometimes run into what's called a *merge conflict*. This means that someone else has edited the same lines of the same file that you have, and that they've already merged their branch into `main` before you got a chance to merge your branch into `main`. When you try to merge your branch, Git isn't sure whether to keep the edits made by the other developer or the edits that you're trying to merge.

To continue with your merge, you first need to resolve the merge conflict. There are several ways to do this. Many people find dedicated Git GUI tools such as Sourcetree (macOS and Windows) or Sublime Merge (Linux, macOS, and Windows) to be the easiest and most intuitive way to handle merge conflicts. Other people prefer to resolve merge conflicts manually, using Git terminal commands and a text editor. GitLab users have another option: you can use GitLab's built-in graphical merge conflict resolution tool. Regardless of what approach you take, you'll have to somehow tell Git which changes to accept, which changes to throw away, and when to continue with the merge.

Let's see how the GitLab merge conflict resolution tool works. Imagine that you're working on the `login.py` file on the `new-login-message` branch. After creating a merge request for that branch and committing some edits, you return to the merge request so that you can merge the branch, only to discover that the MR is blocked by a merge conflict:

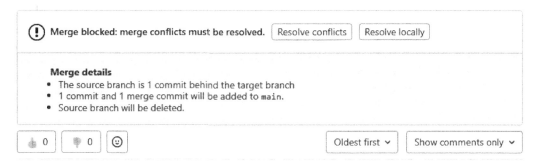

Figure 2.3 – Merge request blocked by a merge conflict

Since you only edited one file, you know that someone else must have edited the same lines of the same file and merged their edits into the `main` branch before you had a chance to do so yourself. Now, Git is understandably confused about whether to accept your edits, their edits, or some hybrid. Until that gets straightened out, it can't merge your `new-login-message` branch into `main`.

GitLab gives you two options to proceed: you can either click **Resolve conflicts** to use the built-in GUI tool to resolve the merge conflict, or you can click **Resolve locally** to manually instruct Git on how to handle the merge by editing files on your computer's copy of the repository and then pushing those edits back up to GitLab. The second of these strategies is beyond the scope of this book, so let's focus on the first strategy: using GitLab to resolve the merge conflict. Note that this option only appears in the GUI during simple merge conflicts such as the one in this example. If you need to resort to complicated edits to combine parts of two separate commits, you will probably need to resolve the merge conflict locally and then push the resolution back up to GitLab.

In this example, you will want to use GitLab's built-in merge conflict tool, so you must click **Resolve conflicts**. You will be taken to a page that shows which lines have conflicting edits. You will see that there's only one line with conflicting edits, with your edit highlighted in green and the edit already made by someone else highlighted in blue. Let's say you've changed the line "We're glad you're here" to "We're really glad you're here," whereas the existing edit changes the same line to "We're super glad you're here!".

Figure 2.4 – Resolving a merge conflict within GitLab

You decide that you like your edit better, so you click the **Use ours** button. This tells GitLab to keep your edit and throw away the existing, conflicting edit. After you enter a commit message and click **Commit to source branch**, GitLab creates a new commit on your `new-login-message` branch that resolves the merge conflict. This new commit triggers a pipeline run on your branch. Once that finishes, you're free to merge the MR just like you normally would. Congratulations – the merge conflict has been successfully resolved and the merge is complete!

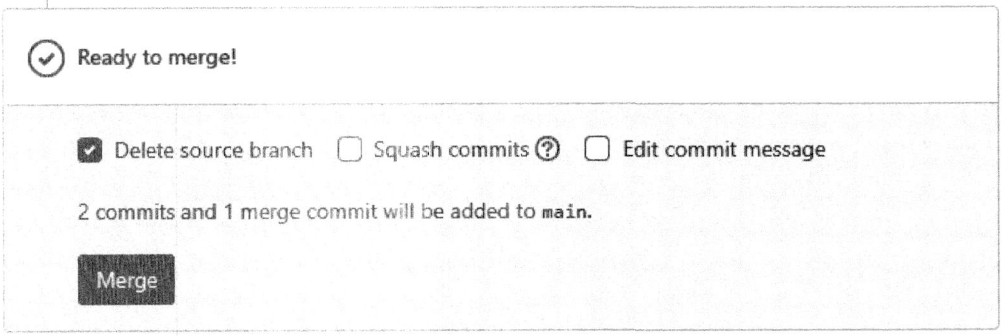

Figure 2.5 – Merge conflict is resolved and MR is unblocked

It would be irresponsible to pretend that all merge conflicts are as straightforward to resolve as this example, but the general approach remains the same no matter how complicated things get: you tell GitLab which edits to keep, which edits to throw away, and how to combine edits when you want to mix and match edits on the same line of code or text. Many third-party, GUI-based Git tools have more powerful merge conflict resolution tools than GitLab offers, so don't be afraid to try a different tool for this task if you find you need more firepower or just a different view of what's going on.

This concludes our explanation of creating, committing to, and merging branches. We hope you now have an idea of why branches are one of Git's most essential and popular features! But branches become even more powerful when you share them with other developers on your team, and when you can get access to branches that they've been working on. In the next section, you'll learn how to work collaboratively with branches.

Syncing local and remote copies of repositories

Git can be a useful tool for solo developers, but it's most often used within a team of developers. As we've already discussed, Git's distributed architecture means that every developer on the team has a complete copy of the project's repository, including all its commits, commit messages, branches, and all the other data and metadata that is included in a repository. Keeping these repositories synced, so that they all have the same information in them, is critically important. If my copy of the repository and your copy of the repository contain different files or different edits to the same files, then I can't see what work you've done and vice versa. And if my copy of the repository doesn't contain the branches that you're adding commits to, I can't review and approve your work. Synchronizing repositories isn't an automatic process: it involves active participation by the developers. This section will explain how to do this.

The "golden" repository

Before showing you the commands for syncing repositories, we need to partially retract something we said earlier. Remember how we explained that one of the advantages of Git's distributed architecture is that there's no central server that all developers need to talk to when doing their work? That's not strictly true. Git's distributed architecture does require every developer to have a complete copy of the project's repository, but the team needs to designate one of those repository copies as what we'll call the **golden** repository. That's the repository that is considered to contain the *latest version of the stable code base* and is the repository where your team releases software. I might be working on a feature on a branch on my computer, and you might be working on a bug fix on a branch on your computer, and we might have completed all of the edits needed to finish those tasks, but until we put our edits into the golden repository, they aren't officially part of the project's stable code base. Because of the special role that this golden repository has, I tend to think of it as a "first among equals" or the "repository of record."

The golden repository is the copy of the repository that lives on the GitLab instance. If your team of 20 developers uses GitLab, there will be at least 21 copies of your project's repository: one on each developer's computer and the golden copy on the GitLab instance. If the computer that hosts your GitLab instance is unavailable for some reason, you could temporarily designate the repository that's on any developer's computer as the team's golden repository. But you would want to revert to using the GitLab instance's copy as the golden repository as soon as it's available again.

When we talk about syncing edits between different copies of the repository, this syncing always happens via the GitLab instance. In other words, if I've made commits to the repository on my local computer and want to make them available to my coworkers, I would *not* send those commits directly to each of their computers. Instead, I would send my commits to the golden repository, and then each developer would retrieve my commits from the golden repository.

The following diagram shows a workflow that allows one developer to share their commits with another developer by pushing and pulling the branch that contains those commits to and from the golden repo:

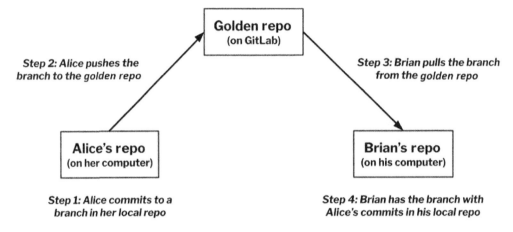

Figure 2.6 – Sharing commits with coworkers via the golden repo

Configuring remote repositories

Before you can sync your repository with the golden repository, Git needs to know that the golden repository exists. Any repository copy that's not on your local computer is called a "remote," so an important prerequisite for syncing commits is to configure remotes.

You can use the following command to see a list of the names and URLs for any remotes that Git knows about:

```
git remote --verbose
```

Earlier, we described two ways to get a repository onto your computer: `git init` and `git clone`. If you're in a repository that you created with `git init`, and you ask Git to give you a list of remotes, it will return no output. It doesn't know about any remotes yet, because you haven't told it about any. But if you copied a repository to your machine using `git clone`, then Git already knows about one remote: the copy of the repository that you cloned from.

Before we get ahead of ourselves, let's discuss how to clone a repository. As we mentioned previously, that's the most common way to get a repository onto your computer, so it's an important practice to be familiar with.

You can clone a repository from a computer that your local computer has network access to, but let's concentrate on cloning a repository that's hosted on a GitLab instance. This example assumes that the repository is hosted by the instance of GitLab that lives at www.gitlab.com. If you're using a self-hosted version of GitLab instead of the **Software-as-a-Service** (**SaaS**) version that we're using in this example, the cloning process is the same, except that the address of the repository you're cloning will look slightly different.

To clone a GitLab-hosted repository, you need to know the address of that repository. There are several forms this address can take, but the two most common forms use the **HTTPS** protocol or the **SSH** protocol. Although either protocol will work, using the SSH protocol is generally preferred. It requires you to configure SSH keys to get started, but then you never need to enter credentials when interacting with that remote: the key infrastructure takes care of all authentications automatically. The HTTPS protocol, on the other hand, requires you to enter a username and password every time you use a Git command that talks to that remote.

You've already seen how to create a repository for our Hats for Cats project using `git init`, but now, let's change gears and assume that there's already a Hats for Cats repository on a GitLab instance, and you want to clone that repository to your computer.

First, you need to create public and private SSH keys using the `ssh-keygen` command in your computer's terminal, and then upload the public key to your GitLab instance. GitLab has excellent documentation on how to do this that's available at https://docs.gitlab.com/ee/ssh, so we'll refer you to that instead of rehashing the instructions here. Note that you only have to do this process once, and then you'll be authenticated whenever you're interacting with any project on that GitLab instance from your same local computer. If you change to a different GitLab instance or a different local computer, you'll need to repeat the process.

Now, you need to find the SSH address of the project. Log in to GitLab and navigate to the project. We haven't formally introduced you to the GitLab GUI yet, so the instructions and the following screenshot may seem a little mysterious, but they'll make more sense later when you're more familiar with GitLab components and navigation.

On the main page for your project, as shown in *Figure 2.7,* click the **Clone** button. In the dropdown that appears, copy the address next to the **Clone with SSH** label:

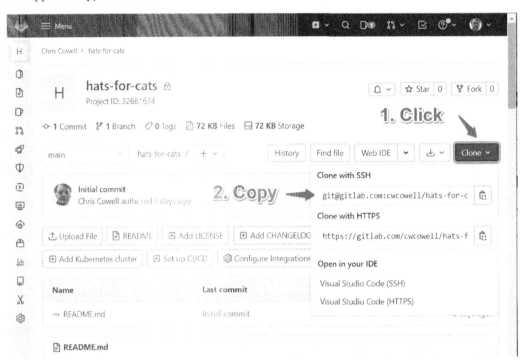

Figure 2.7 – Cloning a repository from GitLab

Now that you've set up a key pair and have the project's SSH address on your clipboard, navigate to the directory on the local filesystem that you want to contain the repository, and clone the remote repository to your computer using `git clone` and the repository's SSH address. Your SSH address will look different from the one shown here:

```
$ cd ~/code
$ git clone git@gitlab.com:cwcowell/hats-for-cats.git
```

The process of cloning defines a remote repository for you: it lets your local copy of the repo know that a remote copy exists at whatever URL you cloned it from. You can see this remote copy listed in the output of `git remote --verbose`:

```
$ git remote --verbose
origin   git@gitlab.com:cwcowell/hats-for-cats.git (fetch)
origin   git@gitlab.com:cwcowell/hats-for-cats.git (push)
```

Here, two remotes have been defined: the first is for getting other people's commits, while the other is for sending your commits. Don't worry about the distinction between these two; you can think of them as a single remote. You'll also notice the word "origin" in the output. The golden copy of any repo is usually referred to as the "origin," for reasons known only to the designers of Git.

If you created a repository using `git init` instead of `git clone`, you'll need to create a Git project and repository on your GitLab instance to serve as the remote repository; then, you can use the `git remote add` command to let your local repo know that this remote repo exists. Because this is a much less common workflow than using `git clone`, we'll let you look up the syntax for this command if you ever need it.

Pushing

So far, we've used the word "send" to describe the process of copying your local commits to the golden repo. But the official Git term is "push." And the command you use to push commits is, unsurprisingly, `git push`.

Let's go back to the scenario where you created a branch on your local repository called **login-feature**. Imagine that you've added a few commits to that branch and now, you want to push that branch up to the golden repository on the GitLab instance so that your teammates can look at the branch and the commits you made to it. To do this, make sure you're in the branch you want to push, and then push it.

Before we show you the command for that, we should explain that there's one wrinkle whenever you push a branch to a remote repository *for the first time*: you must tell the remote repository what to name its copy of your branch. Almost always, you will want the remote copy of the branch to have the same name as the local copy of the branch. The remote copy of your branch on the golden repo is sometimes informally called the "upstream" branch. To tell the remote repo to name the upstream branch `login-feature`, change to the branch you want to push, and then pass a few extra options to `git push`:

```
$ git switch login-feature
$ git push --set-upstream origin login-feature
```

Notice that the word `origin` is included in these options. This tells Git which remote to push to, even though you only have one remote defined at this point. Also, it's important to understand that you only have to set the upstream branch name once. From that point on, you can just run `git push` without any additional options to push the commits of your current branch up to the remote golden copy of the repo.

Fetching

So far, you've seen how to push your edits up to the golden repo so that your coworkers can see them. But how do you get their edits into your local repo? The first command you need to know is `git fetch`. This command talks to the golden repo and finds out if anyone has pushed any new branches or commits to existing branches up to the golden repo. Then, it relays that information to your local repository. *It does not update any branches or files on your local computer.* It simply collects metadata about any edits that have been made on the golden repo and tells your local repo about them, without making any changes to your local repo. This means that `git fetch` is a non-destructive, completely safe command that you can run whenever you want, as often as you want.

This command is useful because it lets you know if your branch is "behind" the golden repo's copy of that branch: is it missing commits that are on the golden repo's copy of the branch? This lets you know if you may experience a merge conflict if you try to push your changes up to the golden repo. If someone else has already changed the same files on the same branch on the golden repo, there's no way you could know that unless you use `git fetch` to learn about changes that have happened there. So, if you're wondering whether you've got all the latest edits on a branch, or you want to know if anyone has added any brand-new branches to the golden repo, `git fetch` is the way to get that information.

It's worth repeating that `git fetch` gives you up-to-date information about the state of branches on the golden repo, but it doesn't update any files on your local computer. To update your local files, you need to learn about one final Git command.

Pulling

To replace all the files on a local branch with updated versions of those files that may exist on the golden repo's copy of that branch, switch to the appropriate branch and then *pull* the changes:

```
$ git switch login-feature
$ git pull
```

If any edits have been made to that branch since you last ran `git pull`, Git will replace any local files on that branch with updated files from the golden repo's copy of that same branch.

Remember that `git pull` only operates on one branch at a time. That is, it will only grab updated files from the golden repo *for the branch that you're currently on*. There's no way to grab all the edits from all the branches with a single use of `git pull`, but there's also no obvious reason why you'd want to.

Let's combine all the sync-related Git commands into a single workflow, to show you how you would keep your copy of the project's repository in sync with the golden copy of the repository:

1. On your local computer, use `git switch` to switch to the branch that you want to do your work on.
2. Use `git fetch` to grab information about whether the golden repo's copy of your branch has any new edits.
3. Run `git status` to see if your local branch is "behind" the golden repo's copy of the same branch.
4. If it is, update your local files with `git pull`.

5. Make and commit edits to the local copy of the branch.
6. Send all the commits on your local copy of the branch up to the golden copy of the branch with `git push`.

Having completed this explanation of syncing repository branches, you're now equipped with all you need to know to do real work with Git! But if you find that you need to learn about concepts and commands we haven't covered here, or if you'd like to see these same topics addressed with different explanations and examples, there are plenty of other places you can look for more information. Now, let's take a look at some of the best alternative resources.

Additional resources for learning Git

A word of caution is needed at this point. You've only seen the most basic usages of the Git commands introduced in this chapter. There are *many* options available to change the behavior of these commands, and there are many different wrinkles and nuances to using them correctly in different situations. We've already mentioned that the important concept of resolving merge conflicts is beyond the scope of this lightning-fast introduction to Git, but some other important concepts and practices are likely to crop up in daily Git usage that we don't have space to cover here, including **rebasing** and choosing between **fast-forward merges** and **commit merges**. We also can't describe common troubleshooting processes when you find your files in an unwanted or unfamiliar condition while using Git. What we can do, however, is point you to some other resources that you can use to continue to expand your knowledge of Git and your repertoire of Git commands and practices.

With that in mind, here are our favorite Git references and learning materials:

- GitLab has a very good four-page PDF cheat sheet that covers the most common Git concepts and commands. This is the first place we look when we need to remember how a basic command works: `https://about.gitlab.com/images/press/git-cheat-sheet.pdf`.
- *Ry's Git Tutorial*, by Ryan Hodson, is a fantastic tutorial for learning Git or refreshing your knowledge of its commands and concepts. It's only available as a free Kindle ebook on Amazon.
- *Pro Git*, by Scott Chacon and Ben Straub, is too dense and dry to use as a tutorial, but it is a good reference. It's where we turn when we need to look up an exotic command or find out all the options available for a common command such as `git commit`. It's a free ebook available on the Git website: `https://git-scm.com/book/en/v2`.
- *Dangit Git!?!* is a website that shows you how to get out of a dozen or so of the most common Git jams. When we've made a mistake with Git commands and need to fix what we broke, this is where we look for guidance: `https://dangitgit.com/`.

Remember that there's no way you can learn or remember all of Git's commands and options. We believe that it's best to learn a handful of commands that you use every day, and then look up the additional commands and syntax for more complicated operations only as the need arises. A reference source such as *Pro Git* or the Git man pages will dazzle you with all the different ways you can configure these commands to make them work differently, and with all the additional commands that Git provides for unlocking the tool's advanced features. But only wade into those waters if you want to; there's no need to understand all the commands or options available to use Git productively. Even if you could somehow learn all of Git, the effort required would be far beyond the point of diminishing returns. Get comfortable with the concepts and commands presented here, practice with throwaway repositories, dip into reference sources as needed, and you'll be all set to be a happy and effective Git user.

Summary

Pause, take a deep breath, and pat yourself on the back. You've learned a lot about a complicated tool in a very short time.

You now understand how and why programmers use VCSs to handle a wide variety of daily tasks and problems, and why Git's features and architecture have helped it become the preferred VCS. You also know about the most used Git concepts and commands.

Now that you've completed this chapter, you can create new Git repositories using `git init` and `git clone`; add file edits with `git add` and `git commit`; tag commits for future reference with `git tag`; list, create, or delete branches with `git branch`; merge branches with `git merge` and resolve any merge conflicts that arise; and sync local branches with branches on the golden repo with `git push`, `git fetch`, and `get pull`.

You also know where to look to learn more about Git, whether you need tutorial steps, reference material, or troubleshooting help.

With this background in Git under your belt, it's time to move from Git to GitLab. In the next chapter, you'll learn how GitLab can make Git easier and more powerful. We'll give you a basic understanding of GitLab's components and GUI so that we can introduce you to the powerful concept of GitLab CI/CD pipelines.

3
Understanding GitLab Components

GitLab is a huge, complicated web app that aims to be a "one-stop shop" for making every step of the software development life cycle easier: it helps you to plan, create, test, secure, and deploy software. And those are just the big tasks it covers! It also helps you track progress using a variety of workflows, document projects, create release notes, store Docker images or other types of software packages, host static web pages, monitor the performance of deployed applications, and watch for suspicious network traffic within Kubernetes clusters. This list could be much longer, but you get the picture: *GitLab helps with most of the tasks involved in the standard software development life cycle.*

In *Chapter 1*, we articulated key problems in the software development life cycle that GitLab was designed to solve. Now, we'll introduce you to the key GitLab concepts and components that you'll need to be familiar with in order to use it effectively. Once you understand these building blocks, you'll be ready to start the work of setting up CI/CD pipelines, which we will begin to address in *Chapter 4*.

In this chapter, we'll discuss projects, groups, issues, branches, and merge requests. We'll then bring those GitLab components to life by showing you how to create, manage, and use some of those concepts in the application's GUI. When you're comfortable with these fundamentals, you'll learn how to use **GitLab flow**, which is a best practice workflow recommended by GitLab's developers for effectively combining the tool's various building blocks as you write, test, secure, and deploy software.

This is how the main topics appear in the chapter:

- Emphasizing the "why" over the "how"
- Introducing the GitLab platform
- Organizing work into projects and groups
- Tracking work with issues
- Editing files safely with commits, branches, and merge requests
- Enabling DevOps practices with GitLab flow

Technical requirements

You'll benefit most from this chapter if you're able to follow along by logging into an account on a GitLab instance. This account can be an account on the instance hosted at `gitlab.com` (also known as a **Software-as-a-Service** (**SaaS**) instance), or an account on an instance hosted by your company (known as a self-managed, a self-hosted, or an on-premises instance). You could even host GitLab on your own hardware at home or on a virtual machine in the cloud, using a service such as AWS EC2, Google Cloud Platform, or Microsoft Azure.

Hosting your own instance is not as far-fetched as it sounds, thanks to surprisingly low hardware requirements—you can even host GitLab on a Raspberry Pi!—and a variety of "Omnibus" Linux packages that contain everything you need for an entire GitLab instance. We'll refer you to the GitLab installation documentation at `https://about.gitlab.com/install` for more information if you want to go down this path.

If you'd prefer to let someone else take care of installation, administration, and upgrade tasks for you, head over to `https://gitlab.com` and sign up for a free account on their SaaS platform. Although there are minor feature differences between the SaaS and self-managed varieties of GitLab, they are so small that we won't discuss them in this book. For all intents and purposes, the feature sets of SaaS GitLab and self-managed GitLab are identical.

As of early 2023, GitLab has three **product tiers**: Free, Premium, and Ultimate. The first of these tiers is open source and free for everyone to use. It also has the most limited feature set. The Premium tier requires a paid license but adds some extra features. The Ultimate tier costs more than Premium but unlocks the entire GitLab feature set. These tiers apply to both SaaS and self-managed installations.

This book will discuss some features that are available in the Free tier, some that are available only in the Premium and Ultimate tiers, and some that are only unlocked with an Ultimate license. If you are on a budget, don't worry. GitLab has plenty of functionality to improve your life as a software developer, even with the lower tiers. Many people find the Free tier to be all they ever need, especially if they mainly use GitLab for personal hobby projects.

Emphasizing the "why" over the "how"

Before we get started, a word of warning. For the most part, this book will not lead you through step-by-step instructions on what to click in the GitLab GUI in order to perform various operations.

First, instructions for most operations are already well covered in GitLab's official documentation, which is remarkably clear and thorough.

Second, because GitLab is in rapid development, its GUI often changes. These changes are rarely radical, workflow-breaking changes, but they are significant enough that screenshots, or even bullet-pointed instructions for how to perform operations, can quickly get stale. This means that any concrete instructions in this book could become confusing or impossible to follow, or potentially even lead to data loss, as the GitLab GUI drifts over time. To avoid that problem, we'll mostly focus on *why* you might want to use different GitLab features. Although we'll give you a general picture of *how* to use those features, we usually won't provide detailed instructions for every configuration option or workflow.

Introducing the GitLab platform

What is GitLab?

The company called GitLab makes a single product: a web application that is also called GitLab. Behind the scenes, the GitLab web application is a complicated collection of tools, databases, queues, and glue code holding it all together, but as far as the user is concerned, it's just a single, web-based tool for building software.

> **Different Meanings of "GitLab"**
> Throughout this book, the term "GitLab" refers to the tool rather than the company, unless we explicitly say otherwise.

As we discussed in the first chapter, GitLab's single-tool model is much easier to install, administer, and upgrade than any collection of separate, more focused tools. It requires only a single set of credentials per user. It offers a consistent GUI for all of its features. It integrates all the software development life cycle tools, allowing data to flow smoothly and without loss or distortion from one feature to the next. It provides a single location to learn about the status of your software as you plan, build, test, secure, and deploy it. To top it all off, it's a lot cheaper than buying separate licenses for a collection of separate tools. And if you find that any of GitLab's individual features don't give you the flexibility or power that you need, you can almost always integrate other tools with GitLab to make it suit your technical needs and preferred workflow.

What problem does GitLab solve?

The purpose of GitLab—the problem it aims to solve—has shifted and broadened over the years. It was created in 2011 with a narrow focus: it wanted to make Git both easier to use and more powerful. In those days, it was not much more than a web-based GUI wrapper around Git and a centralized place to store projects' golden Git repositories.

Since then, GitLab has widened its scope. It now aims not just at Git but at the entire software development life cycle.

To get a sense of how its mission has grown, you first need to understand Gitlab's concept of "stages" in the software development life cycle. GitLab recognizes 10 stages:

- **Manage**: Create audit and compliance reports, and restrict access to resources.

- **Plan**: Divide work into workable chunks that you can prioritize, weight, and assign to team members.
- **Create**: Commit, review, and approve file edits, whether they contain code, configuration information, or other assets.
- **Verify**: Run automated tests to make sure your software does what it's supposed to.
- **Package**: Bundle your software into a deployable format.
- **Secure**: Find any security vulnerabilities in your software or its dependencies.
- **Release**: Deploy your software, optionally using sophisticated techniques such as feature flags and canary deployments.
- **Configure**: Set up the environments where your code will be deployed.
- **Monitor**: Report on performance metrics, incidents, or errors.
- **Protect**: Detect potential security problems in deployment environments such as Kubernetes clusters.

Note that there's nothing magical about this division of the software development life cycle into stages. Another company might have divided it into 9 or 13 stages and might have drawn the boundaries between stages slightly differently. But GitLab's division probably seems reasonable to anyone who has been involved in software development.

Let's return to the question of what problem GitLab aims to solve. Since its humble beginnings as a solution to the difficulties of using Git (that is, early GitLab focused exclusively on the Create stage described previously), it now addresses problems faced by practitioners of all 10 of these software development life cycle stages. Because different stages present different problems, it's hard to give a succinct description of the single problem GitLab is targeting. In fact, it's probably impossible considering that GitLab now targets a myriad of problems from all 10 stages. The shortest, best answer we can give to the question of why GitLab exists is this: *it helps people write better software, more efficiently, and with less risk.*

We're the first to admit that GitLab is not yet equally effective at addressing the problems of all 10 stages. That is to say, some of the features that GitLab offers as solutions to various problems are more mature or more robust than others. As you might expect, the GitLab features that have been around the longest (such as the Git-related functionality) are generally the most mature, and more recently developed features (such as protecting your application from suspicious traffic within a Kubernetes cluster) are significantly more minimal. But GitLab is very transparent about its own assessment of the relative maturity of its solutions to the problems of the various stages, and which features it intends to focus on developing and improving in the near future. So, if you're particularly curious about how full-featured GitLab's solution to a particular software development life cycle problem is, a quick Google search for "GitLab maturity" will probably give you all the information you need to make an informed decision about whether GitLab offers enough power and flexibility to address the problems that trouble you the most.

At this point, you might be wondering how GitLab can compete with specialized tools that focus on just one of the software development life cycle stages. After all, can a single tool really replace a suite of 10 separate tools, each of which is considered "best in breed" for their problem domain?

First, you might find that you don't need as many features or as much power as you initially think you do. One of the authors of this book once took a full-day training course on a Java performance profiling tool. He left the training with his head spinning from all the fantastic features the product offered and the detailed performance bottleneck reports that he would soon be able to present to his manager. But, it turned out his company only needed 2% of the power of that tool and could have gotten away with using a much simpler and cheaper alternative instead. The moral of this story? *GitLab might give you all the power you need, no matter which software development life cycle stage you're concerned with.*

Second, some of GitLab's features are the result of integrating independently developed open source tools that truly are the best tools available for the problems they address. For example, many of GitLab's security vulnerability scanners are highly regarded open source tools. It's true that you could download and use these tools outside of GitLab, but GitLab makes it trivial to enable them in your workflow, and it integrates their output into existing GitLab dashboards in a familiar, easy-to-read format that's consistent with all of GitLab's other reports.

Finally, if you really do find that you need more than GitLab offers to solve a particular software development life cycle problem, you can almost always find a way to integrate outside tools into your GitLab workflow. Some of these integrations are explicitly supported by GitLab, and as a result, have virtually seamless results. Other integrations require more work on your part. But, virtually any tool that you can run from an operating system's command line can be integrated into GitLab. Results may vary, but the number of tools that can't talk to GitLab at all is vanishingly small.

The verify, secure, and release stages

Now that we've established that GitLab has ambitious goals for helping with all 10 stages of the software development life cycle, let's scale things back a bit. This chapter focuses on the middle of the SDLC: the **verify**, **secure**, and **release** stages. These are among the most commonly used stages when writing software, and among the most problematic for all the reasons described in *Chapter 1*. Fortunately, they are also the stages at which GitLab is most effective, and the feature it uses to solve the problems posed by those stages is, as you might guess, CI/CD pipelines. Now you know why so much of this book focuses on exactly that topic!

To understand how GitLab can help with the problems found in those three stages, you'll need to know about a few concepts, terms, and GitLab components. Fortunately, everything you're about to learn in the rest of this chapter will be relevant and useful to many of the other Gitlab stages as well. So, once you understand how to use these concepts, you'll not only be able to move on to understanding GitLab CI/CD pipelines but you'll also be better equipped to understand how GitLab tackles other SDLC stages that are not discussed in this book.

The rest of this chapter will focus on introducing those concepts, terms, and components. Let's dive in, starting with a GitLab component called a **project**.

Organizing work into projects and groups

Projects are the fundamental building blocks of GitLab. A GitLab project represents a single software product that you are working on or a single non-software project that you are working on. Projects are where you store your files, and they are the starting point for navigating GitLab's different features. In short, projects are where you spend most of your time as a GitLab user.

Here are some examples of typical projects, and who might use them:

- A mobile phone app for finding a nearby car wash, used by development team #1
- A desktop version of the same car wash app, used by development team #2
- The documentation used by the technical writing team
- An upcoming conference, used by the event planning team
- Onboarding tasks for new employees, used by the entire company

As you can see, some of these examples are software-related, but others have nothing to do with software. You can use projects to plan, manage, and track the progress of any kind of work. Although it's true that most GitLab projects are focused on developing software, your company might find many non-technical uses for projects as well.

There's no hard-and-fast rule for how to chop up your work into projects. For example, one company might decide to put all its documentation in a separate, documentation-specific project as described in the previous example. Another company might include the documentation files for each software product within the projects created for those products. Use whatever structure works best for you. Often, this requires some trial-and-error experimentation, so don't be afraid to rejigger your use of projects.

It's easiest to understand what a project is by seeing a picture of one. It won't surprise you to know that GitLab is developed using GitLab tools. Here's the project for the open source portion of GitLab:

Organizing work into projects and groups   61

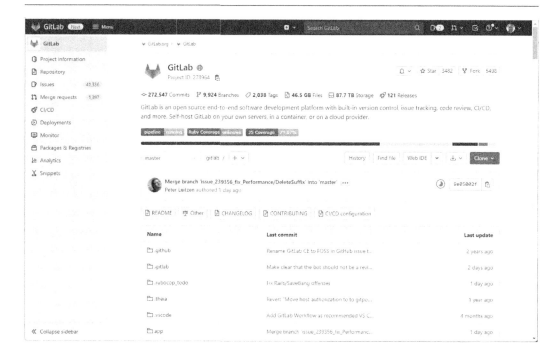

Figure 3.1 – The project for GitLab's open source code

As you can see, the list of files takes up the largest part of a project's screen. What might not be obvious from the screenshot is that those files are actually a Git repository.

You can think of a GitLab project as being a "wrapper" around a Git repository. Furthermore, you can consider the repository that lives in GitLab to be the "golden" copy of the repository, as discussed in *Chapter 2*. Because a project contains a Git repository, the project also gives you access to all the other things that a Git repository normally contains, including Git commits, Git tags, and Git branches. We'll talk about how to view these components later in this chapter.

Sometimes, you'll find that you have a collection of projects that all hang together in some way. Here are some typical examples:

- Projects that all belong to the same team
- Projects for macOS and Windows versions of the same software
- Projects that are all related to database management

When this happens, you can use a **GitLab group** to gather those related projects so they all exist in a single place within GitLab. You can think of GitLab groups as being similar to directories or folders that hold collections of projects.

GitLab groups aren't limited to holding GitLab projects: they can also hold other GitLab groups. You can have up to 20 levels of these subgroups within a GitLab group. You're encouraged to use these subgroups in any way you want to organize your projects into related collections.

Here's a sample structure of groups, subgroups, and projects that might help you understand the relationship between the three concepts. Imagine that there's a company called Acme Anvils, whose IT team oversees developing software for selling its anvils. It also makes separate software that's used for internal purposes such as inventory management. Their group hierarchy might look like this:

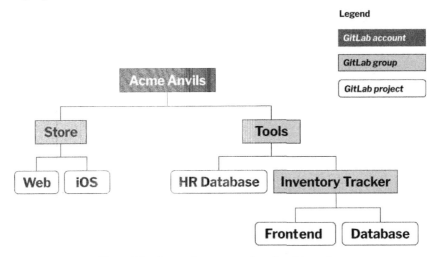

Figure 3.2 – A sample group and project hierarchy

Groups are more than just a way to collect related projects. You can also use them to establish roles and permissions. Using groups, you can do the following:

- Invite other GitLab users to be members of a group.
- Assign them a role within that group.
- Grant a user, group, or role permission to view or edit any projects within that group.

Thus, groups provide a simple way to regulate access control to several users at once.

A group will also roll up components from all the projects within that group. For example, you can go to a single screen to see all the issues in all of the projects within a group.

But, groups don't have to be complicated, and you don't have to use all of their features. They're a great way to simply collect related projects into a single place.

Enough theory about projects, groups, and subgroups. Now, it's time to see those concepts in action.

Example – organizing your Hats for Cats work

Cast your mind all the way back to *Chapter 1*, where we introduced your idea for a Hats for Cats web store. It's time to get serious about setting up GitLab to help you develop that software.

Let's say that you decide that Hats for Cats needs to exist in three different forms: a web app, an iOS app, and an Android app. You decide that although some of the logic will be similar between these three products, there are enough implementation differences so that each deserves its own project.

(Reminder: this chapter won't tell you how to create, edit, or view projects or groups. As discussed at the start of this chapter, the official GitLab documentation is your best source of information for step-by-step instructions for working with any GitLab components or using the GUI. This chapter—and in fact the entire book—focuses on the *why* rather than the *how*.)

Because iOS and Android are both mobile platforms, you decide that it makes sense to collect those under a single group dedicated to mobile development. Then, you decide to collect that group, together with the web app project, under an umbrella group that comprises your entire Hats for Cats concept. Finally, you decide it makes sense to provide online documentation that is entirely platform-agnostic: it should apply equally to the iOS, Android, and web versions of the app. Because it isn't tied to any of the existing projects, you want to create a new project just to hold the documentation.

To realize this structure in GitLab, it's often easiest to work from the top down, starting with groups and finishing with projects. You start by logging in to GitLab and creating the top-level **Hats for Cats** group, using all the default settings. (If you'd like to follow along, please take a look at the official GitLab documentation for explicit instructions on how to do this.) When that's done, GitLab takes you to the home page for that group. Now you decide to create a subgroup called **Mobile** within the **Hats for Cats** group.

Now, it's time to create the projects. (Again, GitLab documentation can explain the exact process for doing this, but fortunately, it's very simple.) Imagine that you do the following in order to begin working on Hats for Cats:

1. Make a project called **Documentation** inside the **Hats for Cats** group.
2. Make a project called **Web** inside the **Hats for Cats** group.
3. Make a project called **iOS** inside the **Mobile** subgroup.
4. Make a project called **Android** inside the **Mobile** subgroup.

When you're done, you end up with a group and project structure that looks like this:

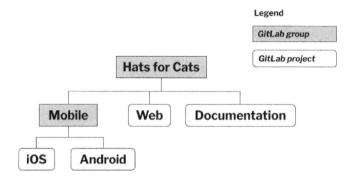

Figure 3.3 – Hats for Cats group and project hierarchy

Let's do a quick review before moving on:

- A project gives you a Git repository in which you can store your code.
- A project is also the central place from which you'll do most of your work in GitLab.
- Several related projects can be collected within a group.
- Groups can hold projects, other groups, or both.
- By organizing your projects within groups and possibly subgroups, you can keep them well organized and easy to find, but you also gain the ability to assign permissions to other team members at the group level and have those permissions apply to all projects within the group.

Time to move on to the next fundamental building block of GitLab: **issues**.

Tracking work with issues

If a GitLab project is where a single product or initiative lives, a GitLab **issue** is where a single chunk of work lives. If you've used tools other than GitLab for planning and tracking work, you might have run across terms such as "story" or "ticket" to describe components that are similar to GitLab issues.

Issues live within GitLab projects, with each issue only belonging to one project (although they can be moved between projects). In addition to being linked to projects, issues are also linked to a huge number of other GitLab components, as you'll see when we introduce you to those components. In fact, these linkages are a big part of what gives GitLab its power to reach across all 10 stages of the SDLC.

The structure of a GitLab issue

GitLab issues consist of several parts, of which these four are the most important:

- A **title**
- A **description**
- Several optional **metadata** fields
- A threaded **discussion**, where team members can comment on the issue

Let's look at each of these issue components in more detail.

The title is a short description of what the issue is about. For example, `Add a FAQ page`, `Fix bug #12`, or `Improve page load performance by 20%` are all reasonable issue titles. You don't need to provide all the details about a feature in its title; that's what the **description** field is for.

The **Description** field can contain as little or as much text as you want. It can contain screenshots or links, and it makes full use of Markdown's formatting features. It can also be edited later as more information comes to light or the exact direction of the issue changes.

Issues have several metadata fields. We won't go over all of them, but here are some of the most important ones:

- **Assignee**: This field identifies the person or persons who own the issue, in the sense that they're responsible for pushing it forward and serving as a point of contact if people have questions or comments about the issue that they don't want to add to the issue's discussion section.
- **Due date**: There are several ways to use due dates in GitLab, but the most straightforward is to assign a due date directly to an issue.
- **Labels**: We'll discuss these in more detail later, but they serve to prioritize, route, or report on the progress of an issue, among other uses.
- **Weight**: This field describes how much work you expect the issue to require. If you're familiar with the Scrum method of project management, you've used the similar concept of "story points." When assigning a weight to an issue, you can either use a concrete metric (for example, person-hours) or a more abstract metric (for example, tiny tasks get one point, medium tasks get two points, and large tasks get three points). Every team has their own philosophy about this, which they develop with time and experience.

In addition to these explicit metadata fields, there's another important piece of metadata about the issue: whether it is open or closed. Every issue starts with a status of **Open**. When someone completes the work required by an issue, they will normally change its status to **Closed**.

Finally, every issue has a discussion section that lets people participate in threaded discussions, as you'd find on Facebook or Instagram. Because it's threaded, people can reply to individual messages, or they can add entirely new messages. Discussions can include emojis, links, or images.

Since a picture is worth a thousand words, here's a sample issue from your Hats for Cats project:

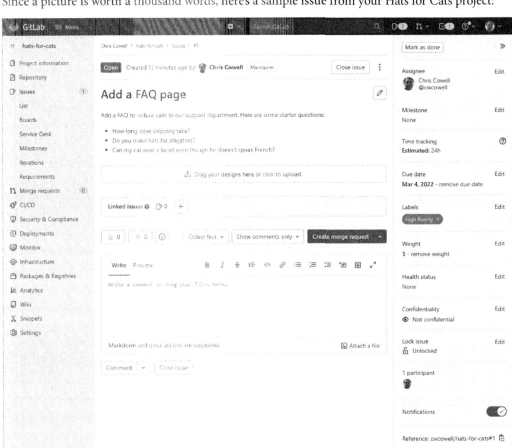

Figure 3.4 – Sample issue

Most projects contain many issues, with both **Open** and **Closed** statuses. GitLab makes it easy to see a list of all the issues in a project and to zoom in on any issues in the list to see the full details of that issue. You can also look at a list of issues from a group level instead of a project level. This view shows a list of all the issues that belong to any of the projects within that group. So, if you want to know how many issues are left to work on for both the iOS and Android versions of the Hats for Cats app, you can go up a level from the individual projects and look at a list of all the issues that have the **Open** status within the **Mobile** group.

The kinds of tasks that issues can represent

You might think that issues are only used to capture work related to software development, but that's just the tip of the issue iceberg. Let's look at the broad range of tasks that you can describe and track with a GitLab issue:

- Add a feature.
- Fix a bug.
- Write automated tests.
- Set up a database.
- Configure a tool for the whole team to use.
- Research technical options.
- Brainstorm solutions to a problem.
- Plan an event.
- Poll the team about preferences for coding standards.
- Report and manage a security incident.
- Propose an idea for a new product or a new feature.
- Ask a question that anyone can provide an opinion on.
- Request T-shirt designs for an upcoming corporate outing.

Of course, there are many more possible uses for issues than are included in this short list. As you can see, they can be used for technical or non-technical work, and they can be used by a single person or an entire company.

To give one more possibly unexpected example, every new hire at GitLab is assigned an issue that includes *Welcome to the company* text and a long list of onboarding tasks for them to complete and check off. The employee's manager and the company's human resources department monitor this issue during the employee's first few weeks to see how they are progressing through the onboarding process. Later, after onboarding is complete and the issue has been closed, the employee can use the issue as a reference source for company policies and procedures.

Labels

Before explaining how you might realistically use issues, we need to introduce you to **labels**. These are colored tags containing a short bit of text. You can apply labels to issues or other GitLab components, such as merge requests (which we'll discuss later), and remove them when they are no longer useful. You can define whatever labels you need for your project or group, and you can always add more labels or delete existing labels. Then, you can apply one or more labels to an issue to "mark" that issue with the contents of the label.

Here are some examples of commonly created labels:

- **High Priority**: Indicates an issue that needs to be worked on immediately
- **QA**: Indicates an issue that is the responsibility of the quality assurance team
- **Status::Healthy**: Indicates an issue that is progressing according to the schedule
- **Status::At Risk**: Indicates an issue that has fallen behind and needs extra resources to be assigned to it

Notice that the last two labels have double colons inside their descriptive text. The double colons have a special meaning: they turn these labels into **scoped labels**, which means they are mutually exclusive. That is, an issue can have the **Status::Healthy** label or the **Status::At Risk** label applied to it, but not both. Non-scoped labels—labels that don't contain a double colon—can be applied in any combination to any issue. For example, you could apply both the **Front-end** and **DB** labels to an issue that needs work from both your frontend developer and your database administrator.

GitLab uses hundreds of issues to prioritize, route, assign responsibility, and track work as it develops the GitLab product itself, so don't be afraid to make and apply whatever issues you need; they're free to create and easy to manage.

Issue workflows

As with many GitLab components, there's no single workflow for using issues that works well for every team in every situation. You're encouraged to experiment and discover the best way to use issues for yourself considering your needs and team culture. But, we can present a *typical* workflow for issues, which you can use as a starting point when exploring possibilities for working with GitLab issues.

Here's a sample workflow for one of your Hats for Cats projects:

1. *Think up some work that needs to be done and figure out which project that work belongs to.* For example, as part of the Hats for Cats iOS project, you need to research the Objective-C and Swift programming languages to figure out which you should use for writing the iOS app.

2. *Create an issue in that project and describe the work inside that issue.* You create an issue titled `Research languages for iOS` and add a description of the possible languages and your initial feelings about which might be the best to choose.

3. *Add a weight to the issue.* You decide to use a metric of the total person-days expected and assign this issue a weight of two.

4. *Set a due date for the issue.* You set the issue to be due in 3 days.

5. *Assign labels to prioritize and route the issue.* You assign the **iOS** and **High Priority** labels to the issue. The former ensures that the right people monitor it, and the latter indicates that work on the issue needs to begin immediately.

6. *Discuss the issue.* People who are working on the Hats for Cats iOS app chime in with their past experiences with the different iOS languages. Other people ask clarifying questions. Someone adds links to outside blog posts that discuss Swift and Objective-C. You add a screenshot of a language comparison table from a developer-focused website.

7. *Assign the issue.* In the discussion, you ask your most experienced developer whether they're willing to tackle this task. When they agree, you assign the issue to them so that everyone knows that they're responsible for working on this issue and updating its progress.

8. *Update labels.* As work progresses, the person to whom you assigned the issue updates its labels. For example, they might remove the **High Priority** label once it's underway, and add a **Status::At Risk** scoped label when they realize that they're unlikely to complete the research by the issue's due date.

9. *Close the issue when it is complete.* The developer to whom the issue was assigned completes their research and posts their findings in the issue's discussion section. Then they close it, signifying that no more work remains to be done on the issue.

This wraps up your introduction to GitLab issues. You've seen what kinds of work you can describe in an issue, what data goes into an issue, and what workflow you might use when working on an issue. It's hard to be an effective GitLab user without creating and using lots of issues, so it's a great idea to practice creating, viewing, and editing issues as you get comfortable with GitLab.

Editing files safely with commits, branches, and merge requests

In the last chapter, you learned about using branches and commits in Git, where a branch is a series of commits, and a commit is a snapshot that consists of edits to one or more files. Because GitLab is in some senses a wrapper around a Git repository (although of course, it's much more than that), branches and commits are also an important part of using GitLab. There's a third, related concept that you'll use frequently in GitLab: the **merge request** (often referred to as an **MR**). In this section, we'll explain what an MR is and show you how to work with all three components in GitLab.

GitLab often gives you more than one way to do something, and that's true of working with commits and branches. You can either type commands into a terminal or use the GitLab GUI to perform most of the operations you're likely to need for these two components. Because MRs are a concept that's specific to GitLab and not Git, you'll see that MRs require you to use the GitLab GUI.

Before you can commit edits to a branch, you need to create the branch. Thinking back to the last chapter, you'll remember that you can make a branch with the `git branch <BRANCH-NAME>` command followed by some form of the `git push` command to copy your branch up to the golden copy of your project's repository. Alternatively, you can work primarily in the GUI by creating a new branch right inside GitLab and then copying that branch to your local copy of the repository (assuming you have a local copy) with a combination of `git fetch` and some form of `git pull`. Because the exact command depends on your situation, you should consult your favorite dedicated Git reference material for full information.

Although normally we won't lead you through explicit instructions for using the GitLab GUI, creating branches, commits, and MRs is so fundamental to working effectively with GitLab that we'll give you an overview of exactly how to work with these through the GUI.

Let's start by creating a branch. Because a branch is a part of a Git repository, and a GitLab project is nothing more than a GitLab repository with a ton of extra features, it makes sense to create a branch within a GitLab project. For example, imagine that you want to add an `allow-password-change` branch to the Hats for Cats Android app so your developers can add a feature that lets users manage their passwords.

Here's how to add that branch:

1. Navigate through your group structure and open the **Android** project.
2. In the navigation pane on the left-hand side of the page, click **Repository** > **Branches**. This takes you to a list of branches that exist in the project's repository.
3. Click the **New branch** button, fill in the branch's name, hit the **Create branch** button, and you're done:

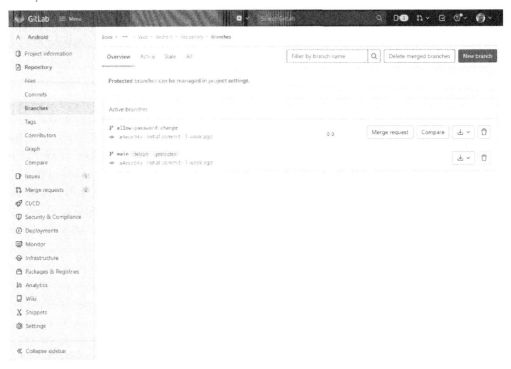

Figure 3.5 – List of branches within a project

After you've created a branch, you can commit edits to it. Once again, there are two ways to do this. You've already learned about the three-command sequence that you can use in a terminal: `git add <FILE-NAME>` followed by `git commit --message "<MESSAGE>"` followed by `git push`. But, if you'd rather work within GitLab, here's what you need to do:

1. Navigate to the project's repository by clicking **Repository** > **Files** in the left-hand navigation pane.
2. Make sure you're working in the right branch by clicking the branch name dropdown near the top left of the page:

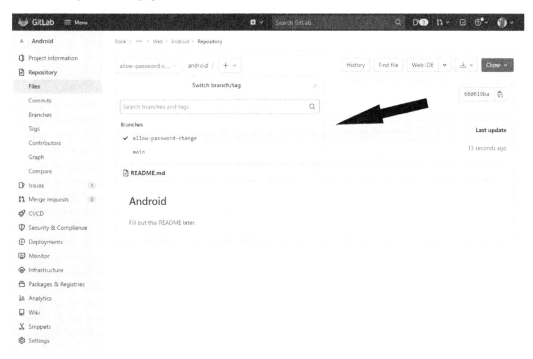

Figure 3.6 – Selecting a branch in a project

3. Within the repository's list of files, click the name of the file you want to edit. This will display its contents.
4. Click **Edit in Web IDE** to open an in-browser editor, and make any changes needed to the file.
5. If you'd like to edit more files within this commit, click on the next file's name in the file browser toward the left of the page and make any edits you want to its contents.
6. When you're done making changes, click **Commit…** and enter a commit message. If you haven't created a merge request for this branch yet, it's usually a good idea to check the **Start a new merge request** checkbox. Click **Commit** and you're done.

7. If you've cloned the repository to your local machine, you might want to use `git checkout <BRANCH-NAME>` followed by `git pull` to copy the commit you just made to your local repository, but you can often get away with doing this occasionally instead of after every commit.

Figure 3.7 – Commit your edits

Editing files and committing changes directly to your project's repository without ever touching a terminal is one of the great joys of using GitLab, so it's well worth practicing this feature until it becomes a part of your normal workflow.

Making branches doesn't do you any good unless you can switch between them, so you can view or edit the contents of whichever branch you want. You've seen how to do this from the command line using `git checkout <BRANCH-NAME>` or `git switch <BRANCH-NAME>`. It's just as easy to switch branches within the GUI: just find the branch dropdown that exists at the top left of many pages and switch to your preferred branch. It can be easy to forget which branch you're on, so it's good to get in the habit of quickly checking this dropdown from time to time to keep yourself oriented.

> **Tip**
> It probably goes without saying, but we'll say it anyway: switching the branch using a terminal command only changes the branch that you're on in your local repository and not the branch that you're on in the golden copy of the repository hosted on GitLab. Similarly, changing the branch in the GitLab GUI only changes the branch that you're on in the GitLab-hosted repository, not the branch that you're on in your local repository. So, don't switch in one location and assume that you've also switched on the other; the local and remote copies of your repository are completely independent when it comes to keeping track of which branch you're on.

Commit history

One of the most common operations with a Git repository is to look at the history of the commits on a particular branch, as seen in *Figure 3.8*. As you learned in *Chapter 2*, running `git log` in a terminal will show you a reverse-chronological history of all commits made to whatever branch you're on in the local repository, along with the author, timestamp, **Secure Hash Algorithm** (**SHA**), and commit message of each commit. You can do the same thing in the GitLab GUI by navigating to the main page of a project, selecting the branch you're interested in from the branch dropdown, and clicking the **History** button:

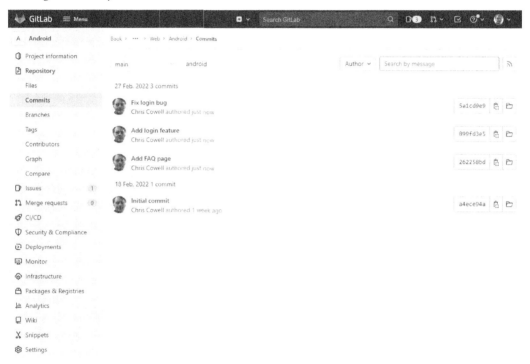

Figure 3.8 – List of commits on a branch

The history is a list of commits on this branch, with the most recent at the top of the list. This list includes the same information about each commit as you would get from the `git log` command. A nice bonus of using a GUI such as this is that you can click on any commit within the list to see every edit made to every file in the commit, displayed in an easy-to-read side-by-side format (switchable to an inline format, if you find that easier to parse visually). Of course, you can get this same information within a terminal with the `git diff` command, but that output is not nearly as easy to read as the output shown in the GitLab GUI.

Merging one Git branch into another

Merging a branch into another branch is the first action that's performed significantly differently in the GUI versus in a terminal. As you will remember, you can merge branch-a into main (to pick two sample branch names) from the command line using git checkout main followed by git merge branch-a. But, doing this same operation in the GitLab GUI requires an MR. This is one of the most important and often used parts of GitLab, so it's a critical thing to understand and get practice with. It's important to understand that a merge request is the *only* way to merge one branch into another from within the GitLab GUI. Here's a sample merge request from one of your Hats for Cats projects:

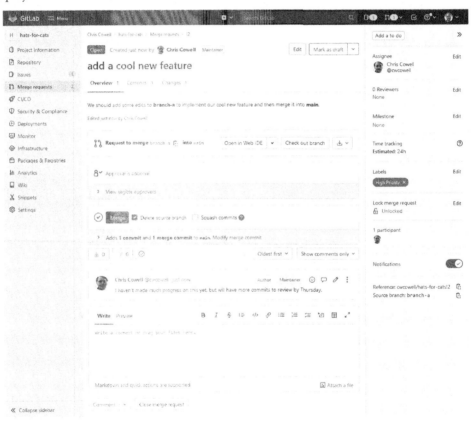

Figure 3.9 – Sample merge request

Merge requests

A merge request is exactly what it sounds like: a GitLab component that represents a request that somebody (maybe you, maybe somebody else) merge one branch into another in the golden copy of the repository on a GitLab instance. A merge request looks a lot like an issue. It contains many of the same fields, including a title, a description, an assignee, and a threaded discussion.

But, merge requests add a few extra fields that don't exist in issues. These include the **source branch** and **target branch** fields. The source branch is the branch that contains new commits that you have been working on, and the target branch is the branch that you want to add those new commits to. For example, if you wanted to merge `branch-a` into `main`, the source branch would be `branch-a` and the target branch would be `main`.

Merge requests also display the Git commits that are on the source branch, and collect all the edits from each commit into a single screen within the MR. This lets you see exactly how merging the source into the target would affect the files of the target branch.

Another aspect of merge requests that separates them from issues is that they contain a special pane that displays the results of the automated tests and scans that the CI/CD pipeline has performed on the code in the branch. We'll talk about this pane in more detail later, but you can think of it as a one-stop shop for showing the overall status of the code that you're developing. Is it doing what it's supposed to do? Does it have security vulnerabilities? Is it introducing dependencies that use unacceptable software licenses? In short, by looking at this pane, you can quickly see whether the work you're doing on the branch is making the overall software product better or worse. This is a very handy feature, for sure!

Finally, merge requests contain a big, impossible-to-miss **Merge** button. The mission of a merge request is to merge one branch's commits into another branch, so it would be useless if it didn't give users a way to perform the merge. There are many reasons this button might be grayed-out and unclickable, thereby blocking the merge from happening.

The following list is some examples of why a merge might be blocked. Note that most of these blocking behaviors are configurable, so you can decide which works best for your team:

- The merge request title starts with `Draft`. This indicates that the branch associated with the merge request is still a work in progress, and the developer does not intend for it to be merged yet.
- GitLab's license scanner (more about this in a later chapter) detects that the merge request is introducing a dependency with a license that's incompatible with the overall project's license.
- Automated tests fail for the most recent commit to the branch associated with the merge request.
- One or more discussion threads in the merge request are unresolved.
- The merge request hasn't received enough approvals, or approvals from the right people, to satisfy the approval rules. We'll describe this in more detail next.

Reviewing and approving code in merge requests

Because merge requests have the power to alter the files in the target branch, and the target branch is almost always `main`, `master`, or whatever branch holds your stable, production-ready code, it's critical that every MR is scrutinized by members of the development team. Fortunately, merge requests have several features to enable code reviews:

- You can **link comments directly to one or more lines in a file**, so it's obvious which lines of code you're referring to when you make suggestions for improving them (or when you praise them).
- You can **propose alternative code** right in the discussion section. These proposals even include a button that allows the original author to accept your suggestions with a single click on the GUI.
- You can **assign reviewers** from your team. They will receive notifications via email saying that you'd like them to review the edits in your merge request. These reviewers are listed in a metadata field in the MR, so everyone on your team knows who has been asked to review the files.
- Team members can **approve your code**. This is a separate concept from reviewing your code. Reviewing is usually a repeated process that consists of a review, followed by the original author making fixes in response to your review, followed by another review, followed by more fixes, and so on. An approval is a single, one-time "thumbs up" that means that the approver considers your edits to be ready to merge.
- You can create **rules for who must approve your MR** before it can be merged. These rules can become quite complicated and can involve several groups of people. Here are three sample rules for who must approve a merge request in order for it to be unblocked:
  - **Rule 1**: Either the tech lead or the architect for your team
  - **Rule 2**: Your development team manager
  - **Rule 3**: Any one of the three members of the quality assurance team, plus any one of two members from the security team, plus two of the three architects

As you can see, MRs are critical to getting your edits reviewed, approved, and merged into the right branch.

Creating a merge request before you commit code

There are several ways to create merge requests, including a few shortcuts that GitLab provides in possibly unexpected (but helpful) places. As we've done previously when describing other GitLab components, we'll ask you to look at the official GitLab documentation for up-to-date instructions on how to use the GUI to create, view, and manage merge requests.

However, we should definitely give you some guidance on *when* to create merge requests. This might sound odd or counterintuitive, but *we recommend that you create a merge request for a branch immediately after creating the branch, before you've committed any code to the branch.*

This advice probably sounds especially strange if you've used tools like GitHub before. GitHub's merge requests (known as **pull requests**) are usually created *after* you've committed all the code you intend to put on a branch. After all, if the purpose of a merge request is to merge the source branch's edits into the target branch, what's the point of opening a merge request when there isn't any code on the source branch to merge?

Using a merge request as a dashboard for your code

There are two reasons why making MRs early in the workflow is such a widely accepted best practice among GitLab users. First, an MR serves as a "dashboard" that lets you know about the overall quality of the code you're adding to the branch. The dashboard answers questions like the following:

- Are automated tests passing?
- Does your code meet performance requirements?
- Has your code introduced any security vulnerabilities?
- If it adds any new third-party dependencies, do they use licenses that are compatible with your overall project license?
- Does your code satisfy style and quality requirements?
- If you distribute your app as a Docker image, are there any known security vulnerabilities in the base Docker image that your code is packaged with?

These results are all available for viewing in other parts of the GitLab GUI, but it's convenient to see them all neatly presented within an MR.

More importantly, when you view the results within the MR, you see a "delta" view of these results. In other words, the results in the MR will tell you how the test and scan results for the MR's associated branch *differ* from the results of the same test and scans as run against your default branch. This is incredibly valuable because it lets you know whether the code that you are contributing to the branch is headed in the right direction. To put it simply, *are your commits to the branch making your software better or worse?*

Of course, if you wait to create a merge request until you're all done coding, you won't benefit from this constant guidance on whether you're on the right track with your commits. This is, all by itself, a great reason to create an MR before you've committed any code to your branch.

Merge requests improve collaboration

But, there's another compelling reason to create your MR early in the development workflow: *merge requests encourage collaboration among team members*. By providing an area for threaded discussions, they let your coworkers review and comment on every commit you make. Are you introducing subtle bugs? Your coworkers can spot them and alert you when they're still easy to fix. Are you starting to code an algorithm that's not as fast as an alternative? Someone can let you know before you commit many hours and lines of code to build the wrong thing. Are you misusing certain idioms in your programming language? If a senior developer can point that out early in the process, you can adjust your style before committing any more code to the branch.

These scenarios all share a common theme: by collaborating early and often, by reviewing small pieces of code that arrive in a single commit, problems become easier to spot and cheaper to fix. MRs are exactly the place where this kind of collaboration can occur.

Anyone who has been asked to review a completed feature that consists of 3,000 lines of code knows the sinking feeling of being unsure where even to begin. Or the despair you feel when you realize that the developer has misunderstood the specifications and not built the feature that the product owner intended. Or the awkwardness that comes from pointing out a programming or style error that the developer has made hundreds of times throughout the feature's code. All these situations can be avoided by frequent reviews of small pieces of code. And, that's only possible when you have a merge request ready to go before the first commit lands.

The frequent collaboration enabled by merge requests not only helps the folks who are reviewing the code but also helps the author of that code. In the same way that automated test failures are easier to troubleshoot and fix when the commit that caused the failures consists of small pieces of code, it's also easier to fix style problems, suboptimal algorithms, or bugs when a code reviewer spots those problems in a 12-line piece of code than it is when they call out those problems in 3,000 lines of code that make up the completed feature or bug fix. It's far better and easier to adjust your coding practices early in the development process than it is to have to go back and make potentially complicated or even destabilizing fixes after you thought you were done coding.

These principles apply to security vulnerabilities as well. A truism in software is that you must take security into account throughout the entire development workflow; you can't just tack it on at the end. The frequent security scan results that show up in merge requests help make it possible to honor this principle by "baking in" security from the very beginning of the development workflow. Code reviews by experienced developers or members of your security team also help achieve this goal, and the MR discussion pane is exactly where that sort of code review takes place. This principle of "shifting left"—which we've discussed earlier in this book—is especially important when it comes to security. This is because security problems sometimes require extensive rethinking and reworking of basic architectural decisions in your software. This kind of repair is much easier, cheaper, and less disruptive when the code base is smaller and simpler, as it tends to be when work has just begun on a new feature.

The three amigos – issues, branches, and merge requests

You now know quite a bit about issues, branches, and merge requests. It's important to understand that these three GitLab components are closely related when they're used to plan and accomplish a programming task.

GitLab recommends a particular workflow for these three components. They suggest that you first create an issue as soon as you've identified work to be done. As soon as that issue is assigned to a developer, the developer should immediately make a branch to work on, and then create a merge request for that branch. The issue, branch, and merge request should all have similar (or sometimes even identical) titles to show that they are related to each other. For example, if you saw these components, you'd know from their titles that they all address the same task:

- **Issue**: `simplify the login process`
- **Branch**: `simplify-login-process`
- **Merge request**: `simplify the login process`

Because issues, branches, and merge requests are so closely related, and because all three are usually required when completing any coding work with GitLab, you'll sometimes see them referred to as the **three amigos**. If you're not sure how to start work on a programming task, a good rule of thumb is to make sure you have the three amigos all lined up before you write any code.

When two amigos are enough

However, it's also worth mentioning that you don't *have* to have all three components for every task. If a task doesn't require you to edit any files in your repository, there's no need for a branch, which means there's also no need for a merge request. You might remember that, earlier, we said that a possible use case for an issue would be to solicit T-shirt designs for an upcoming corporate event. Those T-shirt designs could all be added directly to the issue's discussion section. You don't need to edit any files to satisfy the requirements of that task, so you could get away with not making a branch, and not making an associated merge request. In fact, making a branch and merge request issue would probably be confusing to your coworkers because it suggests that you *do* expect files to be edited while completing this work.

Similarly, there are cases where you need a branch and merge request, but don't need an issue. For example, imagine that you need to fix a tiny, trivial typo in your code. You *could* make an issue describing the problem, but that's probably overkill for such a small edit. It seems more appropriate in this case to simply make a branch and merge request, then make a single commit that fixes the typo, and then ask for review and approval of the MR. Most GitLab users would probably agree that no issue is needed (although no harm would come from making one). Having said that, some organizations might decide that every MR requires a related issue, which is also a perfectly acceptable policy, even if it occasionally leads to some extra work.

How are issues and merge requests different?

You might find yourself wondering how issues and merge requests differ. We've already discussed the extra kinds of information that merge requests contain, but there's a philosophical difference between the two components that's helpful to keep in mind. Think of issues as being the place to present and discuss **ideas**. A merge request, on the other hand, is where you present and discuss **code**. If you use this concept to distinguish the two, that will help you understand when just one of them is needed versus when both are needed. It also helps you understand whether any comments you might have are better suited to the discussion section in the issue (if you're talking about the general idea of the work) or the discussion section in the merge request (if you're talking about the specific code delivered by a developer).

Another difference between issues and merge requests is the different status values they can have. Issues can be **open** or **closed**, whereas merge requests can be **open**, **closed**, or **merged**. In fact, closed merge requests are somewhat rare, as that status is only used when you abort a merge request instead of following through with the merge. That does happen sometimes, but the far more common outcome for a merge request is for it to transition to the **merged** status once its associated branch is merged.

Now, you've seen how to use the GitLab GUI to deal with fundamental concepts such as commits, branches, and merge requests. You've also been shown how issues and merge requests may look similar at first glance, but serve importantly different roles within GitLab. You understand why it's important to create a merge request before you've committed any edits to merge, and how merge requests support close, frequent collaboration among team members. Finally, you know about the three amigos of issues, branches, and merge requests, and you understand how they work together to help you plan work, complete work, and merge any code changes that result from that work. In other words, you've been exposed to all of the fundamental building blocks of using GitLab to write software, even if you're still in the dark about how GitLab verifies, secures, packages, and deploys the software once you've written it. But, we'll get there soon, we promise!

Enabling DevOps practices with GitLab flow

Let's end this chapter by seeing how issues, branches, and merge requests fit together in a realistic example. This shows GitLab's recommended best practice for how to use all the components you've been introduced to in a smooth workflow that works for most situations. In fact, this workflow is so strongly recommended and so well proven over time that GitLab even has a name for this workflow: **GitLab flow**. As always, you're encouraged to treat this workflow as a starting point when developing your own processes and procedures; feel free to tinker with it as needed for your team, product, and organizational culture.

While working on the Hats for Cats web app, you decide to add a feature that lets you filter the hats by cat breed. After all, a cowboy hat for a large-headed Maine Coon might swamp the dainty head of a Devon Rex. Here are all the steps prescribed by GitLab flow to bring that feature into existence:

1. In the **Web** project under the **Hats for Cats** group, you make an issue titled `Filter hats by breed`, leaving all metadata fields empty.

2. In the issue's discussion section, you mention two people who you think might have opinions on whether this feature is a good idea.

3. Both those people add replies to the discussion section. One just leaves a thumbs-up emoji. The other expresses support for the idea but asks whether the app should filter by other criteria as well.

4. You decide that filtering by other criteria is a good idea, but you're not sure what those criteria should be. You make another issue titled `Question: what criteria should we use when filtering hats?` You set this issue aside to deal with later and return your focus to the `Filter hats by breed` issue because you're confident that breed should be one of the criteria.

5. At a team-wide planning meeting, the group decides to assign the issue a weight of 8, which for your team means it's expected to be a 1-week task. You assign the issue to a backend developer named Elizabeth, and you set its due date field to 2 weeks from today.

6. Elizabeth applies a *scoped* **Status::In Progress** label and an *unscoped* **Back-end** label to the issue. This will help the team keep track of whether the issue is on track and understand who is responsible for it.

7. Elizabeth makes a temporary branch called `filter-hats-by-breed` to hold her commits.

8. Elizabeth creates a merge request titled `Draft: Filter hats by breed`. She assigns teammates Alice and Bob to review the merge request. They have nothing to do yet since Elizabeth hasn't added any code to the MR's branch.

9. Now that Elizabeth has the three amigos of issue, branch, and merge request set up, she starts coding.

10. After she finishes a small, testable chunk of code, she commits it to her branch.

11. Elizabeth looks at the MR to see the results of the automated tests, code quality scans, license scans, and security scans that ran against her first commit. They don't report any problems, so she celebrates with a mug of Assam tea with extra sugar.

12. Alice and Bob get email notifications that Elizabeth has committed code to the MR's branch. They look at the MR and review her changes. Both add some comments about what parts of her code they like, and what parts can be improved.

13. Some of the suggestions seem wrong to Elizabeth, so she adds comments in the MR's discussion section explaining her point of view. She continues to talk it out until they all reach an agreement about how she should proceed. Elizabeth adds a new commit with the agreed-upon fixes.

14. Once again, Elizabeth looks in the MR to see the results of automated tests and scans against her last commit. One of the security scans points out a vulnerability that she unwittingly introduced. She quickly adds a new commit that fixes the vulnerability. The scans run again on this fixed code, and this time it's smooth sailing.

15. Elizabeth gets a thumbs-up review from both Alice and Bob on all the code she's committed so far, so her work is done. She removes the **Back-end** label, adds a **Front-end** label, and re-assigns the issue to a frontend engineer named George.

16. George writes some frontend code and adds a few commits to the same `filter-by-breed` branch that Elizabeth was using. Each commit triggers a new run of automated tests and scans, and each is reviewed by Alice and Bob.

17. George realizes that the work is falling behind schedule, so he adds an **At Risk** label to the original issue. The development manager responds to this by assigning another frontend developer named Helen to help George.

18. The cycle of commit-then-review-then-inspect-automated-test-and-scan-results continues for a few more rounds until George and Helen complete the feature. They remove the **At Risk** label. Alice and Bob are satisfied with the code, and both add thumbs-up emojis to the discussion.

19. George removes `Draft:` from the title of the issue, indicating that he considers the code ready to be merged.

20. George mentions the security and QA teams in the MR's discussion so they can approve it. Until they do, the **Web** project's approval rules block the MR from being merged.
21. One member of the security team and two members of the QA team mark the MR as "approved." This re-activates the MR's merge button. With great glee and a feeling of accomplishment, George removes the **Front-end** and **Status::In Progress** labels and clicks the MR's merge button.
22. The whole team goes out to a pub to celebrate and eats an uncomfortable quantity of pizza.

Here's a diagram showing this flow, but with some steps removed for clarity:

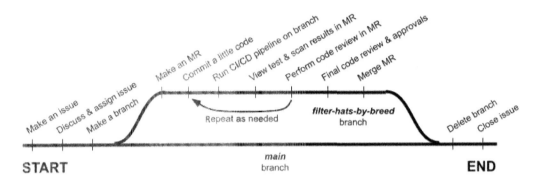

Figure 3.10 – Major steps in GitLab flow

Summary

You've been exposed to an awful lot of concepts and terminology in this chapter, so let's do a quick review.

GitLab is a web application whose mission is to solve many of the problems faced by people involved with any of the 10 stages of the SDLC. So, GitLab doesn't solve just one problem; it solves many problems that exist in many different facets of software development.

Working with GitLab happens mostly within a GitLab project, which represents one software product, one portion of your org chart, or one initiative. Projects that share a similar theme can be collected within GitLab groups, and groups can also contain subgroups.

Each individual task or chunk of work is recorded in a GitLab issue. Issues describe the work to be done, allow team members to participate in a discussion about the issue, and include many fields to store metadata about the issue. Issues usually represent software-related tasks, but can (and should) be used to describe, plan, and track non-technical work as well.

You can create *scoped* or *unscoped* labels to highlight issue statuses or health, or to indicate which person or team is responsible for doing work on the issue. You can assign labels to merge requests as well as issues.

A GitLab merge request is the component you use for merging one branch into another within the GitLab GUI. Each merge request lists a source branch and a target branch, and merging the merge request will cause any commits that were only on the source branch to be added to the target branch. Merge requests look similar to issues, but they serve different purposes: the former is used for describing, discussing, and merging code. The latter is used for describing and discussing ideas and tasks.

You can also use the GitLab GUI for performing many common Git-related tasks besides managing merge requests. For example, you can use the GUI to create a branch, add a commit, show a list of commits on a branch, or assign a tag to a commit.

GitLab flow is the best practice workflow for using all of the GitLab components in a proven, reliable way to build software. You're not required to use GitLab flow, but it's a great starting point for figuring out what workflow and policies work best for your organization or team.

So far, we've been dancing around a central part of GitLab flow: the **CI/CD pipelines** that run countless different checks on your code once you've committed it to a repository. In the next chapter, we'll tackle it head-on, and get to the heart of what is possibly GitLab's most powerful and most helpful feature.

4
Understanding GitLab's CI/CD Pipeline Structure

By now, you have enough knowledge of Git and GitLab concepts to understand how developers can use those tools within the **Create** stage of the **software development life cycle** (**SDLC**) to create, review, and store code. You've also been introduced to some of the problems presented by the **Verify**, **Package**, and **Release** stages that come immediately after the **Create** stage. Now, it's time to get to the meat (or tofu, if you prefer) of this book: how GitLab's CI/CD pipelines can help solve those Verify, Package, and Release problems.

In this chapter, you'll learn what **continuous integration** (**CI**) and **continuous delivery** (**CD**) mean, and how they fit into GitLab Flow. You'll learn how to describe the different parts of a pipeline, including stages and jobs. You'll see how those parts fit together, and how code flows through them. You'll be shown how to view the overall status of a pipeline, and the status of the individual stages and jobs that make them up. You'll learn about the different ways GitLab can trigger pipelines, and why you might want to limit how often your pipelines run. Finally, you'll learn how to configure a simple Hello World-style pipeline for your Hats for Cats software.

Once you're comfortable with these concepts and practices, you will have opened the door to powerful GitLab features that are enabled and configured through pipelines. And when you hit that point, odds are you'll become a devout and committed GitLab user who can't imagine going back to other DevOps tools.

In this chapter, we're going to cover the following main topics:

- Defining the terms "pipeline", "CI", and "CD"
- Parts of a pipeline – stages, jobs, and commands
- Running GitLab CI/CD pipelines
- Reading GitLab CI/CD pipeline statuses
- Configuring GitLab CI/CD pipelines

Technical requirements

As with the previous chapter, you'll get the most out of this chapter if you've got an account on a GitLab instance (self-managed or **Software-as-a-Service** (**SaaS**)) that you can log in to and use to practice and experiment with the concepts discussed.

Defining the terms pipeline, CI, and CD

Since much of the power of GitLab comes from configuring CI/CD pipelines to do various things to and with your code, it's critical to understand what a pipeline even is. So, an obvious place to start a discussion of this topic is to figure out exactly what we mean by pipeline, CI, and CD. We won't start creating pipelines yet—that will come in a later chapter.

Understanding what a pipeline is

A GitLab CI/CD pipeline is a series of steps that are performed on your files whenever you commit edits to the GitLab-hosted copy of a repository. A lot is going on in that sentence, so let's take a more careful look at each part of it.

What do we mean by "a series of steps"? You can think of these steps as *tasks that are performed on your files*. For example, you may want to run various tests or scanners on your files to make sure your code is well-written, is free from security vulnerabilities, uses appropriately licensed dependencies, and satisfies all functional or performance requirements. You may also want to package your code into some deployable format, whether that's a Ruby Gem, installable Red Hat package, Docker image, or any other package type. Of course, you may also need a step that deploys your code into an appropriate environment, whether that be a test environment, a pre-production environment, or your project's actual production environment.

What do we mean by "your files"? Technically, a GitLab CI/CD pipeline can perform the steps we just described on any files included in a GitLab project's repository: source code files, configuration files, README files, and test data files. In short, *you can configure a pipeline to inspect, test, package, deploy, or otherwise manipulate any files in your project*. By far the most common type of files that are targeted by pipeline steps are source code files, but it's important to remember that you can configure pipelines to perform almost any task on almost any file in a GitLab project's repository.

Why did we specify that pipelines run "whenever you commit edits"? Because in the vast majority of cases, *adding a Git commit is exactly what causes a pipeline to run against your files*. Many of the advantages that GitLab brings to the SDLC can only happen if the pipelines run often, against small collections of file changes. To make this happen, the default behavior for GitLab is to run a complete pipeline every time you commit edited files to the GitLab-hosted copy of your project's repository. Committing is not the only way to trigger a pipeline, even if it is by far the most common way. Later in this chapter, you'll learn about starting pipeline runs manually, and also how to prevent a pipeline from running after a commit.

Finally, why is it important to specify that pipelines only work on the GitLab-hosted copy of a repository? That's because pipelines are a GitLab concept, not a Git concept. This means that pipelines can only access files that GitLab knows about, and that means files that are in the copy of your project's repository that is stored on the GitLab instance. In other words, if you edit files on a local copy of your project's repository, GitLab cannot see those versions of the files (at least, not until you sync them with GitLab using `git push`), so it can't run pipelines on those versions of the files. Again: *pipelines can only target the versions of your files that live on your GitLab instance.*

Defining one pipeline per project

Each project defines only one GitLab CI/CD pipeline. However, exactly what happens in that pipeline – the tasks that it includes – might depend on various factors, leading one run of the pipeline to "look different" from other runs of the project's pipeline. For example, the pipeline that runs against edited source code may include many automated tests and packaging the code into a Docker image, whereas the pipeline that runs against edited documentation may involve spelling checks and deployment to a web server. But it's still the same pipeline in both cases. It's just that certain "features" of the single pipeline can be turned on or off, depending on which features make sense for which types of code changes. It's easy to see two pipeline runs from the same project give wildly different outputs and think that they are two completely different pipelines, but that's not the case. *Every GitLab project has just one CI/CD pipeline*. It's just that what that pipeline does can vary from run to run.

Understanding different uses of the term "pipeline"

The term "pipeline" is sometimes used loosely. The most accurate way of thinking about it is to say that a project's pipeline is just a blueprint or recipe for the series of steps that will be applied to the project's file. Performing those steps is not technically a pipeline and is instead called a "pipeline run" or "pipeline instance." But people often refer to individual runs as pipelines. We'll do the same thing in this chapter: we'll often use the shorter term "pipeline" when "pipeline run" or "pipeline instance" would technically be more accurate. Whether we're talking about the blueprint for the pipeline or an individual instance of a pipeline should be clear from the context.

A project can run more than one pipeline instance at a time. If you make two commits just a few seconds apart, and if the pipeline steps take several minutes to complete, then you could have two pipeline instances running at the same time, on the two different commits. Each pipeline run would be performing the same steps but against different versions of your files.

Viewing a list of pipelines

One of the most common things you'll do when using GitLab to build software is look at a list of running and completed pipeline instances. Following the pattern established in previous chapters, we'll focus less on how to do this (since the GUI may change and the official GitLab documentation will always have up-to-date instructions) and more on why you may want to do so.

GitLab's list of pipelines not only tells you the pass/fail status of all of your pipeline runs, but also lets you know if any pipelines are "stuck" or unable to run for some reason. It shows you which version of the code each pipeline is running against, the commit message for the commit or Git tag that triggered the pipeline, who made the commit or tag, when the pipeline started, and how long it took to run (if it completed).

The list of pipelines also provides a GUI control for canceling a pipeline mid-run. Some complicated pipelines can take several minutes (or possibly even hours) to run, and if you have a limited number of pipeline minutes available to your project, you may want to cancel a pipeline that was triggered by some trivial file change to conserve your minutes.

Finally, the list of pipelines also provides GUI controls to rerun any pipeline. You may want to do this if a pipeline failed for what you suspect was an intermittent network problem, for example.

Here's a list of pipelines – both running and completed – for the Hats for Cats project. The table lists pipelines in reverse chronological order, with the most recent pipelines at the top. You can see that two pipeline runs have finished with a "passed" status, one has finished with a "failed" status, and the two most recent pipelines are still running. Don't worry about the icons in each row that depict the status of the different parts of each pipeline; we'll go over those later in this chapter:

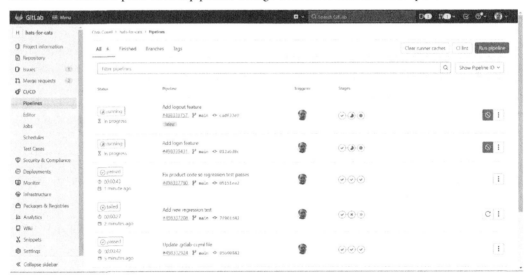

Figure 4.1 – A list of Hats for Cats pipeline runs

You've seen what pipelines are, how the term can be used loosely, how each project has just one pipeline defined, and what sorts of information you can get from a list of pipelines. Now, let's pull apart the terms CI and CD and look at what they mean when applied to pipelines.

CI – finding out if your code is good

Although every GitLab project defines, at most, one pipeline, almost every pipeline consists of two halves: a CI half and a CD half. The CI portion of a pipeline consists of steps dedicated to answering the question, *Is your code good?*

The term **CI** stands for **continuous integration**. This is not just a GitLab term – it's a standard term whose definition is understood and agreed on by most software companies. You can think of it as the portion of the pipeline that makes sure any file edits you are working on will integrate well with your project's stable code base. In other words, when you merge your feature or bugfix branch into the default branch, will any new problems crop up? Spotting these problems early on, as you're working on your code but before you merge it, increases your odds of fixing them easily and cheaply.

The CI portion of a pipeline does this by running tests, scans, and other checks on your code whenever you commit it to the GitLab-hosted copy of your project's Git repository. At least, that's the default behavior for GitLab pipelines. You can override that behavior so that pipelines don't run on *every* commit, and there are some good reasons you might want to do that, but we'll discuss those later.

You've already seen some references to some of the kinds of tests and scans that are run by a pipeline's CI-related steps, but as a refresher, here's a *partial* list of possible CI-focused pipeline steps:

- **Functional tests**: Does your software do what it's supposed to? This category includes the regression tests that **Quality Assurance** (**QA**) teams spend much of their time writing.
- **Security scans**: Does your code introduce any security vulnerabilities?
- **Code quality scans**: Does your code adhere to best practices for class length, white space usage, and other style-related considerations?
- **Performance tests**: Does your code meet performance expectations?
- **License scanning**: Do all of your code's dependencies use software licenses that are compatible with your main project's license?
- **Fuzz testing**: Can you trigger crashes or unexpected errors in your code by passing it unusually long strings, numbers that are outside the expected ranges, or other strange or extreme data as input?

Because GitLab provides first-class support for these types of checks, they are simple to enable within CI pipelines. But *you can integrate almost any tool, scan, or check into a GitLab pipeline*. We'll learn how to do this later, but for now, all you need to know is that any tool that can be run from the command line – whether commercial, open source, or home-grown – can be added to a GitLab pipeline.

Benefits of CI

As you can see, one of the big advantages of CI is that it enables the "shifting left" philosophy that we've discussed previously. The earlier you run tests, the sooner you find problems. And the sooner you find problems, the less of a burden they are to fix. Shifting as many software development tasks as far left as you can on the timeline pays huge dividends.

The other advantage of CI, especially when combined with GitLab's transparent "single pane of glass" approach to monitoring your development life cycle, is that it promotes collaboration. For example, when security tests run frequently, that lets the entire team get a handle on the state of the project's security. Are we adding unanticipated vulnerabilities that we should budget time and people to fix? Do developers need to adjust their coding approach or architecture to reduce the chance of introducing more vulnerabilities when they add new features next month? If the entire team – managers, developers, QA, UX, technical writers, and anyone else involved with the product – can see the state of the project's security, they can all either help directly or adjust their work in whatever way makes sense to either remediate existing security problems or prevent future security problems.

This collaboration principle applies not just to security issues, but also to functional problems, performance problems, usability problems, or any other metric by which you measure your software. CI gives everyone on the team an understanding of the state of your software so that everyone can pitch in to help build or fix the software in whatever ways make sense for their roles.

> **Understanding the Phrases CI Pipeline and CD Pipeline**
>
> Throughout this book, we'll sometimes refer to a *CI pipeline* or a *CD pipeline*, but remember that a GitLab project doesn't have separate CI and CD pipelines – it has just one pipeline that contains some CI-related steps and some CD-related steps. The expressions "CI pipeline" and "CD pipeline" are just shortcuts for the more cumbersome (but more accurate) phrases "CI portion of a project's single pipeline" and "CD portion of a project's single pipeline," respectively.

CD – finding out where your code should go (and putting it there)

Whereas the term **CI** has a standard definition that all companies use, the term **CD** is more ambiguous. GitLab uses the term to mean either **continuous delivery** or **continuous deployment**. We'll get to the difference between these two terms later, but both have to do with deciding what environment your code should be deployed to, and then actually performing that deployment.

This will make more sense if we talk a little about environments. Most software development teams have several environments set up for deploying code. These environments serve different purposes: some are used for conducting functional tests on your software, some are used for performance tests, and some mimic the production environment so that you can spot and fix any integration errors before they show up in production. And of course, every project will have a production environment that hosts the code that real users interact with.

Software developed with GitLab also uses environments, and the CD portion of a GitLab CI/CD pipeline is responsible for deciding which environment code should be deployed to, and then putting it there. Depending on how you've configured your project's pipeline, the tasks that perform this work look at a variety of factors when deciding where to put your code. The most common factor pipelines use is whether they're running against a Git branch or a Git tag, and if the former, what the branch's name is.

Different companies use different naming schemes for their Git branches, but here's a typical example of how the CD portion of a GitLab pipeline may decide where to deploy a project's code. Remember that although this is realistic, it's by no means the only way to configure your CD pipeline:

- If a pipeline runs against a branch with a name such as `add-login-feature`, `fix-password-bug`, or `remediate-cross-site-scripting-vuln`, deploy the code to a **review environment** for testing (more about these in the next section).
- If a pipeline runs against the `main` branch, deploy that code to the **staging** (sometimes called **pre-production**) environment.
- If a pipeline runs against a Git tag in the `production` branch, deploy the code to the **production** environment. This assumes that your team adds a version tag such as `version-1-0` or `version-12-2` to every commit that it intends to deploy to users.

Understanding review environments

Any non-trivial software project needs at least one test environment. This is a machine that the software can be deployed to as it's being developed so that the QA team can use the software in a safe, sandboxed place to make sure it satisfies functional requirements. Some teams have additional, specialized test environments dedicated to performance testing, load testing, scalability testing, or other types of testing. GitLab has a special name for all of these test environments: **review environments**. Every non-default Git branch has a review environment dedicated to just that branch. As soon as that branch is merged into the default branch that holds the stable code base, GitLab destroys the no-longer-needed review environment.

Review environments are one of the most amazing features of GitLab. You don't have to set these environments up yourself. Any time you create a branch in the GitLab-hosted copy of your project's repository, a review environment magically appears, ready for your CI/CD pipeline to deploy to. And when you're done with your branch and either delete it or merge it into your stable code base, the review environment magically disappears. It's truly one of GitLab's very best and most helpful features.

Continuous delivery

We've already said that one of GitLab's meanings for the term **CD** is **continuous delivery**. This means that a GitLab CI/CD pipeline will automatically deploy your code to the right environment, based on whatever factors you configure the pipeline to pay attention to. But there's one important exception: with continuous delivery, GitLab will *not* automatically deploy your code to the production environment. Instead, *it presents a GUI control that asks a human (generally, a release engineer) to manually approve and trigger the deployment to production.* This is a final failsafe that prevents your team from deploying faulty code, or the wrong version of your code, to actual users. This is the most common form of CD for GitLab users.

Continuous deployment

The other thing that **CD** can mean is **continuous deployment**. This is the same as continuous delivery, with one exception: it does away with the final, manual failsafe. Continuous deployment sends your code to the production environment completely automatically, just like it deploys code to any other environment. Getting rid of the human element could be seen as risky by some organizations, but if you have a mature, proven, trusted CI portion of your pipeline, you may feel confident that any code that passes through the gauntlet of tests, scans, and other checks is good enough to deploy directly to customers. This can be a good time-saver for companies with a high level of trust in their CI pipeline.

Packaging and deploying code with CD

A CD pipeline – whether it implements continuous delivery or continuous deployment – sometimes needs to package your project's code into a deployable form before it can be deployed. We'll talk about this more concretely later. For now, just know that the CD phase of your pipeline may involve packaging Java code into a WAR or EAR, packaging Ruby code into a Gem, packaging C code into a Docker image, collecting all of your project's files into a *tarball*, or bundling up your project's code in whatever form makes the most sense for your project's language and deployment strategy.

Of course, there are some cases where no packaging is required. Some projects with simple deployment strategies can deploy a collection of loose, unpackaged files.

Whether or not your CD pipeline packages your project's code, it will always need to send your software somewhere. This could take the form of pushing a Docker image to a repository (either public or hosted by Gitlab, as we'll learn more about later), using a command-line tool to deploy code to an AWS environment, or any of countless other environment-specific deployment techniques. Generally, this is the last task (and sometimes the only task) of the CD part of your project's pipeline.

Benefits of CD

To review, the purpose of CD is to "make releases boring." If your CD pipeline deploys code every time you commit – whether it's deploying code to a review environment, a staging environment, or the production environment – that helps you release code to customers more frequently, with fewer changes, and less risk.

Of course, customers won't see code that your CD pipeline deploys to a review or staging environment, but by deploying to those environments and testing your software there, your team can feel more confident about releasing the code to production when it makes business sense to do so. These non-production deployments can be thought of as trial runs for the real thing, and can help you send your customers frequent, small releases. This approach lets you get features to your customers sooner, allows customers to provide feedback on those features sooner, and reduces the risk that your deployments will need to be rolled back due to unforeseen problems.

GitLab Runners

Now that you understand the high-level concepts of pipelines, continuous integration, and continuous delivery, it's time to briefly introduce a new, critically important concept that makes pipelines possible: GitLab Runners.

As you'll learn in the next section, pipelines ultimately boil down to a series of shell commands that are run automatically, with little or no human intervention. This is a crucial concept to grasp when learning about CI/CD pipelines, so we'll repeat it in different words: a CI/CD pipeline is just a series of commands that are run by a robot, where those commands perform tasks related to building, verifying, and deploying software.

GitLab Runners are the robots that execute those commands. Technically speaking, a GitLab Runner is a small program that is sent commands to execute by the GitLab instance. We'll discuss the role of GitLab Runners in CI/CD pipelines and explain how to install and configure them – and how to tell if you even need to – in the next chapter. We won't go into any further detail here, but it's important to understand that GitLab Runners are where the rubber meets the road for a pipeline: they are what convert your CI/CD configuration code into actual, executing tasks for building, verifying, securing, and deploying your code.

To whet your appetite, here's a quick glimpse into how GitLab Runners fit into the GitLab CI/CD architecture. Think of a pipeline as relying on three components: the CI/CD configuration file that defines the pipeline's tasks, the GitLab Runner that executes those tasks in some environment, and the GitLab instance that manages and coordinates all aspects of the pipeline and ultimately displays the results of the pipeline's tasks. You can picture it all fitting together like this:

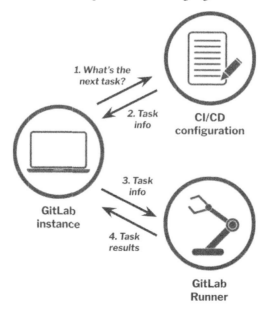

Figure 4.2 – GitLab CI/CD pipeline architectural diagram

You'll learn much more about many aspects of GitLab Runners in the next chapter, but this quick introduction should be sufficient to help you understand the rest of the material in this chapter.

With that, we can conclude our definitions and discussion of the concepts of pipelines, CI, CD, and GitLab Runners. As you've seen, CI/CD pipelines are a series of steps that are automatically performed against the files in your project's Git repository, any time you edit any of those files. By running these pipelines often, and against small file changes, GitLab makes it easy to find problems early, fix them cheaply, and deploy new code to customers frequently and in a low-risk fashion. Other than taking a little time to churn through, pipelines are pretty much all upside, with no real reason not to run them. They're a critical part of your GitLab workflow, and a big reason that developing software with GitLab is so much easier and more efficient than developing software without it.

Now, let's move on to investigate the anatomy of pipelines. What are the components that make up pipelines, how do they fit together, and how does GitLab show you what happens in a pipeline?

Parts of a pipeline – stages, jobs, and commands

That's the big picture of what a GitLab CI/CD pipeline is – how the CI portion of a pipeline differs from the CD portion of the same pipeline and why pipelines are such an important part of the SDLC. Let's zoom in a little and take a look at the structure of a pipeline in more detail. In particular, *how is a pipeline put together from stages and jobs?*

Stages

Every pipeline consists of one or more **stages**. A stage is a collection of pipeline tasks that are thematically related. For example, these are probably the three most commonly used stages:

- **Build**: This stage holds tasks that compile and/or package your source code into a deployable format.
- **Test**: This stage holds tasks that run automated tests, code quality scans and linters, and possibly security scans.
- **Deploy**: This stage sends your code to the appropriate environment, depending on what Git branch or Git tag the pipeline is running against (among other possible factors).

These three stages are so commonly used that GitLab adds them to your pipeline by default. You can, of course, override this default setting by adding, removing, or replacing stages. Regardless of what stages you end up with, we recommend that you always define your stages explicitly, even if you're using the three default stages. This may seem unnecessarily verbose, but we've found that it aids readability, assists with troubleshooting, and prevents confusion down the road.

You can define as many stages as you want. For exceptionally simple projects, you could even make a stripped-down pipeline with just one stage. You can call them whatever you want, and you can include spaces and several other punctuation symbols in stage names. Because long stage names can sometimes be truncated by GitLab's GUI, we recommend keeping them as short as you can without sacrificing clarity.

GitLab has no way of checking that the tasks included within a stage are thematically connected. That's your responsibility. This means you can create truly horrible, messy stages if you want to. For example, you could run automated regression tests in a stage called *Deploy Documentation*, and you could deploy documentation in a stage called *prepare-test-environment*. How you divide your pipelines into stages, and what tasks you put in each stage, is entirely up to you. This freedom is not without cost, however: it's considered a best practice to occasionally review your stage structure and refactor it as needed for clarity and consistency.

Viewing stages in the GitLab GUI

Remember the list of pipeline runs we saw in *Figure 4.1*? If you flip back to that screenshot, you'll notice that each row in the list of pipeline runs includes icons that give the pass/fail status for each stage within the pipeline. Here's a zoomed-in view of the status of the Build, Test, and Deploy stages in the Hats for Cats pipeline:

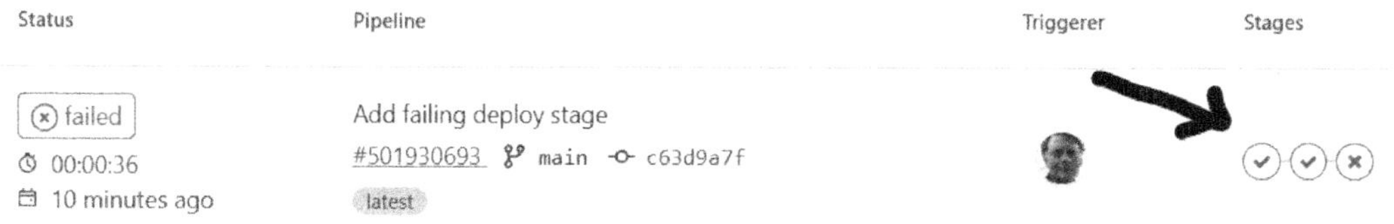

Figure 4.3 – Status icons for a pipeline instance's stages

In this pipeline instance, the first two stages passed, and the third stage failed. You can't see the names of the stages from this view, but if you hover over a stage's status icon, the stage name will appear.

If *all* the stages in the pipeline pass, the pipeline will have an overall status of **passed**. In this case, because the final stage failed, the overall status of the pipeline is **failed**.

If you need more details about what happened in each stage, click on the status icon at the left of the row for a pipeline instance (in this case, the red **failed** icon). That brings you to a zoomed-in view of the pipeline, which gives you more details about each stage. Here's what that view looks like:

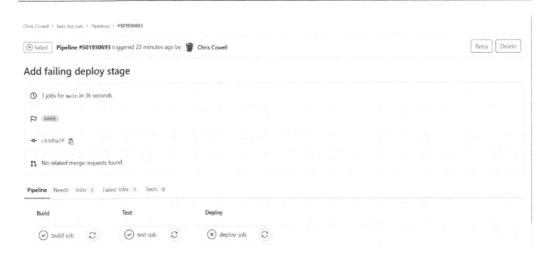

Figure 4.4 – Details of three pipeline stages

You can see the **Build**, **Test**, and **Deploy** stages depicted as columns, with the tasks that occur within each stage listed within the stage's column. But what are those tasks exactly? That's a perfect segue to the next topic: jobs.

Jobs

Throughout this chapter, we've been talking about the "tasks" that happen within a pipeline. Now, it's time to introduce you to the formal name for those tasks: GitLab calls them **jobs**. Each job must have a name that describes the task it performs.

You can think of jobs as the next level down (down from stages, that is) when it comes to the building blocks that make up a GitLab CI/CD pipeline. Each stage contains one or more jobs, and each job is contained by some stage.

If you look at the preceding screenshot again, you'll see that the **Build** stage contains a job called **build-job**, the **Test** stage contains a job called **test-job**, and the **Deploy** stage contains a job called **deploy-job**.

As you may have guessed from these job names, each job typically performs one task. For example, a job may compile all of your Java source code into classes. Another job may reset the data in a test database. Another job may push a Docker image to a registry. But in the same way that GitLab doesn't validate that your stages contain thematically similar jobs, it also doesn't validate that your jobs perform the task that the job's name suggests. In other words, you could make a job called *compile-java* that deletes stray files generated by your automated tests, or a job called *deploy-to-production* that runs a security scanner. So, be careful to name your jobs carefully, and periodically review them to make sure the names are still accurate and readable.

Another thing that GitLab can't validate is whether each job performs a single task. This means there's nothing to prevent you from creating a job called `test` that runs nine different automated test suites, three performance tests, and five security scanners. Of course, that would violate the best practice of having each job perform only one task, so GitLab will let you create jobs that are as broad or narrow in scope as you want.

Commands

Let's address a topic we've only danced around so far: how exactly does a job perform a task? The answer to this is the final building block in GitLab CI/CD pipelines: **commands**. Each job contains one or more commands that let the job *do* something.

A command contained by a job is, well, the same thing as a command that a human may type into a terminal. It is just that: think of a job as a robot that types a command into a Linux bash shell, a macOS Zsh shell, or Windows PowerShell, just like a real person would. Here are some examples of commands that might be included in a GitLab CI/CD pipeline job:

- The `javac *.java` command to compile Java classes
- The `docker build --tag my_app:1.2` command to create a Docker image
- The `mvn test` command to use the Maven build tool to trigger automated Java unit tests

Once again, these commands could be typed in by a person or by a GitLab CI/CD pipeline job; the result is the same. If a person used all of the same commands that are included in a pipeline's jobs, you'd end up with an identical pipeline. The only difference is that the human-run pipeline would be much slower (and possibly more error-prone).

A job can contain as many commands as it needs to perform its task. For example, if a job is in charge of cleaning up an environment by deleting temporary files produced by tests, it may contain three separate commands:

- `rm -f tmp/`
- `rm *.tmp`
- `rm -f /tmp/test_files/`

Instead, you could create three separate jobs called, perhaps, `remove-files-1`, `remove-files-2`, and `remove-files-3`, but since these are all closely related commands that you would always run together, most GitLab users would prefer to include all three commands in a single job.

Fitting the pipeline pieces together

Now that you've been introduced to stages, jobs, and commands, let's review how they all fit together:

- Each GitLab CI/CD **pipeline** consists of at least one **stage**. A stage represents a category of task that the pipeline must perform.
- Each **stage** consists of at least one **job**. A job represents a single task that the pipeline must perform.
- Each **job** consists of at least one **command**, where a command is exactly what a human would type into a shell to perform a pipeline task.

It's probably obvious that different projects will likely define very different pipeline stages, jobs, and commands. But if you look at enough project pipelines, you'll notice certain recurring patterns. As we've already mentioned, most pipelines contain at least the **Build**, **Test**, and **Deploy** stages, and the jobs within each of those stages are often pretty similar (at least for projects that use the same languages and build tools). While these core stages and jobs are fairly common, most non-trivial software projects will define plenty of jobs and sometimes stages that are unique to them. Other projects will have similar or identical needs but accomplish them either using different commands or the same commands organized into different jobs and/or stages. Seeing the variety of ways that teams set up their CI/CD pipelines is part of the fun of using GitLab.

Running GitLab CI/CD pipelines

Whenever a project's pipeline runs, *it's running on some version of that project's files*. This means that in the CI portion of the pipeline, it runs automated tests and scans on just one version of your files. Then, in the CD portion, it deploys that same version of the files to the appropriate environment. You will also see this described as a pipeline running "against" a version of your project's files.

The point of pipelines is to check the status of your code – and then deploy that code – every time you make changes to it. So, running a project's pipeline on yesterday's version of your code may produce one set of results, while running the pipeline against today's version of the code may generate very different results, even though the pipeline consists of the same stages, jobs, and commands. Between yesterday and today, you may have added new automated tests, introduced new test failures by adding buggy product code, or added a dependency with security vulnerabilities. If any of those are the case, the two pipeline runs would produce different reports about the quality of your code.

Branch pipelines

The most common way to run a pipeline is to *commit a change to a branch*. Whenever you do that, GitLab automatically runs a pipeline against whatever version of your project's files exist in that commit. In the list of pipeline instances, you'll see an entry for that pipeline instance that shows (among other information) the branch name and the SHA of the most recent commit in the branch. Here's an example:

Figure 4.5 – Pipelines running against different branches, with different results
(branch names are highlighted)

In this example, the most recent pipeline ran against the **add-login-feature** branch and the second most recent ran against the **fix-password-bug** branch. These branches may contain very different contents inside the same files, or one branch may contain new files that the other branch doesn't have yet. That explains why the test stage failed in the pipeline that ran against **add-login-feature** but not in the pipeline that ran against **fix-password-bug**.

GitLab also lets you manually run a pipeline against any Git branch you want, even if it wasn't the last branch you committed to. Triggering a pipeline against an arbitrary branch is easy: visit the list of pipelines, click the **Run pipeline** button, select the branch you want the pipeline to run against, and click the next **Run pipeline** button, as shown in the following screenshot. In this example, we are about to run the pipeline against the **add-login-feature** branch, but if we were to expand the drop-down box with the branch's name, you would see that it lists all the branches that exist in the GitLab-hosted copy of the project's repository:

Figure 4.6 – Manually running a pipeline against a specific branch
(the branch's name and trigger button are highlighted)

Git tag pipelines

Remember learning in *Chapter 2* that you can add a Git tag called `version-3-1` to the commit that you released to customers as version 3.1 of your product? GitLab also lets you run pipelines against arbitrary Git tags such as that one, even if the tag doesn't point to the last commit on a branch. Just tell GitLab to run a pipeline against any tag using the same manual trigger process that you used to point a pipeline at a specific branch. The dropdown that lists available branches includes entries for all Git tags as well, as shown here:

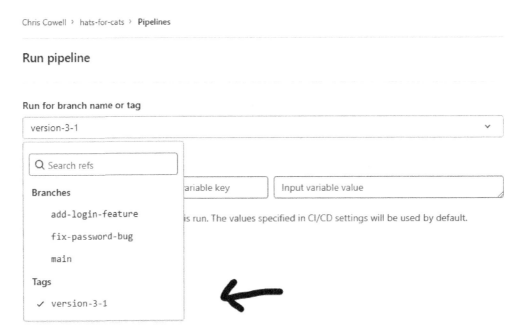

Figure 4.7 – Manually running a pipeline against a specific tag
(the tag's name is highlighted)

Other types of pipelines

You've just seen how to run pipelines against a branch or a Git tag. There are three other types of pipelines that you should be aware of, although they are used less frequently than the branch or tag pipelines:

- **Merge request pipelines** run against the source branch of a merge request, whenever commits are made to that branch.
- **Merged result pipelines** are special kinds of merge request pipelines. Merged result pipelines run against a *temporary merge* of a merge request's source branch into its target branch, whenever commits are made to the source branch. Note that this kind of pipeline doesn't *actually* merge

the two branches; it just runs a pipeline against the collection of files that would have resulted if you *had* merged them. This is a great way to make extra sure that your branch will integrate well into your stable code base.

- **Merge trains** are a special kind of merged result pipeline. Merge trains queue up several merge requests and then perform separate, concurrent merged result pipelines on each merge request in the queue. But instead of performing a temporary merge of just the source and target branches of one merge request, the merge train performs a temporary merge of the source branches from *every merge request that's ahead of the current merge request in the queue*. This is a good way to make sure that multiple branches will integrate well into a rapidly changing target branch when they are merged.

These alternative pipeline types aren't used as often as the standard branch and tag pipelines. Because they are conceptually more difficult to understand, and because they require some extra configuration on your part, we'll refer you to the official GitLab documentation to learn more about whether they might be useful for your projects, and if so, how to get them running.

Skipping pipelines

Even though GitLab's CI/CD pipelines are amazing, powerful, and an enormous help to anyone who builds software, there are times when it makes more sense *not* to run a pipeline. The following are some examples:

- Teams using the SaaS version of GitLab (that is, the instance hosted on gitlab.com) have a limited number of monthly minutes of compute time for running pipelines. If they are running low on minutes, they may want to run pipelines only on the most important commits.

- If you make a trivial change that you know won't affect any of the pipeline tests or scans, and you don't need it deployed immediately, you may not need a pipeline for that commit. Examples of this situation include adding a comment to your code, lightly editing a README file, or fixing a tiny typo in the GUI's text.

- When you're about to make several small commits to the same branch, and you consider all the commits to be low risk, you may want to wait until all the commits are submitted before running a pipeline against all of them. But this should be used sparingly: by increasing the scope of changes, you're giving up some of the benefits of "shifting left" that GitLab provides.

Fortunately, it's easy to prevent a commit from triggering a pipeline run. Just include one of these two phrases anywhere within a commit message, and GitLab will make the commit without running a pipeline against it:

- [skip ci]
- [ci skip]

This pipeline pause applies just to a single commit. The next time you commit to that branch without including one of the two skip messages, the pipeline will resume on the new commit (which, of course, will include any edits you made on the pipeline-less commit).

You've now seen how pipelines can run against Git branches or Git tags, and you've learned about other, more specialized, and less frequently used pipelines that run against temporarily merged branches. You also understand how pipelines can be triggered automatically when you commit edited files, or manually whenever you want to rerun your scans and checks against any version of your code. You even know how to tell GitLab to skip a pipeline for a particular commit, saving time and compute resources. You may not use all of these triggering techniques and pipeline variations in your work, but it's good to know what options are available when special needs arise.

Of course, a pipeline doesn't do you any good if you can't find its results or don't understand what it's reporting. So, in the next section, we'll investigate how to view and interpret the information that a completed pipeline provides.

Reading GitLab CI/CD pipeline statuses

Not only does each pipeline instance have a pass/fail status, but each stage within the pipeline instance has a pass/fail status, and each job within any stage has a pass/fail status as well. There are more statuses available than just **passed** or **failed**. Here are some of the most commonly seen values:

- **running**: The pipeline, stage, or job is in progress.
- **pending**: Waiting for resources to become available to start a job.
- **skipped**: When an earlier stage fails, all later stages are skipped by default.
- **canceled**: Users can cancel any job or pipeline while it's running.

In *Figure 4.3*, you saw how the list of pipeline instances shows the status not only of each pipeline instance but also of the stages within each pipeline. In *Figure 4.4*, you saw how you can zoom in on an individual pipeline instance to see the status of all the jobs within each of the pipeline's stages. GitLab lets you zoom in even further to see the output of the individual commands that are contained within a job, by clicking on one of the job icons shown in *Figure 4.4*. This view shows you what commands GitLab types into a shell while executing that job, and what output is generated by those commands.

For example, the following screenshot shows the command and output for a job that runs a series of Python unit tests. You can see from the output that two tests passed and one failed. Normally, we'd add more logic to the job so that it uploads the unit test results, which would let GitLab display those results within its GUI. But for the sake of simplicity, this example omits that step:

Configuring GitLab CI/CD pipelines

Figure 4.8 – Job for running Python unit tests
(the job's command and output are highlighted)

There are several places within the GUI where GitLab displays the status of pipelines, stages, and jobs. Also, there are several different graphical representations of the project's pipeline structure and the status of each element within the structure. These icons and diagrams are easy to spot as you navigate around GitLab, and most of them can either be hovered over or clicked on to reveal more information about that element.

So far in this chapter, we've covered what pipelines are, how they benefit software development teams, how they are structured, how to run them, and how to interpret their results. But you may have noticed that we haven't explained how to create and configure them yet. That's a big topic that much of the rest of this book is concerned with. However, we realize you might be getting antsy at this point: now that you know so much about pipelines, you're probably itching to try them out in your GitLab instance!

Never fear. We've found that learning GitLab is easiest if you're introduced to its features and components multiple times, in different contexts, and with different sets of background knowledge each time. With that in mind, this is a great opportunity to give you a lightning-fast introduction to setting up a simple CI/CD pipeline for Hats for Cats. We'll go through the material quickly, but don't worry – you'll see these concepts again, repeatedly, in future chapters.

Configuring GitLab CI/CD pipelines

We've mentioned that you can configure your project's CI/CD pipeline to define its stages, jobs, and commands. But how do you do that? All CI/CD pipeline configuration happens within a file called

`.gitlab-ci.yml`, which lives in the root of your project's repository. Look through any public GitLab project, and you're sure to see a file with that name that determines what happens in that project's pipeline.

Every `.gitlab-ci.yml` file uses a domain-specific language that consists of keywords, values, and some syntactical glue. Some keywords define stages and jobs within those stages. Other keywords configure jobs to do different things within the pipeline. Still, other keywords set variables, specify Docker images for jobs, or affect the overall pipeline in various ways. This domain-specific language is rich enough to let you do just about anything you'd like in your CI/CD pipelines, but not so rich as to be overwhelming (at least, once you've had some experience writing and reading these CI/CD configuration files).

There are about 30 keywords available to use in a `.gitlab-ci.yml` file. Rather than trying to memorize the details and configuration options available for each, we recommend that you concentrate on the big picture of what's possible with CI/CD pipelines, and then learn the nuances of the relevant keywords as needed. The official GitLab documentation is the best source of information on these keywords, especially since they change from time to time.

We'll spend much of the rest of this book demonstrating some of the key CI/CD pipeline tasks you can accomplish with these keywords, so this is a good time to dip your toe into the CI/CD pipeline configuration water by looking at a bare-bones `.gitlab-ci.yml` file. The contents of this file will drive an actual pipeline, albeit a simple one. Let's walk through it, explaining each line as we go.

Since `.gitlab-ci.yml` files use the YAML format for structured data, this would be a good time to learn or review the extremely simple YAML syntax. The Wikipedia article on YAML is a good place to find that information. We'll wait for you here until you feel confident using YAML.

Now that that's out of the way, let's get started. Most CI/CD configuration files begin by defining the pipeline's stages. If you don't define any stages, your pipeline will have `build`, `test`, and `deploy` stages by default. If you do define stages, these will replace – not augment – the three default stages. For this simple pipeline, we only need the `build` and `test` stages, so let's define those explicitly in a new file called `.gitlab-ci.yml` at the root level of the `hats-for-cats` project repository:

```
stages:
  - build
  - test
```

We're going to have two jobs in this pipeline, with one job in each of the two stages we just defined. Let's say that this project is Python-based, so both jobs will use Python-related tools. In the next chapter, we'll explain more about how GitLab Runners can run jobs within Docker containers. For now, all you need to know is that we can specify a Docker image within our CI/CD configuration file for jobs to run within. In this case, both of our jobs will need access to Python tools, so we'll tell the pipeline to use a Python Docker image for all jobs:

```
image: python:3.10
```

Our first job will run mypy, which is a tool that makes sure Python source code uses the right data types in its functions and variables. This task could reasonably be put in either the build or test stage, but let's put it in the build stage just so we can have at least one job in that stage. Here's how we define the job:

```
data-type-check:
  stage: build
  script:
    - pip install mypy
    - mypy src/hats-for-cats.py
```

Since the first word on the first line is not a keyword that GitLab recognizes, GitLab assumes it's the name of a new job to be defined. This name can contain spaces instead of hyphens if you prefer, but sometimes, that can be harder to parse visually.

The next line assigns this job to the build stage.

The third line starts with the script keyword, which tells GitLab that we're about to list the commands for this job. And the following two lines do exactly that: the first runs a command to use the pip package manager to install the mypy package into the Python Docker container that the job is running in. The second command runs the mypy command that was just installed on any files that are in the src/ directory. If mypy finds any problems with how our code uses data types, it will fail this job, which will fail the build stage that the job lives in, which, in turn, will fail the entire pipeline instance.

Now, let's define a job for running automated unit tests:

```
unit-tests:
  stage: test
  script:
    - pip install pytest
    - pytest test/ --junitxml=unit_test_results.xml
  artifacts:
    reports:
      junit: unit_test_results.xml
    when: always
```

Since the first line is not a recognized keyword, GitLab knows that this is the name of a new job that we're defining.

The second line assigns the job to the test stage.

Following the script keyword, we define two commands for the job. The first installs the pytest package, while the second runs the newly installed pytest tool on any unit tests that live in the test/ directory. Furthermore, it specifies that pytest should output the results of the unit tests to a file called unit_test_results.xml, which will be in JUnit XML format.

The section that begins with the `artifacts` keyword allows GitLab to preserve the unit test results file when the job finishes, instead of throwing it away. In GitLab terminology, any files that are generated by a job and then preserved are called **artifacts**. *It's important to understand that any files that were generated by a job but not declared to be artifacts are deleted as soon as the job finishes.*

The exact syntax that's used in this example `artifacts` section isn't too important because it can easily be looked up in the GitLab documentation when needed, but here, we are telling GitLab that this artifact contains unit test results in the JUnit XML format, which is an industry-standard format that GitLab requires to ingest and display the test results in the **test** tab on the pipeline details page.

The last line in the `artifacts` section tells GitLab to preserve the results file as an artifact, even if the `unit-tests` job fails. The job will have a **failed** status if there are any test failures, but we want to display the test results every time this job runs, even if (or especially if!) there are any test failures.

Combining all of the configuration code listed previously, the complete `.gitlab-ci.yml` file looks like this:

```
stages:
  - build
  - test

image: python:3.10

data-type-check:
  stage: build
  script:
    - pip install mypy
    - mypy src/hats-for-cats.py

unit-tests:
  stage: test
  script:
    - pip install pytest
    - pytest test/ --junitxml=unit_test_results.xml
  artifacts:
    reports:
      junit: unit_test_results.xml
    when: always
```

The following screenshot shows the pipeline details page after this pipeline has finished. Don't worry about the **unit-tests** job's **failed** status. That's expected whenever any of the tests that it runs fail:

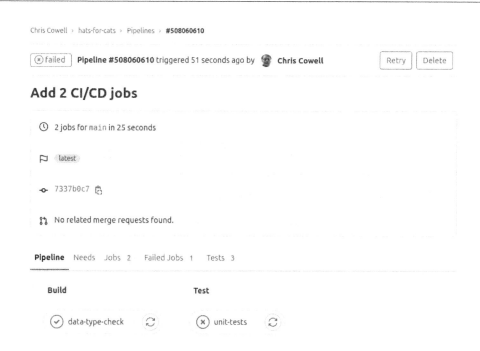

Figure 4.9 – Details page for the completed pipeline that validates Python data types and runs unit tests

Summary

Now that you have a good grasp of the purpose and structure of GitLab CI/CD pipelines, let's review the concepts we covered in this chapter.

Pipelines are a series of steps that are performed against code in your project's Git repository. Each project has just one pipeline, although the various steps that make up a project's pipeline can be run or suppressed, depending on which Git branch or Git tag the pipeline is running against. The term "pipeline" is sometimes used to mean the overall set of tasks that will be run on a project's code, while other times, it's used to mean a single instance or run of that pipeline against a particular version of the repository's files.

The CI, or continuous integration, portion of a pipeline answers the question, *is the code good?* It typically consists of some combination of automated tests, security scans, license compliance checks, and code quality checks. The CI steps of a pipeline enable the *shift left* philosophy, which ensures that problems are found when they are still easy and cheap to fix. It also promotes collaboration among all members of the software development team.

The CD, or continuous delivery/deployment, portion of a pipeline, answers the question, *which environment should the code be deployed to?* It's also responsible for actually deploying the code to that environment. The process of packaging up the code into a deployable format can be considered part of the CD portion pipeline as well. The CD steps of a pipeline promote frequent, predictable, low-risk feature and bugfix releases to customers.

Each project's pipeline consists of one or more stages, where a stage is a collection of tasks that share a similar theme, such as building, testing, or deploying your code. Each stage consists of one or more jobs, where each job consists of a single unit of work, such as compiling Java classes, running automated unit tests, or packaging your application into a Docker image. Each job consists of one or more commands, which are shell commands that a human would type into a terminal if they were to manually perform the same work as a pipeline job. A pipeline ultimately consists of GitLab automatically typing in a series of terminal commands, recording the output of those jobs, and displaying the results to the user.

A pipeline typically runs every time you commit code to your repository, so you always have an up-to-date picture of the state of your code, whether it be on a feature branch, a bugfix branch, or the default branch. Pipelines can run against Git branches or Git tags and can be triggered automatically or manually. More exotic forms of pipelines are available, such as running a pipeline against the code that would result if you were to merge one branch into another.

Each pipeline instance has a pass/fail status (or one of several less-common statuses). Each stage within the pipeline also has a pass/fail status, as does each job within the stages. The status of any pipeline, stage, or job can be viewed within the GitLab GUI.

Pipelines can perform virtually any tasks that a human typing into a terminal could. Each project configures the tasks that make up its pipeline using a special domain-specific language in a file called `.gitlab-ci.yml`.

Much of the rest of this book is dedicated to explaining what sorts of tasks you can configure a pipeline to perform, and what syntax and keywords you can use to do so. But first, we need to introduce you to the tool that performs the work of a pipeline, or that serves as the "robot" that types in the terminal commands defined in your CI/CD pipeline configuration file. In other words, it's time to learn more about GitLab Runners.

Part 2
Automating DevOps Stages with GitLab CI/CD Pipelines

This part is the core of the book: you will learn how to replace the most common manual steps in the software development life cycle with automated equivalents using GitLab CI/CD pipelines. By the end of this part, you will know how to set up your infrastructure to support pipelines. You will also feel confident about configuring pipelines to perform several critical tasks: verifying your code by running quality scans and functional tests, securing your code and its dependencies by running security scans, packaging your code by automatically running the standard build and packaging tools, and automatically deploying your code to the appropriate environments.

This section comprises the following chapters:

- *Chapter 5, Installing and Configuring GitLab Runners*
- *Chapter 6, Verifying Your Code*
- *Chapter 7, Securing Your Code*
- *Chapter 8, Packaging and Deploying Your Code*

5
Installing and Configuring GitLab Runners

In *Chapter 4*, you learned about the fundamentals of GitLab CI/CD. We defined and introduced the vocabulary and concepts around CI/CD pipelines, which included CI/CD pipeline components, different pipeline types, how to observe and interact with pipelines in the GitLab UI, and how to write a pipeline's configuration using the .gitlab-ci.yml file. A few paragraphs were also spent introducing GitLab Runner as the crucial component of GitLab CI/CD, which actually runs pipeline tasks and reports the results back to GitLab.

The sole focus of this chapter will be the topic of GitLab runners. You will learn in this chapter that GitLab runners act as the "muscle" in the CI/CD process. Runners are small programs that are installed separately from the main GitLab application. Their purpose is to receive new CI/CD jobs published by GitLab and follow the jobs' instructions as specified in the .gitlab-ci.yml file. Runners can be installed and configured to work with a variety of types of infrastructure, including standalone servers, VMs, containers, and others.

We'll begin by introducing the runner architecture as well as comparing and contrasting GitLab Runner with other tools that you may be familiar with. Next, we'll describe installing and configuring runners so they can be paired with GitLab to run CI/CD jobs. Finally, we'll end with discussing best practices for using different runner types for different circumstances.

Once you have learned how to install, configure, use, and maintain GitLab runners, you will be well on your way to managing the end-to-end life cycle for building, testing, and deploying your application. Here is how we'll cover the topics in this chapter:

- Defining GitLab runners and their relationship to CI/CD
- The runner architecture and supported platforms
- Installing the Runner agent
- Configuring and registering the runner with GitLab
- Understanding when and why to use the various runner types and executors

Technical requirements

Like the previous chapters, you'll get the most out of this chapter if you have an account on a GitLab instance **software-as-a-service** (**SaaS**) or self-managed). In addition, installing the GitLab Runner agent requires a computer (Windows, Mac, or Linux) on which to install the runner binary. A personal laptop would be fine—the runner is lightweight and its system requirements are minimal. If you are using GitLab.com, CI/CD pipelines can also be run using GitLab's SaaS runners, though be aware of possible usage charges.

Defining GitLab runners and their relationship to CI/CD

Recall that GitLab CI/CD is a series of tasks performed against code in your project, which often include some combination of build, test, and deploy jobs. Importantly, CI/CD pipelines are not run inside the GitLab application, as each job will generally require some specific platform and set of tools to successfully run.

> Note
> GitLab runners are programs that accept CI/CD jobs from GitLab, run the jobs' tasks in an appropriate execution environment, and then report the results back to GitLab.

GitLab Runner is an open source application written in Go

The official repository for the GitLab Runner application lives in a project hosted on `GitLab.com` called `gitlab-runner`. At the time of writing, you can navigate to `https://gitlab.com/gitlab-org/gitlab-runner` to view the project's development and source code. Like the main GitLab application, GitLab Runner follows a monthly release cadence. The latest version of GitLab Runner is *usually* the same major and minor release number as GitLab, though that is not guaranteed to always be the case. Like most of GitLab, GitLab Runner is open source and distributed under the MIT license.

A perusal of the code base referenced in the previous URL shows us that Gitlab Runner is written in the Go programming language. The program is compatible with most major computer architectures (x86, AMD64, ARM, and so on) and operating systems (Windows, macOS, and Linux)—really, just about anywhere that supports installing Go binaries. We'll soon see that installing the runner executable is straightforward and requires few dependencies.

GitLab Runner runs CI/CD jobs specified in .gitlab-ci.yml

Recall from the previous chapter that GitLab CI/CD pipelines comprise stages and jobs defined in `.gitlab-ci.yml`. Each job contains a set of instructions, which is often shell-style commands to be run in sequence. By default, every new commit to a branch where a `.gitlab-ci.yml` file is defined launches a new pipeline run. That means the jobs in `.gitlab-ci.yml` will be scheduled to run following the order and logic specified in the configuration.

During a CI/CD pipeline run, when a job arrives at its "turn," the job will be assigned to an available GitLab runner that is able to run the job's instructions. One job gets assigned to one runner. After the runner receives the job from GitLab, one of the first things it will do is fetch the commit that launched the pipeline, so it has the relevant snapshot of the code base. The runner may then perform steps such as compiling a build, running unit tests, running security scans, or deploying the application to some kind of environment. Remember, the runner just follows the job's instructions from `.gitlab-ci.yml`. Once the runner completes the tasks specified in the job, it will report the results back to GitLab. That will almost always include returning a pass or fail status, as well as any artifacts generated or modified during job execution.

As discussed near the beginning of *Chapter 4* (see the *Viewing a list of pipelines* section), the pipeline status and job execution can be monitored in real time via the GitLab UI. The runner constantly communicates with GitLab, and from the UI, you can view available runners, modify runner settings, intervene with pipeline and job execution, view uploaded artifacts, and more. One way to think about the relationship between GitLab's CI/CD components is to think of runners as the muscles that follow the instructions of `.gitlab-ci.yml` (the brain). GitLab would then be like the nervous system, which coordinates the communication between the brain (the pipeline configuration) and the muscles (the runners doing the heavy lifting of running CI/CD jobs).

The runner architecture and supported platforms

Before going into further details about runner components, installation, and configuration, it's worth clarifying a few pieces of terminology. So far in this chapter, the words *GitLab Runner* and *runner* may appear to have been used interchangeably. However, a bit of nuance is required. *GitLab Runner* refers to the application installed once on a computer. Once the GitLab Runner application is installed, it does not yet communicate with GitLab or run CI/CD jobs. In order to connect to GitLab and run CI/CD jobs, an administrator will need to execute a GitLab Runner command that *registers* individual *runners* with GitLab and specifies the execution environment those runners will use. Each registered runner will then be a dedicated process that checks into GitLab and runs CI/CD jobs.

This setup can appear confusing at first because a single GitLab Runner application will normally support registering multiple runner processes on the computer where it's installed. Moreover, those runner processes might use a variety of execution environments for running their jobs. For example, consider a single, bare-metal Linux server. An admin may install the GitLab Runner application, which they then use to register the following:

- A runner process that executes a job in a shell session on the server OS
- A second runner process that executes a job in a Docker container
- A third runner process that pipes a job's commands to another server over SSH

That is, a single GitLab Runner application installed on a single computer can register multiple runners. The Gitlab Runner application is responsible for starting, stopping, and managing the individual runner processes and picking up CI/CD jobs from GitLab. *Figure 5.1* summarizes the flow of information between GitLab, a runner, and the environment used to execute the job payload:

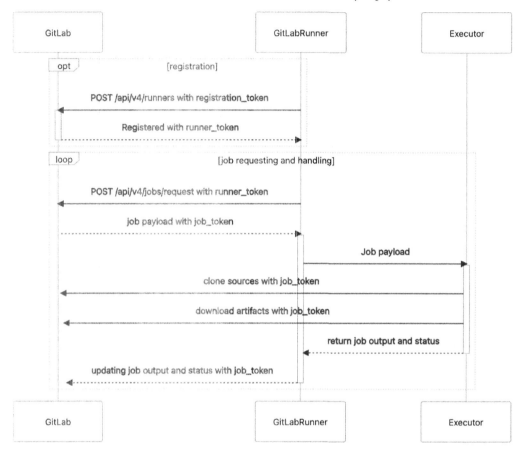

Figure 5.1 – GitLab Runner communication and job execution

For the purposes of this chapter, don't worry too much about the finer details of this flow. Just understand that runners communicate with GitLab in order to receive and run CI/CD jobs in an associated execution environment.

GitLab Runner is supported on most platforms and architectures

At the time of writing this book, GitLab Runner can be installed on every major Linux distribution and architecture, as well as on FreeBSD, Windows, macOS, Docker, and Kubernetes. GitLab also offers a FIPS 140-12 runner binary for those organizations that require it for legal or internal compliance reasons.

Table 5.1 summarizes the supported architectures and operating system platforms as of GitLab Runner 15.3:

Officially Supported Computer Architectures	Officially Supported Operating Systems
x86	Debian
AMD64	Ubuntu
ARM	CentOS
ARM64	Red Hat Enterprise Linux
s390x	Fedora
ppx64le	Linux Mint
	Microsoft Windows
	macOS
	FreeBSD

Table 5.1 – GitLab Runner-supported platforms

This table lists the architecture and OS platforms that GitLab explicitly supports per its documentation. For the Linux distributions listed, GitLab makes official GitLab Runner packages available that can be managed with the distribution's native package manager. However, even if your Linux distribution of choice doesn't appear in the table, you can generally install the GitLab Runner binary manually on any Linux box provided it has a compatible computer architecture.

As previously mentioned, GitLab Runner can also be hosted in a container or container orchestration system, namely Docker and Kubernetes, respectively. Note this refers to the hosting of the GitLab Runner agent itself, as opposed to the executor or execution environment it uses to run jobs. When we discuss executors in detail later in the chapter, we will learn that a runner can be directed to use Docker or Kubernetes as its executor, regardless of where the GitLab Runner agent is installed, provided it has access to the relevant container tools.

Runners can be specific, group, or shared

In *Chapter 3*, we learned that work in GitLab is organized into projects and groups. Projects and groups are intended to represent organizational boundaries such as teams or product lines. Projects normally (though not always) host a Git repository containing source code. Groups are containers that hold projects and other groups, similar to how folders organize files and other folders in a filesystem.

Chapter 4 then introduced CI/CD pipelines. We learned that CI/CD pipelines run inside a project against that project's code. How, then, do we organize and assign runners in GitLab, making them available for CI/CD pipelines to run their jobs? It turns out that we can organize runner availability similarly to how we can organize many other GitLab resources: by making them available at the project, group, or instance level.

Specific runners are enabled for individual projects

Project owners and maintainers may choose to register runners just for their projects. **Specific runners** are assigned to specific projects, and only pick up and run jobs from CI/CD pipelines running in the project they're assigned to.

Using specific runners has a couple of advantages. The first is that specific runners empower project owners and developers to set up the runner infrastructure they need without changing anything outside the project they're working in. For example, a developer might install GitLab Runner on their local laptop, and register a specific runner to a project where they're the lead contributor. The developer won't need to ask IT or platform owners to go through some global change management process. Project-specific runners can be managed under project settings, as shown in *Figure 5.2*:

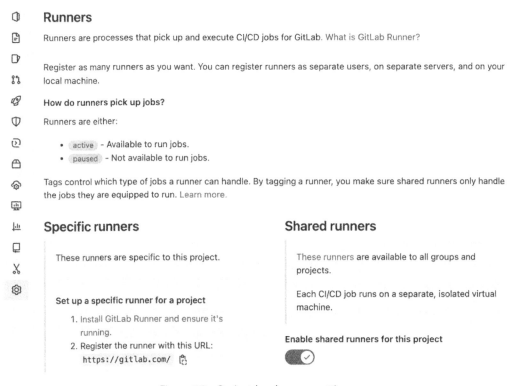

Figure 5.2 – Project-level runner settings

Another advantage of specific runners is the possibility of dedicated or customized tooling for individual projects. Specific runners allow for easier project-level accounting of resource use. Moreover, security and compliance policies may require that certain projects use dedicated infrastructure that is separate from the rest of the organization. A runner registered to one specific project will only run pipeline code from inside that project. Pipelines from other parts of GitLab won't have access to it.

Group runners are available for all projects inside a group

We've learned that some resources in GitLab are only available in projects, some resources are only available in groups, and others can be available in both projects and groups. Runners are an example of that third type of resource. Registering a runner at the group level makes that runner available to all pipelines in all projects within that group and its subgroups. *Figure 5.3* shows that group runners can be registered in a group's CI/CD settings:

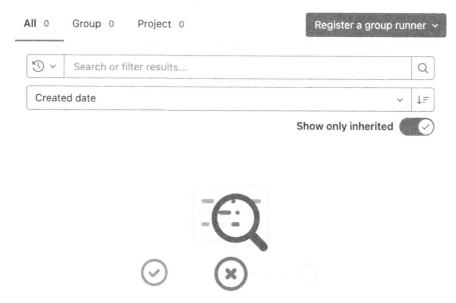

Figure 5.3 – Group runner settings

Group owners can create and manage group runners, which accept and run CI/CD jobs on a **first-in, first-out** (**FIFO**) basis. Group runners are useful for teams that want to share resources or run multi-project CI/CD pipelines, but still need to manage their own runners for accounting or compliance reasons.

Shared runners are available to all projects across GitLab

GitLab instance administrators can choose to register runners that can pick up CI/CD jobs from any project in any group across the GitLab instance. This allows platform owners to abstract away runner management from developers or project managers. Instance admins can also configure CI/CD quotas at the global level that limit the amount of CI/CD pipeline minutes individual projects can use across available shared runners.

> **Shared Runners Only Apply to Self-Managed GitLab**
>
> Administrators can only configure shared runners on self-managed GitLab instances. `GitLab.com` customers can choose to use SaaS runners provided by GitLab, as well as register their own group or specific runners. A certain number of pipeline minutes for SaaS runners are included in each GitLab license tier, with additional minutes available for purchase. There is never a charge to use your own group or specific runners.

Container-based platforms such as Kubernetes are a common executor choice for shared runners in order to provide ephemeral resources that can be quickly scaled. Unlike group runners, which pick jobs on a FIFO basis, shared runners operate via a *fair usage queue*. Projects with the fewest CI/CD jobs using shared runners have priority over those with more active jobs using shared runners. That helps to ensure that a single massive pipeline from one project doesn't hog the entire shared runner infrastructure.

Each runner has a defined executor

Let's review some of the components we have mentioned so far:

- The GitLab application, which schedules and coordinates CI/CD pipelines
- GitLab Runner, the binary installed on a computer
- Individual runners, which are processes that run CI/CD jobs and are managed by the GitLab Runner agent

If you look back at *Figure 5.1*, you will notice an **Executor component**, which receives the job payload and returns the job output and status. The executor refers to the environment that a runner process uses to run a received CI/CD job. A runner's executor is specified when the runner is first registered with GitLab. Recall that multiple runner processes, each with its own executor, can be registered from a single computer that has the GitLab Runner agent installed. *Table 5.2* summarizes the supported runner executors:

Officially Supported GitLab Runner Executors
Docker
Shell
VirtualBox
Parallels
Kubernetes
Docker Machine
SSH
Custom

Table 5.2 – GitLab Runner supported executors

We will describe each executor in turn.

The Docker executor

A runner using the Docker executor runs CI/CD jobs in Docker containers that are launched from a specified Docker image. This provides a reproducible environment containing the tools needed to run the CI/CD job. Using the Docker executor requires that Docker Engine be installed on the same computer as GitLab Runner.

> Note
> Docker is the most common executor used among GitLab users. Docker containers are also the default environment used by the shared SaaS runners on GitLab.com.

The Docker executor makes it easy to ensure CI/CD jobs have the tools they need to successfully run. Those tools are provided in the container image that the runner is instructed to use for the job. The image used for a job can be specified in a few separate places:

- Inside a job definition in `.gitlab-ci.yml`
- Globally in `.gitlab-ci.yml`, so it is used for all jobs in the pipeline
- As the default image used by a runner with the Docker executor if `.gitlab-ci.yml` does not specify an image to use

The image the runner uses can be in a local GitLab container registry, another external registry, or a public container registry such as Docker Hub. For example, if your CI/CD job requires an environment with Python tooling, you might instruct the runner to fetch the `python:3.10` image from Docker Hub, and then launch a container from that image to run the job. Once the job completes, the runner will delete the container until it receives a new job, at which point the runner will run the job in a fresh container.

The Shell executor

The Shell executor runs jobs directly in a shell session on the machine where GitLab Runner is installed. The content of the `script` keyword in each job definition in `.gitlab-ci.yml` is run as if a user were typing commands in a terminal. The key advantage of the Shell executor is that it is simple to get started since it uses the native shell and filesystem of wherever GitLab Runner is installed.

There are, however, a couple of challenges that make the Shell executor difficult to scale:

- The first is that you need to have the necessary build, test, or deploy tools required by the CI/CD job already on the server for the Shell executor to access. Or you would need to have steps in the `script` keyword that install the necessary dependencies.

- The second challenge is the lack of a clean-slate environment for CI/CD jobs. It is easy to leave leftover build and test artifacts since the job will be executed directly in the server's filesystem, rather than in a reproducible environment such as a container.

So while the Shell executor may be the best executor to use as a beginner standing up your first pipelines, it is recommended that you use a different executor for more complicated build environments.

The VirtualBox executor

The VirtualBox executor is a way to provide reproducible environments for CI/CD jobs that may still require full operating system resources. The executor can only be used on computers that have the VirtualBox hypervisor installed. When you register a runner with the VirtualBox executor, specify a **virtual machine (VM)** template that the runner will use to run CI/CD jobs. When the runner picks up a job, it will spin up a new VM from the base template, run the job in a shell session on that VM, report the results back to GitLab, and then tear down the VM.

While useful as a way of ensuring clean-slate environments, the VirtualBox executor may not be necessary unless the job requires access to an operating system running on a Type-2 hypervisor. Consider using the Docker or Kubernetes executor if you would like standardization without the overhead of a VM.

The Parallels executor

The Parallels executor is configured and runs jobs the same way as the VirtualBox executor, the difference being that it uses the Parallels virtualization platform instead of VirtualBox. This allows you to run CI/CD jobs in a Windows VM running on a macOS host machine.

The Kubernetes executor

When a runner is registered with the Kubernetes executor, it runs a CI/CD job in a Pod (that is, a group of one or more containers) in a Kubernetes cluster. This naturally requires you to have a Kubernetes cluster set up, which the runner connects to via the Kubernetes API.

At the time of writing, there are a few different ways that GitLab Runner can connect to a Kubernetes cluster:

- GitLab offers an official **Helm chart** to deploy the Runner agent into a cluster.
- GitLab also includes a broader method to connect a Kubernetes cluster to a GitLab instance, called **GitLab Agent for Kubernetes**. Once the GitLab instance is connected to a cluster, you can then use the agent to deploy a runner with the Kubernetes executor onto the cluster.
- GitLab is actively working on a tool called **GitLab Operator** that further automates the provisioning of GitLab resources in Kubernetes, using container management platforms such as Red Hat OpenShift. Operator will provide another method of deploying a runner with the Kubernetes executor to a cluster. While not yet recommended for production use, Operator can be used to effectively manage resources in your dev and test environments. Refer to the GitLab documentation for more details.

Ultimately, successfully working with container orchestrations requires a high degree of knowledge and experience in networking, storage, and security. If you or your team has Kubernetes expertise, the Kubernetes executor can be a powerful way to implement and scale a cloud-native CI/CD workflow. If not, it is better to stick with previously mentioned executors such as Docker.

The Docker Machine executor

While the Docker executor provisions individual Docker containers for running CI/CD jobs, the Docker Machine executor provisions the entire host (VMs) that has Docker Engine instead. Those hosts themselves then support the launching of Docker containers. Docker Machine is normally used with a cloud provider with autoscaling, so you can quickly and flexibly launch container-compatible hosts as demand requires.

> **Note**
> Docker (the company) is no longer actively developing Docker Machine in favor of Docker Desktop. GitLab maintains a fork of Docker Machine in order to continue supporting the Docker Machine executor.

You can somewhat think of the Docker Machine executor as a combination of the VirtualBox/Parallels executor and the Docker executor, with additional autoscaling support included. Docker Machine can also be useful to ensure isolated resources for each job, by ensuring containers run on their own dedicated VMs. In fact, GitLab uses Docker Machine for its own Linux SaaS runners, offering users runners that are both scalable and properly isolated on the multi-tenant platform.

The SSH executor

Sometimes you might want to run CI/CD jobs on a piece of infrastructure where, for technical or compliance reasons, you are unable to install GitLab Runner. If that infrastructure supports SSH access from a computer where you *can* install GitLab Runner, you can use the SSH executor to run CI/CD jobs on the remote host.

When you register a GitLab runner using the SSH executor, you will also specify the remote host to run the CI/CD job, and the SSH identity file used to connect to that host. When the runner receives a CI/CD job, it will then "pipe" the commands over SSH so they are executed on the remote host. While the SSH executor currently only supports Bash commands and scripts, you might find it useful if you do not want to install the GitLab Runner program on every machine on which you want to run CI/CD jobs.

So far, we've described the major components of GitLab runners: the GitLab Runner agent, its individual registered runner processes, and the executor each runner process might use to run its jobs. There is one more element of runner configuration worth discussing, and that is runner tags.

Runner tags restrict which runners can pick up which jobs

Runner tags are labels placed on GitLab runners that match them with job definitions that also include that tag. Tags can represent the runner's platform or available tools, such as `apache`, `rhel`, or `ios`. Tags can also represent the runner's intended use in a certain stage in the CI/CD process, such as `build`, `staging`, or `prod`. When you also specify one or more tags in a CI/CD job definition, you can ensure that the runner has the proper tooling and environment needed to run that job.

For example, consider the example following job in a `.gitlab-ci.yml` file:

```
deploy-to-staging:
    stage: staging
    script: ./deploy-staging.sh
    tags:
        - windows
        - staging
```

The `windows` and `staging` tags, as included in the CI/CD job definition, ensure that the `deploy-to-staging` job will only ever be assigned to runners that have both the `windows` and `staging` tags also assigned to them. By default, runners that have tags will not run untagged jobs – that is, jobs that do not have tags matching them to a certain tagged runner. This default can be overwritten in the runner's settings, where you can permit tagged runners to run jobs that do not have tags, and therefore presumably do not care where they are run.

> **Runner Tags ≠ Git Tags**
>
> The word "tag" in GitLab can seem confusing because the term is used in a few different contexts. In this discussion, "tag" is simply a label put on runners that matches them to CI/CD jobs with the same tag or tags. These are not Git tags, which are descriptive labels placed on Git commits, and are also found in GitLab. Runner tags are unrelated to tags used in Git version control.

By now, we've covered all the essential information around GitLab runners, how they work conceptually, and the different supported platforms and executors. It is time to walk through the runner installation process.

Installing the Runner agent

This section will be most helpful if you follow along and install and register a runner on your own computer. You will find that the installation steps will differ slightly depending on your system type: Windows, macOS, Linux with a supported package manager, or a generic Linux system. Regardless of platform, the same two-step process holds:

1. Install the GitLab Runner agent.
2. Register a runner with GitLab.

Installing GitLab Runner

As previously mentioned, the method of installation will differ slightly depending on your operating system. For major Linux distributions, the documentation (https://docs.gitlab.com/runner/install/linux-repository.html) will direct you to add the runner repository to your system, and then use your native package manager to install the `gitlab-runner` package. For Windows, macOS, and other Linux distros, you will use `curl` to get the program directly from GitLab, make it executable, then install and start the runner agent.

Let's take the example of a Red Hat Linux Enterprise server with an *x86_64* architecture and RPM-based package management system. The GitLab documentation directs us to first download and execute a shell script that adds the `gitlab-runner` repositories to our system's package manager:

```
sudo curl -L "https://packages.gitlab.com/install/repositories/runner/gitlab-runner/script.rpm.sh" | sudo bash
```

If you were to examine the content of the shell script, you would see that all it does is detect the operating system platform, and then run the relevant package management comment to add the `gitlab-runner` repository. You can verify that this step has been completed by checking your list of available repositories (`sudo dnf repolist` in RHEL). You should see `gitlab-runner` in the list alongside the primary OS repositories.

We've added the runner repository, but have not yet installed GitLab Runner. We can easily do so by installing the `gitlab-runner` package:

```
sudo dnf install -y gitlab-runner
```

Once the installation completes, GitLab Runner should automatically start in the background (you will need to manually start GitLab Runner if you installed it on Windows or macOS, or installed it manually on Linux). You can verify that the GitLab Runner agent is started and running with:

```
sudo gitlab-runner status
```

You should see confirmation that the agent is running, and also that there are not yet any runners registered with GitLab. Registering runners is what we will do next.

Registering a runner with GitLab

We have so far installed the GitLab Runner agent on a computer, where it runs as a background service. However, there are not yet any runners communicating with GitLab. The way we set up runners to communicate with GitLab and run CI/CD jobs is by *registering* one or more runners.

Recall the previous discussion on shared, specific, and group runners. When you register a runner with GitLab, you bind runners to an entire GitLab instance (shared runners), a group (group runners), or a project (specific runners). Registration instructions and runner settings after registration appear in the respective part of GitLab where you register the runner (instance, group, or project). For example, recalling *Figure 5.2*, we see that we can find these details under **Settings | CI/CD | Runners** in the *Hats for Cats* project:

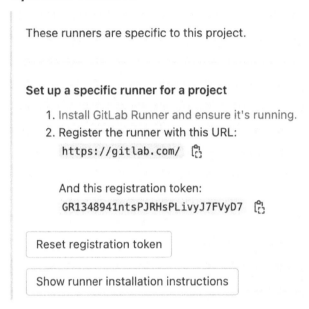

Figure 5.4 – Project-level runner settings

In addition, take note of the registration token shown in *Figure 5.4*. The runner registration token is generated by GitLab and is used by the runner to authenticate to the correct area of GitLab where it is registered:

1. If you are following along on a demo system, copy the registration token to your clipboard, as we will need it when we register a runner from the computer where we have GitLab Runner installed.

2. Next, return to the computer where GitLab Runner is installed. From a Terminal session, run a prompt-based runner registration script:

    ```
    sudo gitlab-runner register
    ```

3. GitLab will first prompt you for the URL of your GitLab application instance. For SaaS, this will be `https://gitlab.com`. Otherwise, it will be the URL you use to reach your self-managed instance. In this example, we will stick with `gitlab.com`:

    Enter the GitLab instance URL (for example, `https://gitlab.com`)**:**
    https://gitlab.com

4. Next, the script will ask for the runner registration token. This is the token shown in *Figure 5.2* and will be different depending on the project or group with which you are registering a runner. Put another way, the registration token authenticates the runner to GitLab and ensures that it is registered to the correct project or group:

   ```
   Enter the registration token:
   GR1348941Xi_koNdj8AjJMjSzQyYY
   ```

5. You can then provide an optional description that will show up in the runner's metadata in the GitLab UI. This example might presume the runner is a Linux server where developers can build and test their code:

   ```
   Enter a description for the runner:
   [localhost] Linux dev server
   ```

6. The next message prompts you to enter any optional runner tags. Recall that tags are label metadata that you assign to a runner. Tags advertise the runner as being able to pick up CI/CD jobs that have those same tags. For example, a build job might include the `rhel` tag to indicate that the job requires tooling provided by Red Hat Linux. Only runners with that tag will be allowed to pick up the job. Tags can be assigned on runner registration, as shown here, and can also be modified via the runner settings in the GitLab UI:

   ```
   Enter tags for the runner (comma-separated):
   dev,rhel
   ```

   The optional maintenance note is another area of descriptive metadata that doesn't otherwise configure the runner behavior:

   ```
   Enter optional maintenance note for the runner
   <leave blank in this example>
   ```

   At this point in the script, the newly created runner process will reach out to GitLab to confirm that it can communicate and authenticate:

   ```
   Registering runner...
   succeeded                       runner=GR1348941Xi_koNdj
   ```

7. Lastly, the runner will ask for the execution environment it should use to run CI/CD jobs. Also, remember that the executor depends on having the necessary tooling available; for example, selecting Docker requires that Docker Engine is installed and available on the server. In this example, we'll select `Shell`, as it's the easiest executor with which to get started and requires no dependencies:

   ```
   Enter an executor: parallels, docker-ssh+machine,
     kubernetes, custom, docker, docker-ssh, docker+machine,
   ```

```
shell, ssh, virtualbox:
Shell
```

8. The script will finally confirm that runner registration has succeeded. A runner process is now running on the computer, managed by the local GitLab Runner agent, and ready to pick up a CI/CD job from the GitLab instance:

```
Runner registered successfully. Feel free to start
it, but if it's running already the config should be
automatically reloaded!
Configuration (with the authentication token) was saved
in "/etc/gitlab-runner/config.toml"
```

We can verify successful registration and communication in a couple of ways. From where GitLab Runner is installed, you can view the configured runners with the following command:

```
sudo gitlab-runner list
Runtime platform                                      arch=amd64
os=linux pid=30148 revision=32fc1585 version=15.2.1
Listing configured
runners                              ConfigFile=/etc/gitlab-runner/
config.toml
Linux dev
server                                         Executor=shell
Token=ZLXwxp4KWrQp2jjZRxjj URL=https://gitlab.com
```

A runner with a description of `Linux dev server` is listed, along with its executor, registration token, and the GitLab instance the runner is registered to.

We can also verify that the runner is properly registered from the GitLab side. The runner we just registered is registered with our *Hats for Cats* project. *Figure 5.5* shows that if we return to the project via **Settings | CI/CD | Runners**, and look under **Specific Runners**, we see `Linux dev runner` registered and available to the project:

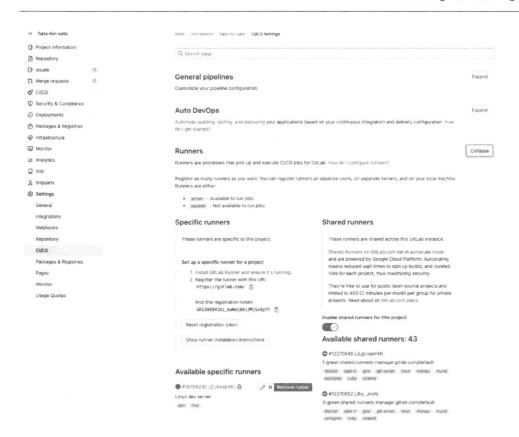

Figure 5.5 – Specific runner successfully registered with GitLab

The GitLab UI shows a couple of other interesting features from our specific runner. The `dev` and `rhel` tags are shown alongside the runner ID and description. The lock icon next to the runner ID indicates that the runner is locked to the specific project to which it is registered, and it cannot be assigned to other projects. The pencil icon will take us to runner settings that we can adjust in the GitLab UI, and the pause button will "pause" the runner. Pausing the runner will keep it registered with GitLab, but will prevent the runner from accepting new jobs while it is paused.

We can view existing runner settings and statistics by clicking on the hyperlinked runner ID. *Figure 5.6* shows information from the runner we registered earlier, which can be viewed in the GitLab UI. This information includes the runner's architecture and networking details, its activity status, and assignable attributes such as runner tags, its protected or unprotected status, description, and ability to be assigned to other projects:

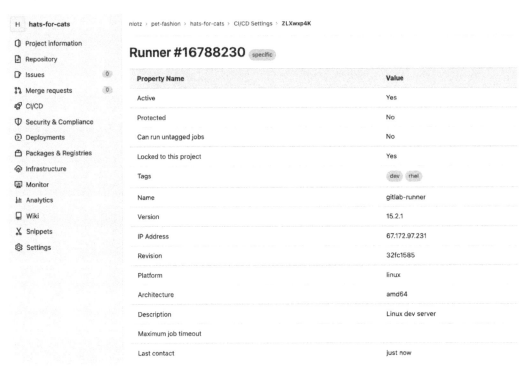

Figure 5.6 – Runner information in the GitLab UI

If we return to the runner settings (as shown in *Figure 5.5*) and select the edit (pencil) icon, we arrive at a page that shows additional runner details as well as attributes we can set from the UI. These settings include protecting the runner and modifying the description and runner tags, as shown in *Figure 5.7*.

The maximum job timeout field tells the runner to report a job as failed by default after a certain period elapses. Be careful with this option; if you set it, make sure it is a value larger than the maximum amount of time you would expect one of your builds to take.

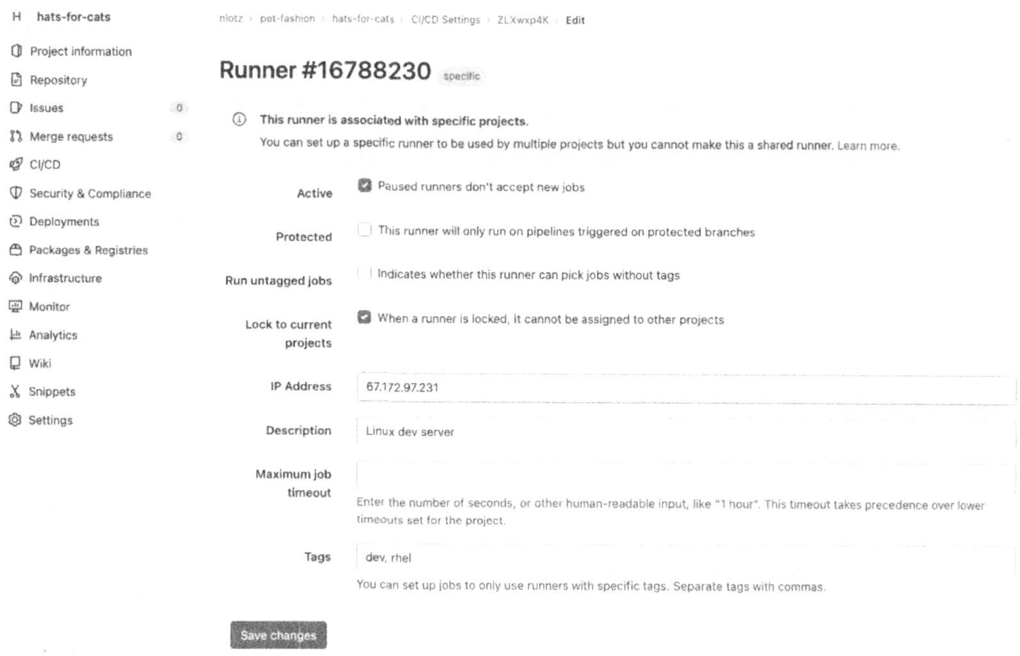

Figure 5.7 – Runner settings in the GitLab UI

At this point, your runner is registered, active, and ready to start picking up CI/CD jobs. The topic we will next turn to is considerations around the runner configurations and executors based on your or your organization's needs.

Considerations regarding the various runner types and executors

We've learned that there are many types of runners, configuration options, and execution environments. In this section, we will discuss some performance, security, and monitoring considerations to help guide your decision-making regarding which runners to use, and when to use them.

Performance considerations

As a developer or operator, you want to make sure that pipelines run as efficiently as possible. Key performance considerations around CI/CD job execution are runner availability and resources, repository size, and how you handle job and application dependencies.

Runner availability

Consider the three scopes of runners discussed earlier in this chapter:

- Shared runners configured at this instance level (if using self-managed GitLab), available to all projects in the instance
- Group runners available to all projects in a group and its subgroups
- Specific runners registered only to designated projects

The way each of the types of runners handles CI/CD jobs can affect pipeline efficiency and execution times. Specific runners are a fairly straightforward case. Use specific runners when you know you need dedicated resources for a project. That said, you may gain pipeline efficiency at the expense of the efficient use of resources. Idle server time can be a consequence of widely using specific runners. Moreover, pooling resources together in group and shared runners can also allow you to take advantage of autoscaling features offered by cloud services in a way that may not be economically feasible with specific runners. So, if your application's resource use and demand are predictable, look to use specific runners. If you expect fluctuation in resource requirements, consider group or shared runners.

Regarding group and shared runners, they may appear to be roughly equivalent in practice, especially if your GitLab instance has a single top-level group storing all your projects. However, group and shared runners are quite different in the way they pick up their respective jobs. Group runners process jobs on a FIFO basis. This means a single resource-intensive pipeline can "hog" a set of group runners as its jobs are queued, especially if there are many jobs in a single stage.

Specific runners, on the other hand, operate via a fair usage queue. That is, projects on the GitLab instance with the fewest jobs already using shared runners are given priority. That may be desirable in some cases, as it suggests more equitable pipeline execution across all your projects in GitLab. In practice, some projects may be more important than others, and you will want those projects to have priority execution, where pending jobs aren't sent to the back of the line because others in the project have already run. In that case, group runners with their FIFO assignment may be your best bet.

Repository size

GitLab's documentation describes a "large" repository as containing more than 50,000 files in the working tree (that is, in the collection of checked-out files). When repositories are large, a rate-limiting step in the pipeline can be the runner cloning or fetching the project repository.

GitLab Runner already has some optimizations in place to minimize the time and resources it takes to pull down project files. If the project has previously been cloned to the runner's execution environment, the runner will perform an incremental fetch so that the entire repository isn't pulled down for each job. Moreover, runners will by default perform a shallow clone, copying down only the latest 20 commits from the project (this setting can be adjusted with the `GIT_DEPTH` variable in your `.gitlab-ci.yml` file).

For some more advanced configuration, you can use the `pre_clone_script` keyword in your `.gitlab-ci.yml` file to set Git configuration commands that run before the runner clones the repository.

Caching dependencies

The considerations around dependency and artifact caching are conceptually similar to the discussion around large repositories. The idea is that we want to minimize the need for runners to repeatedly download the same files, and download only the files they need for the CI/CD job currently assigned to the runner.

The `cache` keyword in `.gitlab-ci.yml` is where you specify file paths that should remain on the runner between jobs. We recommend combining the `cache` keyword with runner tags so that jobs such as tooling are assigned to runners that have those dependencies pre-cached.

By default, each runner will also download all artifacts for every job that has previously run in that pipeline. You can use the `dependencies` keyword to select which jobs' artifacts should be downloaded. For example, if you have separate Windows and Linux build jobs, and separate test jobs for your Windows and Linux builds, it makes sense for the test jobs to only download the artifacts from their respective build job.

Finally, if your pipelines are container-based, you might spend heavy amounts of networking resources pulling container images from public registries to run your jobs. GitLab has a feature called Dependency Proxy, where you can configure a local registry to cache Docker images, so the runner executor does not need to pull from a public source on each run. Rather, the runner will pull from the local registry, and pulling from the public source will only need to take place for updating the container versions in the cache.

Security considerations

There is far more to discuss concerning security and GitLab than can be covered in this book. However, two considerations are immediately implicated by your choices in installing and configuring runners. Those considerations are the choice of runner executor, and how you handle secrets in your CI/CD pipelines.

Your choice of runner executor

Remember that CI/CD pipelines are fundamentally the execution of commands on a remote host – that is, hosts where GitLab Runner is installed. You, therefore, run the inherent risk of performing operations not just on your source code but also on the underlying infrastructure hosting the runner.

In general, some runner executers can be thought of as "safer" than others. Using the shell executor, while convenient, exposes your server's filesystem to the runner, and operations performed against the filesystem may persist across jobs. For example, a CI/CD pipeline job for project A might be able to access files from project B if a pipeline for project B recently used that same runner. The gitlab-runner user will run under the authority of whichever user registered the runner. If sudo was used for registration, that means the runner will have full root access. Therefore, we recommend using the shell executor only for specific runners in projects you trust.

The Docker executor can be thought of as somewhat safer because containers are an additional abstraction layer away from the host system. The runner clones project code and runs job commands inside an isolated container, and then tears down the container after reporting the results back to GitLab. Of critical importance, though, is making sure the containers run in unprivileged mode. That is, the jobs must be run by non-root users to ensure job execution does not involve access to the host system.

The VirtualBox/Parallels executor can be considered among the safest of the runner executors because jobs are run inside an ephemeral VM with an isolated OS and filesystem. CI/CD jobs will not have access to the underlying hypervisor, and there is minimal risk of information unintentionally being shared between jobs. Consider using these executors if you are otherwise unsure of your ability to secure shell or Docker environments.

Secret management

Managing secrets and avoiding their unintentional disclosure is a topic with a larger scope than the focus of this chapter. However, because runners receive both repository information and environment variables from GitLab, it is important to understand how poor secret management can cause your runners to be a vector for exposing sensitive information.

Never, under any circumstances, hardcode secrets (passwords, cloud credentials, deploy keys, and so on) into your project repository. The nature of Git version control is that once information is committed to the project, it is a part of the repository's immutable snapshot history. Simply removing the secret with a future commit does not remove it from previous commits. Because runners clone project repositories with a certain depth of historic snapshots, secrets accidentally left in a project are propagated to the runner infrastructure.

Chapter 7 will cover how you can use GitLab's Secret Detection tool to perform historic scans on your repository for potentially hardcoded secrets. Ultimately, the solution to the "I accidentally committed sensitive information" problem is to consider that information irrevocably exposed, and to therefore reset or rotate the affected credentials or keys.

A similar situation arises with CI/CD variables. Variables used in GitLab CI/CD are exported as environment variables to a runner's shell session. Unmasked and unprotected variables that store secrets run the risk of ending up on runners that execute untrusted builds. To guard against this possibility, store variables as masked and protected variables at the project or group level, ensuring they can only be used on protected branches, and ensuring their values are not exposed on the runners.

Monitoring considerations

Recall that GitLab Runner runs as a separate application on infrastructure outside the GitLab instance. Monitoring the data around your runners and pipelines is essential to ensure proper security and resource utilization.

Considerations regarding the various runner types and executors   133

The three key areas of consideration around monitoring your runners are as follows:

- The analytics available in the Gitlab UI
- The runner logging system
- The exportable metrics produced by the runners themselves

Self-managed GitLab has in-depth logging and monitoring facilities. Most monitoring can be managed by the built-in Prometheus server, and logs can be exported to aggregation systems such as **Splunk**. Similarly, GitLab Runner generates log entries that can be managed in the local operating system as well as by external or web-based tools.

GitLab UI analytics

General CI/CD analytics can be found at the project level under **Analytics | CI/CD**. *Figure 5.8* shows statistics for the public GitLab project hosted on `GitLab.com`:

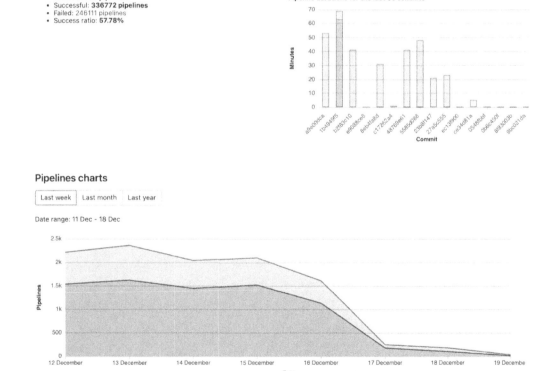

Figure 5.8 – CI/CD analytics for the GitLab project

The metrics shown in the UI here only account for general pipeline trends, namely overall pipeline success and failure rates. However, this data can serve as a useful starting point from which you can determine whether pipeline failures are caused by logic errors in source code or issues with the underlying infrastructure (that is, your runners). If runners appear to be the culprit, you can then dive deeper into runner-specific logs and metrics, as discussed in the next few paragraphs.

Runner logging

GitLab Runner does not have a dedicated log file. Rather, messages are published to the general system log file. Normally that would be `/var/log/syslog` in Debian-flavored operating systems (such as Ubuntu) and `/var/log/messages` in Fedora-flavored operating systems (such as Red Hat Linux). Errors in the runner service, its configuration, or its ability to communicate with GitLab will be logged in these files.

A useful way to confirm that the runner has a valid configuration and that it can communicate properly with GitLab is to run the `gitlab-runner verify` command as shown:

```
$ sudo gitlab-runner verify
Runtime platform                     arch=amd64 os=linux pid=84209 revision=32fc1585 version=15.2.1
Running in system-mode.
Verifying runner... is
alive                                runner=ZLXwxp4K
```

In the preceding output, you can verify the runner's architecture, version, process ID, registration ID, and ability to talk to GitLab.

Runner Prometheus metrics

Self-managed GitLab has in-depth logging and monitoring facilities. Most monitoring can be managed by the built-in Prometheus server. Similarly, GitLab Runner includes an embedded HTTP server that can advertise its metrics to an available Prometheus server.

In order to expose the runner's metrics, you first need to edit the runner's main configuration file, `config.toml`, which can normally be found in `/etc/gitlab-runner`. Add the `listen_address` parameter to tell the metrics server which port to listen on. An example `config.toml` file with the `listen_address` parameter added may look like this:

```
concurrent = 1
check_interval = 0
listen_address = "localhost:9252"
[session_server]
  session_timeout = 1800
. . .
```

After you edit the configuration file, restart the GitLab Runner service with `sudo gitlab-runner restart`. An available Prometheus server will then be able to read in and instrument the runner metrics.

Summary

In this chapter, we described the part that runners play in GitLab CI/CD pipelines. We learned that runners can be thought of as the "muscle" of CI/CD executing jobs specified in `.gitlab-ci.yml`. Runners can be installed as standalone programs on most computer platforms and can be shared with all projects in GitLab, or with only certain projects or groups. Moreover, wherever you have a runner installed, you can choose the execution environment it uses to run CI/CD tasks.

Regardless of your role, it is helpful to understand how runner settings can affect pipeline performance, application security, and observability in the development life cycle. We encourage you to practice the process of installing and registering runners, even if maintaining the runner infrastructure is not part of your day-to-day responsibilities. A confident knowledge level of runner architecture and workflows will make you a better software practitioner as you continue your GitLab journey.

The next chapter will build upon what we've learned so far and will introduce you to building out a robust test infrastructure using GitLab CI/CD. Application verification, and later, security, will serve as core topics whose coverage will enable you to continuously improve the efficiency, sustainability, and security of your DevOps workflows.

6
Verifying Your Code

For most projects, the first thing a **GitLab CI/CD** pipeline should do is *verify the code*. Different projects will rely on different tasks to perform this critical step, but they usually involve some combination of checking the code quality and running automated functional tests. As a prerequisite for certain kinds of verification, some projects will need to build their code first. This chapter focuses on building and then verifying your code.

We'll first discuss whether building the code is necessary, and if so, how to configure a GitLab CI/CD pipeline to carry out that task. Then, we'll talk about how to use a pipeline to run GitLab's built-in code quality scanner. Next, we'll explain how to run automated functional tests within a pipeline. Then, we'll cover a fascinating variety of automated testing called **fuzz testing**, which can find problems that traditional automated functional tests might miss. We'll touch on GitLab's accessibility testing, which ensures that your code can be used by a wide range of people. Finally, we'll briefly mention a few other ways that you can verify your code, though we won't have room to describe them in detail. By the end of the chapter, you'll have an array of tools at your disposal for making sure your code is well written and does what it's supposed to.

These are the main topics of this chapter:

- Building code in a CI/CD pipeline
- Checking code quality in a CI/CD pipeline
- Running automated functional tests in a CI/CD pipeline
- Fuzz testing in a CI/CD pipeline
- Checking accessibility in a CI/CD pipeline
- Additional ways to verify your code

Technical requirements

As with the previous chapters, you'll get the most out of this chapter if you've got an account on a GitLab instance (*self-managed* or *Software-as-a-Service*) that you can log in to and use for practicing and experimenting with the concepts discussed.

Building code in a CI/CD pipeline

At the risk of oversimplifying some of the mechanics that happen behind the scenes when you run software, we can generally think of *interpreted* computer languages such as Python or Ruby as executing raw source code, whereas *compiled* languages such as Java, C, or C# must convert that source code into a runnable form by compiling it, and then execute the compiled version of the program.

This is an important distinction to keep in mind when configuring a pipeline to verify your code because it means that if your project contains any code written in a compiled language (even if it's only a small portion of your overall project), you probably need to include a build job in your pipeline before any verification jobs take place. We say *probably* because some of the jobs that typically run during the verification stage of a pipeline (for example, Code Quality) look directly at source code, whereas others interact with code as it runs. So, if your pipeline only uses verification scans that focus on source code, you can omit the build step no matter what language you're using. If you want to include automated functional tests or fuzz testing in your pipeline, you *will* need to build your code first, so read on!

Every language builds its code in a different way, using different tools. Even within a single language, there are sometimes multiple tools or techniques for building code. Let's look at two different ways to compile Java code and one way to compile C code.

These examples are meant to give you the big picture of how to build code within a GitLab CI/CD pipeline. They are not meant to be comprehensive examples of all the ways to accomplish this task. There are so many different languages and tools that we can only give you a few bare-bones examples and then let you adapt and expand them to work with your own languages, tools, constraints, and preferences.

Compiling Java with javac

Outside of simple training applications, real-world Java projects rarely use the `javac` compiler to convert Java source code (i.e., files with the `.java` extension) into compiled Java classes (i.e., files with the `.class` extension). Using the `javac` tool is effective when you're only dealing with a few files, but it can become cumbersome as projects grow in complexity. But just like peanut butter and jelly sandwiches can be a great introduction to cooking even though they'd never be served at a formal dinner at Buckingham Palace, `javac` is a great way to introduce new GitLab users to the concept of using CI/CD pipelines to compile Java code.

Adding your Java application

Let's keep things simple by creating a single file application and a single Java package called com.hatsforcats. You can use GitLab's Web IDE editor to create a directory called src/com/hatsforcats to store your source code. Inside that directory, use the Web IDE to create a file called Login.java. Add this trivial Hello World-style Java code to that file:

```
package com.hatsforcats;
class Login {
    public static void main(String [] args) {
        System.out.println("Welcome to Hats for Cats!");
    }
}
```

Configuring your pipeline

Now that your app has been added to the project, it's time to configure your pipeline. Start with an empty .gitlab-ci.yml file in the root of your project's repository and define a build stage for your pipeline using the stages keyword:

```
stages:
    - build
```

Next, you'll define a pipeline job that lives within the *build* stage and runs javac. Let's stipulate a few extra requirements for this example:

- All the Java source files belong to the com.hatsforcats Java package.
- Your team's coding standards require you to put all source code within a src/ directory that lives in the project's root directory.
- Compiled files should end up in a target/ directory that lives in the project's root directory.

To compile your code while satisfying these criteria, you'll need to define a job in .gitlab-ci.yml to do the work. Call it something obvious and put it in the *build* stage:

```
compile-java-with-javac:
    stage: build
```

Within that job definition, you'll want to specify which Docker image the job should run within. The job will need access to the javac compiler, so a good image to use is the latest version of openjdk. Add this to the job definition (remember to watch your indentation):

```
    image: openjdk:latest
```

Finally, the job needs to invoke the Java compiler. Any commands that you list under the `script` keyword will run when the pipeline executes that job:

```
script:
    - javac src/com/hatsforcats/*.java -d target/
```

No doubt you can figure out the syntax of the `javac` command from the requirements given earlier, but if not, feel free to refer to the Java compiler's documentation.

Believe it or not, that's all you need in order to compile Java code within a GitLab CI/CD pipeline!

But to demonstrate that the job works as expected, let's add more lines to the `script` section of the `compile-java-with-javac` job. The first line will show the contents of the `target/` directory after `javac` has worked its magic. If the compiler worked, this command will display the compiled version of your Java source file when the job runs:

```
    - ls target/com/hatsforcats
```

The next lines will execute your compiled `Login.class` code to prove that it has compiled correctly. Normally, you wouldn't run your code in a job that's dedicated to building it, but you're doing it in this case simply to demonstrate that the compile actually happened:

```
    - cd target
    - java com.hatsforcats.Login
```

Here's the complete text of `.gitlab-ci.yml` that you have assembled. If you're following along, make sure that your version of that file contains exactly this text:

```
stages:
    - build

compile-java-with-javac:
    stage: build
    image: openjdk:latest
    script:
        - javac src/com/hatsforcats/*.java -d target/
        - ls target/com/hatsforcats
        - cd target
        - java com.hatsforcats.Login
```

Commit this file and navigate over to the list of pipelines in your project. Zoom in on the pipeline run that was automatically triggered by your commit, zoom in on the `compile-java` job, and see whether you can find text similar to this snippet at the end of the job's output:

```
$ javac src/com/hatsforcats/*.java -d target/
$ ls target/com/hatsforcats
Login.class
$ cd target
$ java com.hatsforcats.Login
Welcome to Hats for Cats!
Cleaning up project directory and file based variables
Job succeeded
```

You can see that the `javac` command ran without emitting any errors, the `ls` command shows a compiled version of `Login.java`, and the class produced the expected output when it was executed. Success!

Compiling Java with Maven

Let's try a slightly more complicated, albeit probably more realistic, way of compiling the same Java project you set up in the previous section. Instead of using the Java compiler directly, let's use **Maven** to build your code. If you haven't used Maven before, it's a powerful tool for Java projects that manages dependencies, compiles source code into classes, runs automated tests, and performs other tasks. In this example, you'll use it to convert your `*.java` file into a compiled `*.class` file.

Configuring Maven

Maven is configured via a special file called `pom.xml`. There's no need to get into the structure or content of that file here, but if you're curious about what each section does, the Maven documentation can give you all the details. Copy this bare-bones content into a new `pom.xml` file in your project's root directory:

```xml
<project>
   <modelVersion>4.0.0</modelVersion>
   <groupId>org.hatsforcats</groupId>
   <artifactId>login</artifactId>
   <version>1.0-SNAPSHOT</version>

   <properties>
      <maven.compiler.source>17</maven.compiler.source>
      <maven.compiler.target>17</maven.compiler.target>
```

```
    </properties>
</project>
```

Adding your Java application

If you're re-using the same project from the preceding `javac` example, you already have a Java program added to the project's repository. If you're using a new project, add this Java code to a new file called `Login.java` in a new `src/com/hatsforcats/` directory:

```
package com.hatsforcats;
class Login {
    public static void main(String [] args) {
        System.out.println("Welcome to Hats for Cats!");
    }
}
```

Configuring your pipeline

Either make a new `.gitlab-ci.yml` file in your root directory or replace all the content in your existing `.gitlab-ci.yml` file with this configuration code:

```
stages:
  - build

compile-java-with-maven:
  stage: build
  image: maven:latest
  script:
    - mvn compile
    - ls target/classes/com/hatsforcats
    - cd target/classes
    - java com.hatsforcats.Login
```

You'll notice that the pipeline configuration code for a Maven-powered build is similar to the configuration code for a Java-compiler-powered build, but with a few key differences:

- A different value after the `image` keyword means that the GitLab Runner will execute the job within a Maven-based Docker image instead of a Java-based Docker image.
- The command to compile the code uses mvn instead of `javac`.

- Maven puts compiled classes in a different directory than the source code by default, so you don't have to explicitly tell it to do so like you did with `javac` (although notice that its default directory for compiled files isn't quite the same as the one you specified with `javac`).

After committing this configuration code, you can view the details of the pipeline that is automatically triggered and zoom in on the `compile-java-with-maven` job. You should see something similar to this snippet at the end of the output:

```
[INFO] Compiling 1 source file to /builds/cwcowell/hats-for-
cats/target/classes
[INFO] ------------------------------------------------
[INFO] BUILD SUCCESS
[INFO] ------------------------------------------------
[INFO] Total time:  4.069 s
[INFO] Finished at: 2022-04-11T21:22:28Z
[INFO] ------------------------------------------------
$ ls target/classes/com/hatsforcats
Login.class
$ cd target/classes
$ java com.hatsforcats.Login
Welcome to Hats for Cats!
Cleaning up project directory and file based variables
Job succeeded
```

The Maven-driven compile worked correctly, the compiled class appears where you expected it to, and the class gives the expected output when you run it. You'll never need to run the `mvn compile` command manually again!

Compiling C with Gnu Compiler Collection (GCC)

Let's take a look at building a project based on the C programming language. Normally, you would use a tool such as Make to build your C project, just like you use Maven to build a Java project. But to keep this example as simple as possible, you'll rely on the good old GCC to compile some C code directly.

If you're following along at home, you can either make a new project for your C program, or you can re-use the project that you used for the two earlier Java examples.

Adding your C application

Navigate to your project's repository in the GitLab GUI, add a new file at the root directory called `login.c`, and paste this simple C code into it:

```c
#include <stdio.h>

int main(void) {
    puts("Welcome to Hats for Cats!");
    return 0;
}
```

Configuring your pipeline

Setting up a pipeline to use GCC to compile C code isn't terribly different from what you saw in the Java examples. Here are the main differences:

- The job runs in a Docker image that includes the GCC tools.
- The job definition's `script` keyword specifies using `gcc` instead of `mvn` or `javac` to build your code.
- The job runs the compiled code directly instead of invoking a JVM with the `java` command.

The basic CI/CD configuration code for building and running a C program with GCC could look like this:

```yaml
stages:
  - build

compile-c:
  stage: build
  image: gcc:latest
  script:
    - gcc login.c -o login
    - ./login
```

To repeat something we said earlier, you normally would not run your code in the same job as you built it—in fact, you might not run it at all in a pipeline. But you're running it here just to demonstrate that compiling worked as expected.

And here's a snippet from the output of this job, showing that your C program compiled and ran correctly:

```
$ gcc login.c -o login
$ ./login
Welcome to Hats for Cats!
Cleaning up project directory and file based variables
Job succeeded
```

Storing built code as artifacts

There's one more keyword you need to know before you can move on to pipeline stages that test the code that you just built: the `artifacts` keyword.

Any files that a pipeline job creates—including compiled versions of files that are generated during a build job—are deleted as soon as the job completes. This is very different from how build tools work on the command line. If you type `javac MyApp.java` in a terminal, the `MyApp.class` file that is generated will stick around on your filesystem until you delete it. But in a GitLab CI/CD pipeline, every job operates in its own, self-contained environment. This means that if you compile some files in a `build-java` job and then try to test them in a `test-java` job that lives in a later stage, the `test-java` job will *not* be able to see the files that you so carefully built earlier.

Fortunately, the `artifacts` keyword gives you a workaround. This keyword lets you specify certain files or directories that GitLab should preserve from one job and make available to all later jobs. For example, to preserve the executable `login` file that you generated in the `compile-c` job, you could add these two lines to the bottom of the `compile-c` job definition:

```
artifacts:
  paths:
    - login
```

You can specify more than one file to preserve, and you can specify one or more directories to preserve in addition to any individual files. You can also specify subdirectories or files to exclude from the list of artifacts. For example, to save the entire contents of the directory that Maven puts compiled files in, except for files that start with `Test` that exist in any subdirectory, you could add these lines to the bottom of the `compile-java-with-maven` job from earlier:

```
artifacts:
  paths:
    - target/classes/
  exclude:
    - target/classes/**/Test*
```

The `artifacts` keyword is one of the most important keywords that you'll use when configuring CI/CD pipelines, and forgetting to use it when it's needed is a common mistake. If your pipeline isn't working the way you expect it to, one of the first troubleshooting steps you should try is to check whether you're specifying artifacts in all of the jobs that generate files that you want to access in later jobs.

Now that you've learned when and how to build your code in a CI/CD pipeline, let's move on to what is typically the next pipeline step: *checking the quality of your code*.

Checking code quality in a CI/CD pipeline

One of the many scanners that GitLab makes available to CI/CD pipelines is a special feature that makes sure your project's code adheres to certain quality standards. GitLab calls this feature, unsurprisingly, **Code Quality**. If you've used any sort of linting tool before, you can think of this feature as a turbocharged linter.

The Code Quality feature relies on an outside service called **Code Climate**. Although this service can scan code written in all the major computer languages, it can't handle every language out there. You can refer to Code Climate's official documentation to see a list of supported languages, but rest assured that it works just fine with Java, Python, Ruby, JavaScript, and most other commonly used languages.

What sorts of problems does the Code Quality feature look for? The general categories it's interested in include performance, style, complexity, security, and smells (i.e., patterns that indicate a high risk of bugs). The exact violations that it detects vary from language to language, but here are some concrete examples of quality violations it can spot:

- Functions that take too many parameters
- Functions with too many exit points
- Functions or classes that are too long
- Overly complex logical expressions
- Too much or too little vertical whitespace
- Duplicated code

In addition, if your computer language has an established set of stylistic conventions—think of the PEP-8 standard in Python, or the Rubocop rule set in Ruby—the Code Quality feature can be configured to include those rules.

Enabling Code Quality

It couldn't be easier to add Code Quality to your CI/CD pipeline:

1. Make sure your pipeline has a `test` stage defined (hint: it almost certainly already has this stage, so you probably won't have to do anything).

2. Include a GitLab-provided template (i.e., a file that contains additional CI/CD configuration code) called `Code-Quality.gitlab-ci.yml`, which adds a Code Quality job to your pipeline.

Step 1 will look like this in your project's `.gitlab-ci.yml` file:

```
stages:
  - test
```

And *step 2* will look like this:

```
include:
  template: Code-Quality.gitlab-ci.yml
```

Note that if you had already defined other stages, in *step 1*, you would simply add the `test` stage to the existing stages—you wouldn't delete any existing stages. Similarly, if your pipeline configuration code already includes other templates, in *step 2*, you would add this new template to the existing templates instead of replacing them.

The Code Quality feature is smart enough to detect all of the computer languages used in your GitLab project and run the appropriate scanners for each language. However, it's important to understand that because these scanners are all developed by different people or teams outside of GitLab, there's no guarantee that the scanners will find exactly the same problems in all supported languages. For example, the scanner for one language might be especially good at detecting duplicated code snippets, whereas the scanner for a different language might be especially adept at calling out complex code that should be simplified.

Viewing Code Quality results

Let's see a concrete example of Code Quality in action. Imagine that you have a file called `hats-for-cats.py` in the root directory of your project's repository, containing this code:

```
def register(username, password, phone, city, state, zip):
    # TODO finish this code
```

There are two problems with this code that you would expect Code Quality to catch: the function has too many arguments, and the `TODO` comment should be acted on and removed.

If you enable Code Quality on the project's pipeline and then run the pipeline, the pipeline details page will include a new tab called **Code Quality**, which reveals the results of the Code Quality scan:

148 Verifying Your Code

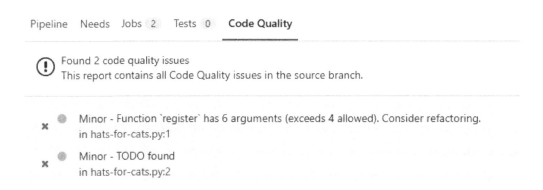

Figure 6.1 – Code Quality results in a pipeline details page

There's another place you can see the same information: in a **merge request**. However, the report in a merge request differs from the report in a pipeline details page in one important way. Whereas the pipeline details report shows all the code quality problems found on whatever branch the pipeline ran on, the merge request report shows the difference between code quality problems on the merge request's source branch and the merge request's target branch. Since the target branch is almost always your project's default branch (i.e., main or master), the merge request report shows you whether the work on your source branch is adding new code quality problems or fixing old code quality problems, compared to your stable code base. In other words, it shows whether the commits on your branch are making the project's code better or worse.

To illustrate this, imagine that you make a branch, make a merge request for that branch, and commit a change to the branch that removes the TODO comment and adds a new FIXME comment. You'd expect the Code Quality report on the merge request to show that one old problem (TODO) has been fixed and one new problem (FIXME) has been added. And that's exactly what appears in the merge request report:

Figure 6.2 – Code Quality results in a merge request

Both report locations—the pipeline details page and the merge request—have an entry for each detected problem. These entries tell you the name of each problem, the filename, and the line number on which the problem occurred. This should be enough detail to let you decide whether to fix or ignore each code quality problem. You may decide to ignore some problems either as false positives or as genuine problems that are too small to be worth fixing.

Code Quality is one of GitLab's best and most valuable CI/CD features. It's such an important tool for keeping your code readable and maintainable that GitLab makes it available on all license tiers of the product, including the Free tier. It's fast to run, reliable, and effective. There's really no reason not to use it on all of your projects.

Running automated functional tests in a CI/CD pipeline

One of the most common tasks in a CI/CD pipeline is running automated functional tests to make sure your code does what it's supposed to do. For example, you might want to use the `pytest` framework to run a collection of unit tests written in Python to test your Python-based Hats for Cats app. Let's see how to do that with GitLab.

> **Note**
>
> If you're not familiar with `pytest`, don't worry. The syntax for `pytest` unit tests is extremely simple and can be understood by anyone with even a little experience of writing automated tests in any language.

Enabling automated functional tests

Imagine that you've written three `pytest`-based unit tests to make sure the Hats for Cats app's login feature works as expected. You might have a file called `test/test_login.py` with these contents:

```
def test_login():
    # add code that tries to log in with good credentials
    assert True


def test_login_bad_password():
    # add code that tries to log in with a bad password
    assert True


def test_login_no_password():
    # add code that tries to log in with no password
    assert False
```

Obviously, these sample tests have placeholder code that forces the first two tests to pass and the third to fail. Real tests would have actual logic that exercises the login feature in various ways, but these simplified examples make GitLab's automated test feature easier to demonstrate.

To run these automated tests in your pipeline, add a job that triggers them just like you would from the command line:

```
unit-tests:
  stage: test
  image: python:3.10
  script:
    - pip install pytest
    - pytest test/
```

This job definition specifies that the job belongs to the `test` stage, and that it must run within a Docker container that has version 3.10 of Python installed. The commands that it runs first install the `pytest` package using the `pip` package manager, and then call the newly installed `pytest` command to run all unit tests that are in the `test/` directory.

After adding this job and running the pipeline, you can inspect the job's output and see that the tests did indeed run. You can even see the pass/fail results of each test. But the job's output is hard to parse and a little cryptic. Wouldn't it be nice if the results of the automated tests showed up in an easy-to-read table somewhere in the GitLab GUI? Fortunately, GitLab can do exactly that. You just need to tweak the job definition a little so that it stores the output of the unit tests in a particular format, and then saves that result file as a GitLab artifact. Adding this code to the end of the existing `unit-tests` job definition will do the trick:

```
  artifacts:
    reports:
      junit: unit_test_results.xml
    when: always
```

This code tells GitLab to preserve the `unit_test_results.xml` file produced by the `pytest` framework. It also designates this file as a report that contains test results that are stored in the JUnit format, which is an industry-standard format that GitLab knows how to ingest and display. Finally, it tells GitLab to hold on to this file regardless of whether any of the tests fail. This last step is important because a failing test will cause the whole `unit-tests` job to have a **failed** status, which would normally cause the artifact to be discarded. But we want to see the results even if—maybe *especially* if—any of the tests fail.

Viewing automated functional test results

After adding the additional code we've just described and running a new pipeline instance, a new tab marked **Tests** will appear on the pipeline details page. Lo and behold, clicking that tab shows you an overview of how many automated tests passed and how many failed:

| Pipeline | Needs | Jobs 2 | Failed Jobs 1 | **Tests 3** |

Summary

| 3 tests | 1 failures | 0 errors | 66.67% success rate | 3.00ms |

Jobs

Job	Duration	Failed	Errors	Skipped	Passed	Total
unit-tests	3.00ms	1	0	0	2	3

Figure 6.3 – Overview of automated test results

This table shows one row per job that triggers automated tests. Clicking on any row breaks down the results further, so you can see exactly which tests passed or failed:

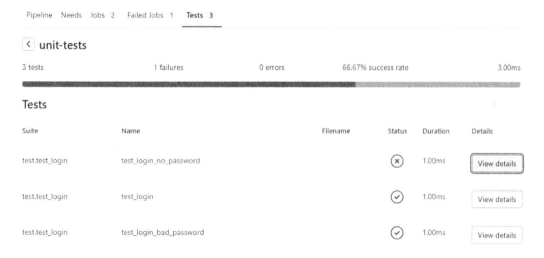

Figure 6.4 – Individual automated test results

As you might expect, the **View details** button next to each test shows you more information about that test, including the line of code that generated the failed assertion and the history of how often that test has failed in the past. This information helps you debug your product code—or your test, if that's where the problem lies.

test.test_login

Name	test_login_no_password
Execution time	1.00ms
History	Failed 12 times in main in the last 14 days
System output	

```
def test_login_no_password():
>       assert False
E       assert False

test/test_login.py:8: AssertionError
```

Figure 6.5 – Details of a single automated test

Looking at functional test results in a pipeline details page shows you all the test results for the code in the branch that the pipeline ran against. Sometimes that's exactly what you want. Other times, you want to know whether the code on a branch is experiencing any new test failures (or has fixed any failing tests) compared to the code on your project's default branch. In other words, is the feature branch fixing broken code, is it breaking code that used to work, or is it doing some of each?

Fortunately, the automated functional test report that appears in a merge request shows you exactly this information. Imagine that you're working on a branch and you manage to fix one test that was failing on the default branch, break one test that was passing on the default branch, introduce one new test that passes, and introduce one new test that fails. The merge request for that branch would present a report that looks like this:

Figure 6.6 – Merge request's delta view of automated functional test results

This shows that two tests are failing, including the old test that you broke on this branch and one of the new tests that you added to this branch. It also shows that one test failed on the default branch but has been fixed on this branch. The merge request report does not mention the new test you added that is passing, other than to include it in the count of five total tests. This is because you are usually more interested in knowing which tests are failing than in knowing which are passing. If you do want to see the status of all tests—both passing and failing—the **View full report** button will give you that information.

Running automated tests is often the very first task that a development team configures new pipelines to perform. If you stopped right there, you'd still get a huge amount of value out of GitLab CI/CD pipelines. But there are so many more ways you can verify your code with a pipeline! Let's look at fuzz testing next.

Fuzz testing in a CI/CD pipeline

Fuzz testing is an alternative, less traditional way of finding bugs in your code. Put succinctly, this advanced testing technique sends semi-random data to your code's functions in an effort to trigger bugs. Although it takes a little more work to set up than the other scanners, it can pay off by spotting bugs that you probably never would have found using other methods.

> **Reminder about GitLab versions and features**
>
> Fuzz testing, like many other features discussed throughout the book, is only available if you're using GitLab with an Ultimate license. You can find out whether your license tier includes a particular feature by looking up that feature in the official GitLab documentation. Features are often made available in lower tiers after they've been restricted to higher tiers for a few years.

There are two ways of performing fuzz testing in GitLab: **coverage-guided fuzz testing** and **web API fuzz testing**. In this book, we will only discuss the former, but the two techniques are similar enough that if you understand one, you'll easily be able to learn about the other using GitLab's documentation. From this point forward, whenever we refer to fuzz testing, we're talking specifically about the coverage-guided variant.

The architecture and workflow of fuzz testing

There are four architectural components you need to understand in order to use coverage-guided fuzz testing: the **code under test**, the **CI/CD job**, the **fuzz engine**, and the **fuzz target**. Let's look at each component and then see how they all fit together in the fuzz testing workflow.

The code under test

Fuzz testing targets a single function in your code. That function can be written in any of the languages supported by GitLab's fuzz tester, and it can be of any length. It must take at least one parameter, but there's no upper limit on the number of parameters it expects. The function can call other functions, and if a bug is triggered anywhere within that call stack, the fuzz tester will report it.

Consider this Python function to be your code under test. Imagine that it's in a file called name_checker.py:

```python
def is_bob(name: str) -> bool:
    if len(name) == 0:
        return False
    return name[0] == 'b' and name[1] == 'o' and name[2] == 'b'
```

This simple function takes a string as a parameter. It immediately returns False if the string is empty. Otherwise, it returns True if the string is bob and False if it isn't.

This is, of course, a terrible algorithm to use for this simple task, but we'll ask you to restrain your urge to mutter insulting things about the author of this code and play along for the sake of the demo. Just pretend it was written by a terrified intern on his first day on the job.

The intern is not only awful at designing algorithms, but he's also not a very good coder. You've probably already spotted the function's obvious bug: it doesn't validate that the string that's passed in is at least three characters long. As a consequence, if the string is only one character long and that character is b, the function will throw an unexpected IndexError when it tries to read the non-existent second character of the string. Similarly, if the only two characters in the string are bo, it will throw an IndexError when it tries to read the third character.

It would be easy for the developer or QA team member responsible for writing tests to forget to test these cases. Let's see whether fuzz testing will save the day by finding this bug.

A CI/CD job

Next, you need to define a job in your CI/CD pipeline that's dedicated to fuzz testing the code under test. You can fuzz-test several different functions in one pipeline, but you'll need a separate pipeline job for each function to be tested. In this case, your code under test consists of just one function, so you'll define a single CI/CD job.

Before we get to the job definition, we should explain that the fuzz testing job *must* extend a job called .fuzz_base, which is defined in a template provided by GitLab. Before defining the job, you'll need to include that template by adding a new line to the includes: section of .gitlab-ci.yml:

```
- template: Coverage-Fuzzing.gitlab-ci.yml
```

The .fuzz_base job that we'll be extending expects to run in a new stage called fuzz, which would have to run after the build stage so it can perform fuzz tests on compiled, runnable code. Let's add that to our list of stages. Assuming that we've already defined build and test stages, the stages: section of .gitlab-ci.yml would look like this:

```
stages:
  - build
```

```
  - test
  - fuzz
```

Now we're ready to add a job definition to `.gitlab-ci.yml` that will kick off the fuzz test for our code under test:

```
fuzz-test-is-bob:
  image: python:latest
  extends: .fuzz_base
  script:
    - pip install --extra-index-url https://gitlab.com/api/v4/projects/19904939/packages/pypi/simple pythonfuzz
    - ./gitlab-cov-fuzz run --engine pythonfuzz -- is_bob_fuzz_target.py
```

This job, called `fuzz-test-is-bob`, first specifies that it should run in a Docker image that includes the latest version of Python. This is needed because the fuzz engine, fuzz target, and code under test are all written in Python.

Next, it inherits job configuration details from a parent job called `.fuzz_base`. This parent job is provided by GitLab, and there's no need for you to know or care what configuration details it provides to your job.

Then your job specifies two commands to run. The first installs a Python-based fuzz engine from a GitLab-hosted package registry. The second runs a binary called `gitlab-cov-fuzz`, pointing it at the correct fuzz engine and fuzz target. This binary is what actually starts up the fuzz test. You'll get a better sense of how the fuzz test proceeds from there when we look at the entire fuzz test workflow in the next section.

The fuzz engine

The fuzz engine is a GitLab-supplied binary that sends streams of random bytes to the fuzz target. These bytes serve as the basis for input data that the fuzz target will feed to the code under test—but more on that topic is coming in the next section.

Truth be told, it's more accurate to call these bytes *semi-random* instead of *random*. This is because the fuzz engine looks at which lines of the code under test were exercised by the last round of data and attempts to mutate that data in such a way that when the mutated data serves as the *next* set of random bytes, it will exercise different lines in the code under test. So, it's random, but it's also influenced by the previously used sets of random data. This is where the term *coverage-guided* comes from: the fuzz tester uses code coverage data to influence how it generates the random data to send to the code under test.

The fuzz target

The fuzz target is a small piece of code that you must write in the same language as the code under test. It serves as a translator or intermediary between the fuzz engine and the code under test. The fuzz target has two tasks:

- Transform the random bytes sent to it by the fuzz engine into the data type that the code under test expects to receive for its input parameter(s). For example, it might need to transform the bytes into an array of integers, a string, or an instance of a class.
- Call the function in the code under test, passing it the transformed random bytes.

For this example, the fuzz target needs to convert the random bytes sent by the fuzz engine into a string, and then pass that string to the is_bob function in name_validator.py. You can call the file that the fuzz target lives in anything you want, but there's a fair amount of boilerplate that you must include in order to make it callable from by the fuzz engine. Let's assume that you call your fuzz target file is_bob_fuzz_target.py and you include this content in the file:

```python
from name_checker import is_bob
from pythonfuzz.main import PythonFuzz

@PythonFuzz
def fuzz(random_bytes):
    try:
        random_bytes_as_string = str(random_bytes, 'UTF-8')
        is_bob(random_bytes_as_string)
    except UnicodeDecodeError:
        pass

if __name__ == '__main__':
    fuzz()
```

Let's look at what's happening here. The first line makes the code under test available so the fuzz target can pass it random data.

The next two lines declare a function called fuzz, which takes random bytes as input. This is required boilerplate: you have to include these lines.

Next, the fuzz target takes the random bytes that were sent to it by the fuzz engine and tries to transform them into a string, which is the data type that the code under test expects as input. For many (in fact, most!) collections of random bytes that are passed into the fuzz target, this conversion will fail due to at least one of the bytes falling outside the range of values that map to letters, numbers, punctuation, and other symbols. The `try` and `except` lines take care of this problem: if any of the bytes can't be converted, the fuzz target simply returns without calling the code under test.

If the bytes *are* successfully converted into a string, the fuzz target exercises the code under test by passing the newly generated string to the `is_bob` function.

The final two lines are more boilerplate that you must include in any Python-based fuzz target.

Remember that the fuzz target must be written in the same language as the code under test. Although the concepts used in non-Python fuzz targets are very similar to what is demonstrated here, the boilerplate and data transformation code will look slightly different in other languages.

A fuzz testing workflow

Here's how the four components work together to perform fuzz testing whenever you run your project's pipeline:

1. The CI/CD job called `fuzz-test-is-bob` triggers as part of the `fuzz` stage. It downloads the `gitlab-cov-fuzz` binary and the Python-based fuzz engine. It then runs the `gitlab-cov-fuzz` binary, pointing it at the Python fuzz engine and the fuzz target that lives in `is_bob_fuzz_target.py`.

2. The fuzz engine generates a series of random bytes and passes them to the `fuzz` function in `is_bob_fuzz_target.py`.

3. The fuzz target transforms the random bytes into a string, since that's the data type that the `is_bob` function (i.e., the code under test) expects as input.

4. The fuzz target passes the string to `is_bob`.

5. If `is_bob` handles the random string gracefully—that is, without crashing or throwing any unexpected exceptions—the fuzz engine looks at which lines of code were exercised by the last series of random bytes and generates a new series of random bytes that are designed to exercise different lines in `is_bob`. This cycle continues, with the fuzz engine generating new bytes with each pass through the cycle.

6. If, on the other hand, the random string causes `is_bob` to crash or throw an unexpected exception, the fuzz engine reports that to the `fuzz-test-is-bob` CI/CD job, which reports that the fuzz test has found a bug in the code under test. Success! Well, success at triggering a failure, anyway.

Viewing the results of fuzz testing

When the fuzz test finds a bug, it displays this information in three places:

- The vulnerability report, which you can navigate to by clicking **Security & Compliance | Vulnerability Report** in the left navigation pane. This only shows any problems that fuzz testing found on your project's default branch.
- The **Security** tab on the pipeline details page. This shows any problems that fuzz testing found on whatever branch that pipeline instance ran against.
- In a merge request. This shows a *delta* between problems that fuzz testing found on the default branch and problems it found on the source branch of the merge request. If nothing has changed between the default branch and the source branch, the merge request will report that the fuzz test found no problems at all, no matter how many problems actually exist on both branches.

Although the exact bugs reported will vary according to the type of report you're looking at, the type of details provided by each report will be almost identical. For example, here's a page from the vulnerability report that presents details about the bug that fuzz testing found in the `is_bob` code under test:

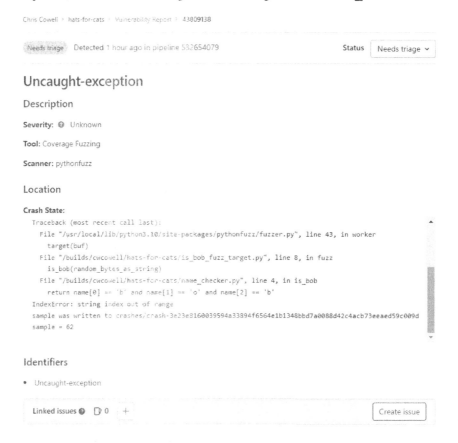

Figure 6.7 – Fuzz testing bug report

Notice that this report includes a stack trace showing what error was thrown (`IndexError`), and which line threw it (the line with the `return` statement). The report also tells you which random bytes—also called a "sample"—triggered the problem. In this case, the fuzz engine generated a single byte: 62. It turns out that 62 in UTF-8 corresponds to the lowercase letter of b. If you look at the `is_bob` function in the code under test, you should be able to see exactly why an input string consisting of a single letter, b, would expose this bug. Isn't it satisfying when a complicated system such as the fuzz tester works exactly as expected?

Extra considerations when fuzz testing

Compared to the predictable, logical nature of the other ways you can validate your code with GitLab, fuzz testing is like your erratic uncle who shows up to family gatherings wearing mismatched socks and spewing mysterious comments that could be either deeply profound or utter nonsense, depending on the day. Fuzz testing's random nature means that its results can be unpredictable. You might run the same fuzz test on the same code under test on 2 different days and find a bug within 10 seconds on the first day, but find nothing after 10 minutes on the second day. You never quite know what fuzz testing will turn up, if anything at all. This isn't anything to worry about, since a new fuzz testing session will happen every time you run your project's pipeline; even if it doesn't find anything today, it might find an important problem tomorrow.

Keeping in mind that fuzz testing increases its chances of finding problems the longer it runs, some teams choose to run it asynchronously rather than as a normal pipeline job that blocks later stages in the pipeline. This technique is beyond the scope of this book, but GitLab's documentation explains how to set this up if you'd like to experiment with it.

Another way that fuzz testing differs from other tests or scanners is that it stops as soon as it finds a single problem, whereas other tools typically continue to run until they've found and reported on every issue they're capable of unearthing. Again, this is normally not a problem since most projects will run fuzz testing tens, hundreds, or thousands of times over the course of their development. But it's good to understand that just because fuzz testing found a bug today, it doesn't mean there are more bugs lurking in your code that it might find on subsequent runs.

Remember that although you can fuzz-test as many functions in your code under test as you'd like, you must create a separate CI/CD job and a separate fuzz target for each function. This can add up to significant overhead when you're getting fuzz testing off the ground. Fortunately, once everything's in place and fuzz testing is working as expected, there's usually no need to change either the jobs or the fuzz targets.

Fuzz testing with a corpus

Fuzz testing has a special, optional feature that you can use called a **corpus**. This is a list of random bytes that the fuzz tester can use for two purposes. First, if a particular series of random bytes caused a bug or crash in the code under test, and then your team fixed that bug, it could be useful for future fuzz tests to send exactly the same random bytes to the code under test to make sure that it hasn't regressed. In other words, once your team fixes a bug, it's a nice safety measure for the fuzz test to make sure that it stays fixed. If you add the troublesome bytes to the corpus, then all future fuzz test runs will use that series of bytes as one of the values sent to the code under test.

The second use of a corpus is to help the fuzz tester find bugs more quickly. When it generates truly random bytes as input to the code under test, it can take a long time to find bugs—if it ever finds them at all. But if you load up the corpus with one or more series of bytes that constitute valid input (i.e., input that the code under test can handle gracefully), then the fuzz test can mutate that valid data and use the mutated data as its next series of input to the code under test. Mutating valid data often results in finding data that triggers bugs far more quickly than relying on truly random bytes as input to the code under test.

Setting up a corpus can be somewhat complicated, especially if you want to make use of a clever GitLab feature that automatically updates the corpus every time the fuzz test finds a bug. The GitLab documentation will lead you through this process if you think a corpus might be useful. We do recommend experimenting with this optional feature because it can hugely increase the power of fuzz testing.

Next, we'll move on from the powerful and somewhat exotic bug-finding tool of fuzz testing and look at an important but often-overlooked way of checking the quality of your code: **accessibility testing**.

Checking accessibility in a CI/CD pipeline

Not all applications include web interfaces, but whenever you do write a web app, we strongly recommend you use your GitLab CI/CD pipeline to make sure your interface is accessible for people with a range of disabilities. Fortunately, GitLab makes it easy to test your website against the **Web Content Accessibility Guidelines** (**WCAG**) laid out by the World Wide Web Consortium.

These guidelines address a wide assortment of characteristics of websites that could cause accessibility problems. Here are just a few of the things that the WCAG covers:

- Pages that require scrolling both vertically and horizontally
- HTML heading tags such as <H1> that contain no text
- Text that doesn't contrast strongly enough with its background
- Images that lack an alternative text description
- Button controls that have no name available for screen readers

You might be surprised both at how many accessibility problems this scanner finds in your web interface, and also at how easy it is to fix many of these issues. Don't feel bad if it finds several accessibility bugs on your site; try pointing the scanner at any popular website and you'll probably be amazed at the number of basic accessibility violations it exhibits!

Enabling accessibility testing

To add accessibility testing to your pipeline, you first need to create a new stage called `accessibility` in your `.gitlab-ci.yml` file:

```
stages:
  - accessibility
```

In all likelihood, your project will already have a `stages` section defined, in which case you should just add the new `accessibility` stage to the existing section instead of defining a whole new `stages` section (which would produce a malformed `.gitlab-ci.yml` file).

Next, include the GitLab-provided template that contains the accessibility-related job definitions:

```
include:
  - template: "Verify/Accessibility.gitlab-ci.yml"
```

As we said before, if you've already defined an `include` section, simply add this template to it instead of defining a new `include` section.

Finally, set a global variable that tells the accessibility scanner which website to inspect. This could be your web app in its production environment or in any pre-production, staging, or review environment. It can also be fun (and instructive) to point the accessibility scanner at any site on the web, even if it's not one you own. Here, we'll point it at a pretend URL where the Hats for Cats website runs in production:

```
variables:
    a11y_urls: «https://www.hats-for-cats.com»
```

Once again, if you already have a global `variables` section, simply add this new variable to it instead of creating a second `variables` section.

Believe it or not, that's all you need to do. To get accessibility testing up and running in your pipeline. The accessibility scanner doesn't offer any other configuration options, which makes it extremely simple to set up.

Viewing accessibility testing results

The accessibility scanner doesn't integrate its results into a GitLab dashboard like you saw with the automated functional test results. But it does generate an easy-to-read HTML page that describes all of the less severe problems (called **warnings**) and more severe problems (called **errors**) it finds.

To see this page, run a pipeline with accessibility testing enabled and visit the pipeline details page. You'll see a job called `a11y`, which is the job that runs the accessibility scanner. Click on that job to see the terminal output from the job. You can ignore that output, but in the **Job artifacts** pane on the right, you'll see a button for browsing any artifacts produced by the job:

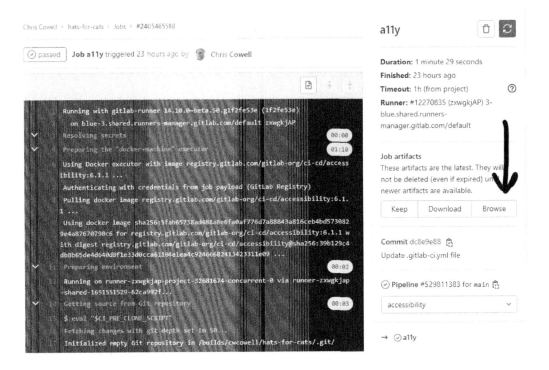

Figure 6.8 – Finding the accessibility scanner's artifacts

Clicking this button will show you both JSON and HTML reports generated by the accessibility scanner. These reports both contain the same information about any accessibility violations found on the targeted website. The JSON output can be downloaded, parsed, and integrated into any other dashboard you may have set up. The HTML report is human-readable within your browser and lets everyone on your team see what accessibility-related work you might want to carve out into issues so it can be tracked and managed.

There's another way to see the findings of the accessibility scanner, other than by looking at one of its two artifacts. Remember how a merge request's versions of Code Quality reports and automated functional test reports show the difference between code quality or test results on the default branch and code quality or test results on the merge request's source branch? The merge request report on accessibility violations works in exactly the same way.

If you have a branch with a corresponding merge request, the merge request will show any accessibility violations that were found on the latest pipeline that was run against that branch, as long as those violations are *not* also found on a pipeline run against the default branch at the time the branch was created. In other words, the merge request shows you whether the pipeline's branch is making your project's code better (by fixing accessibility problems that were on the default branch) or worse (by adding new accessibility problems that were not on the default branch). This is a great report to have if you're working on a feature branch and want to make sure your boss doesn't yell at you because you're adding more problems than you're fixing!

Additional ways to verify your code

We've covered some of the most common ways to verify your code. GitLab offers even more features that help you test your code further. We don't have enough space to cover all of them in detail, but here's a quick description of three additional methods you can use to test code. Details for enabling and configuring all of these tools are available in the official GitLab documentation.

Code coverage

Automated functional tests make sure that your code is doing what it's supposed to do. Having tests in place is a critical part of every software development project, but it's easy to get a false sense of confidence from seeing that all your tests are passing if you don't know how much of your code base those tests cover. After all, having 100 passing tests doesn't do you much good if all of those tests execute the same 5% of your application's code.

Code coverage reports give you confidence in the value of your test results. You can configure GitLab to use an appropriate, language-specific code coverage tool to determine exactly which lines of your product code are exercised by your tests. This report is integrated into the GitLab GUI, so it's easy to tell which lines of code you should target as you write new tests.

Browser performance testing

Since so many of today's applications are run in a browser, and since browser-based applications are generally much slower than traditional desktop applications, it's important to keep track of how quickly the various pages of your website load, and to know whether changes you're making to the code are making those load times better or worse.

GitLab can measure page load times and display the results in merge requests so developers can understand how their proposed code changes affect the performance of their web app. It can even raise a special alert whenever performance degrades beyond a particular user-configurable threshold. The report lets developers fix any performance-related problems that their code has introduced before their code is merged into the stable code base.

Load performance testing

While browser performance testing tells you how quickly the frontend GUI of your web app loads, GitLab's **load performance testing** helps you track the performance of your applications' backend code. Although this feature can exercise your application in various ways, it's most commonly used to target your application's API. For example, it can hammer your application with tens, hundreds, or thousands of simultaneous calls to one or more of your application's REST API endpoints, and then monitor how quickly your application responds to those calls. You can also use this tool to perform long-running soak tests to see whether your application develops memory leaks or other problems over time.

The load performance test feature displays its findings in merge requests so developers can understand how any code changes on the branch associated with that merge request affect their applications' backend performance.

Summary

Once again, you covered a lot of ground in this chapter. You saw how to build code within a GitLab CI/CD pipeline, using a variety of different methods and languages. This doesn't cover every possible way you could compile or otherwise build your code—we've barely scratched the surface of that topic—but you should have a good idea of the general steps involved regardless of what language or tools you use. You also learned that certain kinds of code verification tools require that you build your code first because they interact with your code as it runs. Other tests don't require this step because they simply scan your source code without running it.

Next, you saw how to use GitLab's Code Quality feature within your pipelines to make sure your code follows best practices for coding style, adheres to common coding conventions, avoids unnecessary complexity, and doesn't exhibit any *code smells* that indicate the possible presence of bugs or unexpected behavior.

Then you learned how to integrate automated functional tests into GitLab CI/CD pipelines. You saw not only how to trigger these tests from within a pipeline job but also how to ensure that the results can be seen in two different reports within the GitLab GUI. You also discovered how to use the *delta* view of test results within a merge request to learn whether the code on that merge request's branch is helping or hurting the pass rate of your product's automated tests.

Next up was fuzz testing, GitLab's most complicated but perhaps most interesting bug-finding feature. You learned about the four different components that make up the fuzz testing architecture, and you saw how random data flows from one component to the next in an attempt to trip up your code and cause crashes or unexpected exceptions. You became familiar with fuzz testing's various idiosyncrasies and learned how to accommodate them. Finally, you saw how to use a corpus not only to catch functional regressions in your code but also to speed up fuzz testing and make it more likely to find problems.

The final tool you got to watch in action was GitLab's accessibility testing feature. This helps you ensure that your web applications are usable by people with a range of disabilities, maximizing your possible user base.

These tools are a great place to start when it comes to validating your software projects, but GitLab offers several additional ways to inspect your code even more thoroughly. You got a lightning-fast tour of the code coverage tool, browser performance testing, and load performance testing. All of this will reward further exploration using GitLab's official documentation and some experimentation of your own.

Once your code has been verified, you can deploy it to a production environment for customers to use, right? Nope. You first need to make sure it doesn't contain any security vulnerabilities, which is the topic we'll explore in the next chapter.

7
Securing Your Code

Now that you know how to configure your GitLab CI/CD pipeline to verify that your project's code is meeting its requirements, the next step in constructing a pipeline is to add jobs that look for security vulnerabilities. This is an optional step, but since GitLab makes it easy to add security scanning to your pipelines, and since there's virtually no downside other than adding a few minutes to your pipeline's runtime, *we recommend that you enable all security scanners that are relevant to your projects.*

We'll start this chapter by providing an overview of GitLab's general strategy around using security scanners; several aspects of security scanning are helpful to understand before you start learning about individual scanners. Then, we'll explain the purpose of each of the seven types of security testing that GitLab offers: **Static Application Security Testing (SAST)**, **Secret Detection**, **Dynamic Application Security Testing (DAST)**, **Dependency Scanning**, **Container Scanning**, **License Compliance**, and **Infrastructure as Code (IaC) Scanning**. We'll show you how to enable each type of scanner in your pipelines, and then discuss some sample configuration options and techniques you can use to adjust their behavior to best suit your needs. Finally, we'll cover three additional GitLab features that make security scanners easier to use and more powerful: reading scanner reports, tracking scanner findings using vulnerability management, and integrating outside security scanners.

By the end of this chapter, you'll have learned some critical skills for keeping your code safe and your data secure. You'll understand how to identify which GitLab-provided security scanners are relevant to your project. You'll know how to add them to your CI/CD pipelines and configure their behavior to suit your needs. You'll have a solid grasp of the different types of security reports that GitLab provides. You'll also be able to track your team's progress in remediating any security vulnerabilities. Finally, you'll understand how to add third-party security scanners to your pipelines. In short, you'll feel confident that your code is as secure as possible.

The following topics will be covered in this chapter:

- Understanding GitLab's security scanning strategy
- Using SAST to scan your source code for vulnerabilities
- Using Secret Detection to find private information in your repository

- Using DAST to find vulnerabilities in web applications
- Using Dependency Scanning to find vulnerabilities in dependencies
- Using Container Scanning to find vulnerabilities in Docker images
- Using License Compliance to manage licenses of dependencies
- Using IaC Scanning to find problems in infrastructure configuration files
- Understanding the different types of security reports
- Managing security vulnerabilities
- Integrating outside security scanners

GitLab uses the same handful of configuration techniques for all of its security scanners. To avoid repetition, we'll discuss these in detail only in the section dedicated to the first scanner type (SAST). When we discuss configuration techniques for the other scanners, we'll refer you back to the SAST section.

While we're on the subject of scanner configuration, it's important to understand that most of these scanners offer *many* configuration options, and it is impossible to discuss all of them – or even most of them – in this book. Instead, we'll show you how to get each scanner up and running in a fairly basic form, give you a sample of the kinds of configuration options that exist for each scanner, and point you to the official GitLab documentation as the best source of up-to-date information about the full range of configuration settings for each type of scanner. Fortunately, the documentation on this subject is both clear and comprehensive.

Finally, note that many of these scanners are only available to users with a GitLab Ultimate license. However, GitLab has a history of making Ultimate-only scanners available to Premium or Free license users in later releases. At the time of writing, SAST, Secret Detection, Container Scanning, and Infrastructure as Code Scanning are available to all users regardless of license tier, albeit sometimes in a feature-limited (but still useful) form. So, if you find your favorite scanner is not yet available for your license, there's a chance that it will become available in the future, even if you never upgrade your license.

Technical requirements

As with the previous chapters, you'll get the most out of this chapter if you have an account on a GitLab instance (either self-managed or **Software-as-a-Service** (**SaaS**)) that you can log in to and use for practicing and experimenting with the concepts discussed.

Understanding GitLab's security scanning strategy

There are a few fundamental principles underlying GitLab's security scanners that will be useful for you to know before you learn about what each scanner does. Let's look at those now.

GitLab uses open-source scanners

It might surprise you to learn that all the security scanners discussed in this chapter are **third-party, open-source tools**; none of them are developed in-house by GitLab. For example, IaC scanning is performed by the open-source tool **Keeping Infrastructure as Code Secure** (**KICS**), and Dependency Scanning is handled by the open-source tool **Gemnasium**.

That doesn't mean that these third-party scanners are inferior to GitLab-developed software in any way. They are all rigorously researched and vetted by GitLab before they are adopted as official GitLab scanners. Furthermore, GitLab frequently reviews new open-source security scanners to see whether they should replace or supplement any of the product's current scanners. So, don't worry – these scanners are all first-rate additions to your pipelines, even if their code wasn't written by GitLab developers.

Security scanners that are developed by organizations or companies that are dedicated solely to security are likely to have fewer bugs than proprietary software developed by companies for whom security is not their primary focus. As the saying about open-source code goes, *"given enough eyeballs, all bugs are shallow."* Making bugs shallow – and then fixing them – is especially important for security-related tools: using a poorly designed security scanner that gives you the false impression that your code is secure is worse than knowing nothing about your product's security at all.

Since these scanners are open-source software, what's stopping you from downloading them yourself and running them independently of GitLab? Nothing! But it's hard to see why you'd want to. The scanners that are blessed by GitLab are simple to integrate into GitLab CI/CD pipelines, and GitLab automatically updates them to ensure that your pipelines always run the latest versions (unless you specify otherwise), with no action on your part required. If you have CI/CD pipelines set up in GitLab already, and if your GitLab license tier gives you access to the scanners you need, we advise that you use these tools within GitLab rather than running them independently. You would have nothing to gain and a fair amount to lose in the form of extra system administration and maintenance if you were to download and run them on your own.

> **Which languages do GitLab's security scanners support?**
>
> To see a list of all the languages supported by each type of GitLab security scanner, as well as the names of the open-source tools that are used, consult the official GitLab documentation (https://docs.gitlab.com/ee/user/application_security/sast/#supported-languages-and-frameworks). Keep in mind that these details do change from time to time, so it's wise to revisit the documentation periodically to see which new languages are supported by the different scanner types.

Scanners are packaged as Docker images

When a security scanner runs in your GitLab CI/CD pipeline, it runs within a Docker container. This is irrelevant for most GitLab users, but there are three implications that you should know about.

First, because the pipeline job that runs a scanner has to pull down the Docker image for that scanner, this will add a minute or so to the job's runtime. Of course, the exact delay depends on your network speed and on whether the image has been cached somewhere. This usually isn't a big problem since many scanners take a few minutes to run, even after their Docker image has been downloaded. Also, most non-trivial pipelines run in minutes rather than seconds, so you probably won't notice any short delays caused by pulling down security scanner Docker images.

Second, any security scanning jobs must run on a GitLab Runner that uses Docker or Kubernetes executors. You can refresh your memory about GitLab Runner executors by referring to the previous chapter if you're not sure what this means. If your organization uses the SaaS version of GitLab (that is, you use the instance at gitlab.com), this problem is solved for you: all SaaS-provided GitLab Runners use one of those two executors. If you're using a self-managed instance of GitLab, you probably have a GitLab administrator who is in charge of setting up all the GitLab Runners that your team needs. Just make sure they understand that at least some of those Runners must use Docker or Kubernetes executors if you intend to add security scanning to your pipelines.

Third, because your jobs download security scanner Docker images every time they run, you never have to worry about updating your security scanners. GitLab makes sure that the latest version of each scanner is included in the Docker image pulled down by each job. That's one less maintenance chore for you to keep track of.

Some scanners use different analyzers for different languages

Some scanners, such as SAST and Dependency Scanning, rely on different open-source tools for scanning code written in different computer languages. GitLab calls these language-specific tools **analyzers**. For example, when you enable SAST in a project that contains only Go code, GitLab will run an open-source, Go-aware SAST analyzer called **Semgrep**. But when you enable SAST on a Ruby-based project, GitLab runs a different open-source analyzer called **Brakeman**, which knows how to scan Ruby code.

You don't need to tell GitLab which analyzers to run – it detects the computer languages in your project automatically and only runs the analyzers that work with those languages. It does this by looking for **trigger files**, which are files with certain names or extensions in your project's Git repository. For example, if it finds any files that end in .py, it assumes that your project contains Python code and runs Python-based analyzers for any security scanners you've enabled. It also looks for certain configuration files that are traditionally used with various languages, such as Gemfile or Gemfile.lock in Ruby projects, requirements.txt in Python projects, and pom.xml in Java projects that use the Maven build tool. Most of the time, you don't need to worry about making your computer languages easy for GitLab to detect – it's smart enough to do the right thing with almost all projects. But if you find that it's not recognizing languages as it should, you can see lists of trigger files in the official GitLab documentation for each security scanner type, and make sure that you have at least one trigger file for each language in your project.

It's fine to use multiple computer languages in the same project. GitLab will detect all languages in the project's repository and run the appropriate analyzer for each, assuming that an analyzer exists for that scanner type and language.

For some combinations of scanner type and language, GitLab has more than one analyzer available. When this occurs, it runs all of the relevant analyzers. For example, if you enable SAST on a project with Python code, it will run both the **Semgrep** and **Bandit** analyzers. If both of the analyzers detect the same problems, you may see duplicate results in the scanner reports, with one result from each analyzer. This might clutter up your reports somewhat, but it's better to be safe than sorry. Also, since every open-source analyzer is written by a different development team with a different focus or area of concern, and since different analyzers have different levels of comprehensiveness or maturity, running multiple analyzers is a great way to maximize the number of vulnerabilities found.

If running more than one analyzer for a particular language is producing too much noise, you can configure most scanners to disable individual analyzers. For example, you could tell GitLab to run only the Bandit analyzer and not the Semgrep analyzer when performing SAST scans on Python code. However, we generally recommend that you keep as many analyzers enabled as possible to reduce the chance of vulnerabilities slipping through. And there's no need to disable analyzers for languages that are not included in your project: GitLab is smart enough to run only the analyzers that support the languages that it detects.

Not all analyzers for a particular scanner type will find the same problems. For example, if you have a divide-by-zero vulnerability in Go code and the same vulnerability in Ruby code, one of the two analyzers might report this as a potential problem, while the other analyzer might ignore it. Again, this is the result of different open-source analyzers being written and maintained by different teams of developers.

Vulnerabilities don't stop the pipeline

The default behavior for most GitLab jobs is to abort the pipeline as soon as the stage containing the failed job completes. After all, if your tests fail in an early stage, there's no need to deploy your code in a later stage. GitLab's security scanners sort of follow this standard… and sort of don't. Let's explain what we mean by that.

Every security scanner that runs successfully marks its pipeline job as *passed*, regardless of whether it detected any vulnerabilities. In other words, seeing that a security scanner's pipeline job has a *passed* status simply means the scanner ran to completion – it doesn't tell you anything about whether the scanner found vulnerabilities. So even if your pipeline's scanners find a huge number of vulnerabilities in your code, their jobs will be given a *passed* status and the pipeline will continue to later stages.

This might seem counterintuitive. Isn't detecting a vulnerability similar to having an automated test fail? Well, yes and no. Vulnerabilities are typically something that your team should look at carefully, but as you'll learn later when we talk about GitLab's vulnerability management feature, you might decide not to fix the vulnerability. GitLab doesn't want to presume that you will fix all the vulnerabilities before deploying your code to production, so it continues running pipelines even after vulnerabilities are found. This approach equips development teams with all the information GitLab can provide about the security of their code, without asking the tool to make any assessments about whether that code is suitable to be deployed.

Findings appear in three different reports

Any vulnerabilities or other problems discovered by GitLab's security scanners appear in reports that consolidate the results from all the different scanners. There are three of these reports in different places within the GitLab GUI. Each report shows subtly different information than the others, and it's important to understand the purpose of each so that you don't misinterpret the results. We'll discuss this topic in more detail later in this chapter, but for now, we'll just introduce you to the vulnerability report, which you can find by clicking **Security & Compliance** in the left navigation pane and then clicking **Vulnerability report**. When we discuss the security scanners in the rest of this chapter, we'll include screenshots of sample findings from each scanner as they appear in the vulnerability report.

Pipelines can use non-GitLab-provided scanners

Although GitLab's built-in scanners might give you all the protection you need from security vulnerabilities, it's possible to supplement your security testing by adding many other third-party scanners to your pipelines. We'll discuss how to configure this type of integration in a dedicated section (*Integrating outside security scanners*) toward the end of this chapter.

Now that you understand some of the concepts that underly all of GitLab's security scanners, let's look at each scanner to learn what kinds of problems it can spot and how to use them.

Using SAST to scan your source code for vulnerabilities

Let's start our survey of scanners with **SAST**. *We encourage you to read this section carefully, even if you don't intend to use SAST*, because many of the principles and practices involved with using SAST carry over to the other scanners as well. Understanding how to use SAST gives you a huge head start in terms of enabling, configuring, and reading the findings of other scanners.

Understanding SAST

SAST looks at your project's source code, as opposed to interacting with your code as it runs. Sometimes, this approach is referred to as *white-box scanning*, meaning that the scanner looks *inside* your app to inspect its code instead of staying *outside* the app and simply analyzing its behavior.

This scanner looks for bad coding practices, anti-patterns, or the hallmarks of poorly designed or structured code, which are sometimes referred to as *code smells*, that could potentially result in exploitable security problems. For example, consider this single line of Python code:

```
temp_dir = '/tmp'
```

It looks harmless, but non-Python programmers might be surprised to learn that it's considered a security vulnerability. A Python best practice is to use the language's built-in `tempfile` module to create and manage temporary directories and files. Any directories or files created with this module are automatically deleted when the program finishes executing, which ensures that no sensitive data is accidentally left on the computer's filesystem. Creating a directory to hold temporary files is dangerous because it's easy to forget to clean up after yourself by deleting this directory when the program no longer needs it. This is exactly the kind of problem that SAST is designed to detect.

As mentioned in the previous section, different SAST analyzers for different computer languages will look for different security vulnerabilities. The GitLab SAST analyzer for a different language might not detect a similar problem in code written in that language, either because the code isn't considered to be a vulnerability in that language or because the analyzer might not be as mature or robust as GitLab's Python SAST analyzers.

Enabling SAST

There are two ways to enable SAST in a GitLab project's pipeline: manually, or with the GitLab GUI. They boil down to the same thing since they both result in adding a few lines of content to the `.gitlab-ci.yml` file that configures your CI/CD pipeline. Let's look at both approaches.

Enabling SAST manually

To enable SAST manually, you need to do two things to your project's `.gitlab-ci.yml` file:

- Make sure the pipeline has a `test` stage defined
- Include a template called `Security/SAST.gitlab-ci.yml`

The code looks like this:

```
stages:
  - test

include:
  - template: Security/SAST.gitlab-ci.yml
```

The first of these steps is easy since pipelines usually already have a `test` stage defined by the time you must add security scanning. But if you're adding security scanning before you've added any other test-related jobs, just add the first two lines in the preceding snippet. Of course, if you already have other stages defined, don't delete them when adding your `test` stage – just add `test` to the existing stages.

> **Note**
> Remember that the order in which you list stages matters because that's the order in which GitLab will run them in your pipeline.

The second step involves adding a template to your CI/CD configuration. A template is a file provided by GitLab that contains CI/CD code that defines new job definitions or adds other features. By including a template in your CI/CD configuration file, you can add job definitions that perform tasks such as SAST scanning without having to know how those jobs work.

In this case, the template adds a job definition for each GitLab SAST analyzer. It also adds logic to detect which languages exist in your project so that it knows which of the SAST-related jobs to run. If you imagine that your `hats-for-cats` project contains only Python code, you would expect this template to run two new jobs in the project's pipeline: one for Bandit and one for Semgrep, which are GitLab's two Python SAST analyzers.

Sure enough, if you commit this change to `.gitlab-ci.yml` and look at the details of the pipeline triggered by that commit, you'll see that those jobs are now included in your pipeline, under the `test` stage:

Figure 7.1 – Python SAST jobs on the pipeline details page

Remember that if your project contains code in a language other than Python, you'll see different job names and potentially a different number of jobs on this page. And if your project contains code in Python and another language, you'll see jobs for the SAST analyzers for each of those languages.

Enabling SAST with the GitLab GUI

Strangely enough, using the GUI to add SAST scanning to your pipeline is a more involved process than doing so manually:

1. Start the process by navigating to the **Security and Compliance** option in the left pane and then selecting **Configuration**. This will direct you to a control panel for enabling and configuring most (but not all) of GitLab's security scanners.

2. The exact GUI controls sometimes change with new GitLab releases, but there will be a button that lets you enable SAST. Clicking that button will take you to a new page for configuring SAST.
3. You can usually keep all the options set to their default values and click the button at the bottom that creates a merge request. That will take you to a merge request creation page.
4. Once again, you can usually leave all the fields at their default values and click the button at the bottom to create the merge request.
5. Navigate to the merge request and merge it to complete the process. Your `.gitlab-ci.yml` file should now include the `test` stage if it didn't do so already, as well as include the SAST template described in the previous section. You can see how simply editing that file manually would have probably been much easier!

Once you've enabled SAST using the GUI, you should see the same results as if you'd enabled SAST manually: two new jobs will be added to each run of your pipeline, corresponding to the two Python-based analyzers that GitLab supports for SAST.

Configuring SAST

Now, you know how to add SAST to your GitLab pipeline. But what if you want to change SAST's default behavior? The techniques you can use for configuring SAST are also used to configure most of the other security scanners. We'll discuss these techniques in detail here and then refer you back to this section instead of repeating this information when we introduce you to the other scanners.

There are three ways to configure SAST or any other security scanner:

- In `.gitlab-ci.yml`, set a global variable
- In `.gitlab-ci.yml`, override a job definition that was originally added by the template you included, and set a job-scoped variable for that job
- Use the GitLab GUI

Which of these three techniques you use to configure SAST or any other scanner depends on what configuration option you want to set. Unfortunately, you don't get to pick which of these techniques you'd like to use to set a particular configuration option – you have to refer to the GitLab documentation to see which technique or techniques you must use to set the configuration option you're interested in.

Let's see some examples of configuring SAST.

Configuring SAST with a global variable

First, say that you want to disable the Semgrep SAST analyzer for Python. You can do that by setting a global variable within `.gitlab-ci.yml`:

```
variables:
  SAST_EXCLUDED_ANALYZERS: "semgrep"
```

If you add this variable to your CI/CD configuration file and then rerun your pipeline, you'll notice that the `semgrep-sast` job you saw in the preceding screenshot is now gone.

Of course, if your CI/CD configuration file already has a `variables` section, you should add this new variable to any existing variables instead of creating an entirely new `variables` section.

Configuring SAST by overriding a job definition and setting a job-scoped variable

Next, imagine that you want the Bandit SAST analyzer not to scan certain directories, such as a directory that contains test code. Perhaps you know that your tests are filled with security vulnerabilities, but you don't care because customers will never use that code. You can set that configuration option by editing `.gitlab-ci.yml` to override the definition of the job that triggers Bandit, and setting a job-scoped variable within the new job definition:

```
bandit-sast:
  variables:
    SAST_BANDIT_EXCLUDED_PATHS: "*/my_tests/*"
```

Don't be thrown by the strange-looking value of the variable. This particular variable expects a value written in the slightly odd `fnmatch` syntax. That's the kind of detail you'll learn about when you consult the GitLab documentation to learn more about various configuration options for this and other scanners.

If you add this code to your CI/CD configuration file and rerun your pipeline, the Bandit analyzer will stop reporting any vulnerabilities it finds in the `my_tests` directory. We haven't talked about how to view the results of these analyzers yet, but don't worry – that will come later in this chapter.

Configuring SAST with the GUI

Finally, you can use GitLab's GUI to set certain configuration options for some scanners. For example, on the same GUI page that you used to enable SAST, you can configure SAST to use an analyzer from an alternative Docker image, change the pipeline stage it runs in, or change the depth of directories it searches when detecting the languages in your project. You can also use that GUI page to disable certain language-specific SAST analyzers if you find that they are unhelpful or produce findings that duplicate the results generated by other analyzers.

Compared to other scanner types, SAST makes an unusually large number of configuration options available from the GUI. The GitLab documentation can give you more information about which options are available in the GUI for other scanners, and which options must be set by editing `.gitlab-ci.yml` instead.

Viewing SAST's findings

Once you've enabled and, optionally, configured SAST, it will run the appropriate analyzer(s) for whatever language(s) it detects in your project, and will display its findings in GitLab's three security reports. For example, here's the finding for the vulnerability related to temporary directories that was described previously, as shown in GitLab's **Vulnerability Report** area:

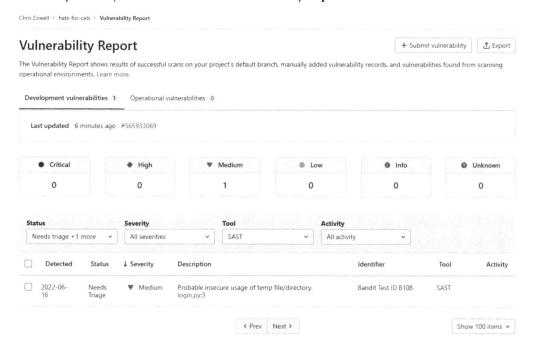

Figure 7.2 – SAST finding

This wraps up our summary of SAST. Let's move on to a separate but related security scanner: Secret Detection.

Using Secret Detection to find private information in your repository

You can think of Secret Detection as a special, focused version of SAST that's dedicated to finding secrets that are accidentally lurking in your source code, such as United States social security numbers or AWS deploy keys. It operates in the same way as SAST – that is, by scanning your source code rather than by interacting with your executing application.

Secret Detection used to be part of GitLab's SAST feature but was eventually spun off to become its own first-class security scanner. We are mentioning this so that you won't be confused if you run into references in old documentation or blog posts suggesting that Secret Detection is performed by GitLab's SAST scanner.

Understanding Secret Detection

Secret Detection looks for a wide variety of strings that represent secrets that should not normally be stored in files in a Git repository. In addition to the social security numbers and AWS deploy keys already mentioned, here are just a few of the 50 or so kinds of secrets it looks for:

- Short- and long-lived Dropbox API tokens
- GitLab personal access tokens
- Heroku API keys
- Private SSH keys
- Stripe access tokens

For example, Secret Detection should find and report on all three of the secrets contained in this snippet of Python code:

```
MY_SSN = '123-45-6789'

MY_GITLAB_ACCESS_TOKEN = 'glpat-txQxy1frpAJodkxJYL8U'

MY_PRIVATE_SSH_KEY = '''
-----BEGIN OPENSSH PRIVATE KEY-----
b3BlbnNzbmUAAAAEbm9uZAwAAAAtzc2gt==
-----END OPENSSH PRIVATE KEY-----
'''
```

Secret Detection is based on **regular expressions** (or **regexes**): the scanner has a regex for each type of string it tries to detect and reports any string literals that match those regexes.

The use of regexes means that Secret Detection is completely language-agnostic. Since it just scans files to see whether any strings match regexes, it doesn't care what computer language is used in your repository. This means that, unlike SAST, Secret Detection doesn't require separate analyzers for different languages: it uses one analyzer for all source code files. Secret Detection is even file type-agnostic: it will scan configuration files, README files, plain text files, and any other non-binary files in your repository. It can look for strings that match regexes in a JSON configuration file just as easily as it can look for strings in a Go source code file.

While regexes are a powerful tool, Secret Detection's reliance on them does mean that the scanner has an important limitation: it can't detect passwords. This sounds surprising at first but makes sense once you realize that a well-written password should be difficult to capture with a regex. It's hard to think up a regex that would capture any possible password without also matching non-secret text such as a sentence in documentation or a series of words in a GUI element. But other than this one case, Secret Detection does a great job at ferreting out strings that should be kept in a more secure location than a Git repository.

There's one fantastic feature that Secret Detection is the only GitLab scanner to offer: **historic mode**. If you enable this mode, Secret Detection will scan all the commits in your repository to see whether there have *ever* been any secrets committed to it.

Why is historic mode important? Since one of the goals of version control systems such as Git is to allow you to go back to the state of files as they were at any point in time, it's easy to see any secrets that have ever been committed, even if they were immediately removed in the very next commit. Once a secret is in a Git repository, it's always retrievable. So, whenever Secret Detection discovers a secret, the entry it creates in any of the security scanner reports always mentions that the secret should not just be removed, but *revoked*. Any secret that makes its way into a Git repository should be considered to have been exposed to the world, and should no longer be used.

This is an extremely important point! If Secret Detection finds a password, you should immediately retire that password and set a new one (which, of course, you shouldn't check into Git). If it detects a deploy key, you should cancel that key and create a new one. This principle holds for any kind of secret. If Secret Detection spots it, simply removing it from the repo is not sufficient. It should be considered no longer usable and should be replaced as soon as possible.

Enabling and configuring Secret Detection

Since Secret Detection used to be a part of SAST, it's not surprising that you can use the same manual or GUI-based methods to enable both scanners.

To enable Secret Detection manually, make sure you have a `test` stage defined in your pipeline. Then, include the GitLab-provided template that contains the Secret Detection-related job definitions:

```
stages:
  - test

include:
  - template: Security/Secret-Detection.gitlab-ci.yml
```

That's all there is to it! The next time you trigger a pipeline, you will notice that a Secret Detection job is now running under the `test` stage.

To enable Secret Detection using the GUI, you can use the same process as for SAST: click the **Security and Compliance** option in the left navigation pane and select **Configuration**. From there, you'll see an option to enable Secret Detection. Clicking that allows you to create a branch and associated merge request that edits your `.gitlab-ci.yml` file to include the Secret Detection template described previously. If you merge the request and trigger a new pipeline run, you'll find that Secret Detection is now enabled in your pipeline. As with SAST, many people find this process more cumbersome than simply editing `.gitlab-ci.yml` manually, but your experience may vary.

Like most GitLab security scanners, Secret Detection has several configurable options. You can learn about all of the options and how to set them in the GitLab documentation, but two are especially worth highlighting here.

First, you might want to enable the special **historic mode** discussed previously to scan an existing repository that you've just imported into GitLab. Second, you can ask Secret Detection not to scan certain directories in your repository. For example, you might store fake social security numbers for testing purposes within a `test/` directory, and have fake deploy keys stored in a `docs/` directory. You would probably want to prevent Secret Detection from flagging these as security vulnerabilities by excluding those directories.

You can set both of these configuration options by overriding the `secret_detection` job definition that's provided by the Secret Detection CI/CD template and then setting job-scoped variables:

```
secret_detection:
  variables:
    SECRET_DETECTION_HISTORIC_SCAN: "true"
    SECRET_DETECTION_EXCLUDED_PATHS: "tests,docs"
```

With Secret Detection already configured and enabled, let us now view its findings.

Viewing Secret Detection's findings

Once you've enabled and configured Secret Detection to your liking and it has run successfully in a pipeline, you can see the results in the **Vulnerability Report** area, just like you did with the SAST results. For example, here are the results that are generated by running Secret Detection on the Python code provided previously:

Detected	Status	↓ Severity	Description	Identifier	Tool
2022-06-16	Needs Triage	● Critical	SSH private key detected; please remove and revoke it if this is a leak. constants.py:6	Gitleaks rule ID SSH private key	Secret Detection
2022-06-16	Needs Triage	● Critical	GitLab Personal Access Token detected; please remove and revoke it if this is a leak. constants.py:3	Gitleaks rule ID gitlab_personal_access_token	Secret Detection
2022-06-16	Needs Triage	● Critical	Social Security Number detected; please remove and revoke it if this is a leak. constants.py:1	Gitleaks rule ID Social Security Number	Secret Detection

Figure 7.3 – Secret Detection findings

Now that you've got a handle on Secret Detection, it's time to look at the next security scanner in the GitLab arsenal: DAST.

Using DAST to find vulnerabilities in web applications

Let's move on to the next type of security scanner: **DAST**. This scanner interacts with your code as it runs instead of looking at your source code. If SAST and Secret Detection are examples of "white-box" testing – they look inside your app to see how it works – then DAST is a form of "black-box" testing – it just sends input and looks for potential problems or security vulnerabilities in the output, without knowing how your application performs that transformation of input into output.

Understanding DAST

DAST tests either **web application URLs** or **Web API endpoints**. If you feed DAST the URL of a website's home page, it will visit that page, identify any links or clickable GUI elements on the page, follow those links or click those elements, and repeat the process. It will continue this "spidering" procedure until it has visited every page that it can reach within your app. At each step, it checks the results returned by the web application to see whether it finds any problems. Here are just three examples of the sorts of things it looks for:

- Exposure of private personal information
- Missing cross-site request forgery tokens
- Accepting sensitive information such as passwords through query strings

If you tell DAST to scan a Web API endpoint, it sends information to the endpoint and analyzes the response, looking for the same sorts of problems.

Regardless of whether it targets URLs or Web API endpoints, DAST can operate in either **passive** or **active** mode. Every time DAST runs, it performs a passive scan, which means that it makes benign, non-malicious requests similar to the requests sent by a real user. If you want a deeper analysis of your web app, you can enable a so-called **full scan**, which adds active attacks to the passive requests that it normally makes. These active attacks are more aggressive and could be considered malicious if they were directed at a website or Web API that you don't own. However, they are invaluable in that they mimic the types of attacks that actual hackers might use, and therefore reveal many weaknesses that could be exploited by malicious actors.

Enabling and configuring DAST

DAST has a plethora of configuration options. We'll cover a handful of the most commonly used options, which will be enough to get you up and running with DAST. As usual, the official GitLab documentation has full details on all of the ways you can configure DAST to behave in non-default ways.

It's easiest to enable and configure DAST using the GUI. The exact details of this process may change in future GitLab releases, so we'll cover the high-level concepts without going too far into specific details.

You can start enabling and configuring DAST by visiting the same security scanner configuration page you used for SAST and Secret Detection: click the **Security and Compliance** option in the left navigation pane and select **Configuration**. From there, you'll be able to click a button to enable DAST, though the button will first take you to another page that lets you set up some configuration options that DAST needs to go through.

First, you'll need to set up a **scanner profile**. This tells DAST whether to use only passive scans or to perform active scans as well. You can also set timeout values to limit the amount of time DAST spends spidering a website. GitLab will let you name this profile so that you can use the same profile later with several different URLs or Web API targets.

Second, GitLab will guide you to create a **site profile**. This profile contains the URL of the website's home page or Web API endpoint that you want to scan. If you're scanning a website, you can optionally add authentication credentials to the site profile. These allow DAST to sign in to the website like a user would, which typically exposes additional URLs to be scanned.

After you've created the two profiles, the GUI will present a code snippet that you can copy and paste into your project's `.gitlab-ci.yml` file. This is a slightly different workflow than the merge request-driven workflow you use to enable SAST or Secret Detection through the GUI, but the result is the same: you add a few lines of code to your CI/CD configuration file, instructing DAST to run in your pipeline.

> **Which URLs can you target with DAST?**
>
> Although you can create a site profile with the URL of any website or web API, we strongly recommend that you only target websites and API endpoints that you own and manage. This is especially true if you are using DAST's **full scan** option, which conducts more aggressive scanning. Furthermore, we recommend that you run DAST only against your application as it runs in a review, staging, or pre-production environment. Running DAST against the production version of your application could destabilize it, degrade performance for real users, or even knock it out completely.

If you prefer to enable and configure DAST manually, you'll need to add a `dast` stage to your pipeline *after* the `deploy` stage. You must also include the DAST template, set a global variable with the URL that you'd like DAST to scan, and set any additional global or job-scoped variables that you need to modify DAST's behavior:

```
stages:
  - deploy
  - dast

include:
  - template: DAST.gitlab-ci.yml

variables:
  DAST_WEBSITE: https://example.com
  DAST_FULL_SCAN_ENABLED: "true"
```

You might have noticed that DAST is the first scanner we've run across that expects to run in its own dedicated stage. The reason for this becomes obvious once you remember that DAST scans executing code and not source code: it can't execute your code until it has been built and deployed. Those tasks usually take place in the `build` and `deploy` stages, so DAST must occur in a stage that falls after those stages in the pipeline.

Because DAST can sometimes take a long time to work its way through all the pages of a website, and because you don't always want to hold up your pipeline while DAST does its thing, GitLab also allows you to run DAST scans on demand or according to a schedule. The process of triggering an on-demand scan or creating a scanning schedule is quite straightforward: in the **Security & Compliance** option in the left navigation pane, select **On-demand scans** and let the GUI wizard guide you through the process.

As mentioned previously, DAST offers an unusually wide array of configurable options. There are far too many to describe here, but the options we've discussed so far are enough for you to get useful vulnerability findings in most cases. If you need to set timeout values for the spider process, disable particular vulnerability checks, set login credentials for the target website, or adjust DAST's behavior in other ways, you can find all the information you need in the official GitLab documentation.

Viewing DAST's findings

The results of a DAST scan show up in the **Vulnerability Report** area, just like the results for SAST and Secret Detection. Since we don't have a full **Hats for Cats** app available to run DAST against, here are some sample results from running a DAST passive scan against `https://example.com`. You can see that all of the results concern header fields, which is the most common type of finding resulting from passive scans:

	Detected	Status	↓ Severity	Description	Identifier	Tool
☐	2022-06-17	Needs Triage	Medium	Content Security Policy (CSP) Header Not Set	CWE-693 + 1 more	DAST
☐	2022-06-17	Needs Triage	Low	Strict-Transport-Security Header Not Set	Strict-Transport-Security Header Not Set + 1 more	DAST
☐	2022-06-17	Needs Triage	Low	X-Content-Type-Options Header Missing	CWE-693 + 1 more	DAST
☐	2022-06-17	Needs Triage	Low	Server Leaks Version Information via "Server" HTTP Response Header Field	Server Leaks Version Information via "Server" HTTP Response Header Field + 1 more	DAST

Figure 7.4 – DAST findings

That concludes your introduction to DAST. Now, let's change gears and investigate Dependency Scanning, a type of security scan that looks at code that you've imported into your project from some outside source.

Using Dependency Scanning to find vulnerabilities in dependencies

Why write your own functions when someone else has already written, tested, and documented a library to perform exactly what you need? It's often easy to find third-party Python modules, Ruby gems, Java JARs, or other open-source software packages that speed up the development of your project. Unfortunately, these third-party dependencies can contain security vulnerabilities, and if you include them in your project, you inherit those problems. This is where GitLab's Dependency Scanning feature steps in – it ensures that any dependencies you use are free of known vulnerabilities.

Understanding Dependency Scanning

Like SAST, Dependency Scanning supports many languages – including all of the major languages you'd expect – but not every language under the Sun. You can consult the GitLab documentation to see an up-to-date list of supported languages.

Dependency Scanning knows how to parse the configuration files used by the package managers of each supported language, and it uses this information to determine which dependencies your project relies on. For example, it might scan `Gemfile.lock` in a Ruby project, `requirements.txt` or `requirements.pip` in a Python project, or `pom.xml` in a Java project that uses the Maven build tool. As you can see from the fact that we mentioned two different Python configuration files, the scanner is smart enough to know that some languages use several different files to list their configurations and it can parse all the most commonly used files in each language. Just like SAST, Dependency Scanning can handle projects that contain several different computer languages. It will parse the dependency configuration files for any languages that it detects, and look for vulnerabilities in all of them.

For example, if your Hats for Cats website is built on an old version of the Django web framework, your project might contain a `requirements.txt` file with just one entry:

```
django==4.0
```

The scanner looks not just for the names and version numbers of dependencies that your project declares explicitly but also for the names and version numbers of any dependencies that those dependencies have. In other words, it looks recursively through the dependency tree to detect transitive dependencies, as well as direct dependencies. It reports on vulnerabilities found on *any* dependencies within the tree, which means that you might see vulnerabilities reported in dependencies that you didn't even know your project used.

Once Dependency Scanning knows the names and version numbers of each dependency in your project, it looks up each dependency name and version number in a database to see whetherthere are known vulnerabilities in that particular version of that particular library. It's important to understand that Dependency Scanning does not do SAST-style scanning of the dependency code – that is, it does not analyze the code within the dependencies, trying to detect new vulnerabilities. Instead, it uses a much more straightforward strategy. It simply determines whether the database contains any information about vulnerabilities that have *already been discovered* in that version of that dependency. This may sound like an unsophisticated approach, but it turns out to be extremely useful and is quite good at revealing problems with commonly used libraries.

Dependency Scanning has a special feature that isn't always available but can be a nice time-saver when it is. If the scanner detects a vulnerability in an old version of a library and knows that the vulnerability has been fixed in a later version of the same library, it will sometimes offer to create a merge request that rewrites your project's dependency configuration file so that it uses the later, fixed version of the library. This only happens under some circumstances and with some languages but is worth taking advantage of when it's offered.

Enabling and configuring Dependency Scanning

You have the same GUI or manual options for adding Dependency Scanning to your project's pipelines as you do for SAST, Secret Detection, or DAST. To enable it through the GUI, click the **Security & Compliance** option in the left navigation pane, select **Configuration**, and find the control for enabling Dependency Scanning. This will create a merge request that adds two lines of code to your .gitlab-ci.yml file, which enables the scanner. Merge the merge request, and you're done.

Enabling it manually is even simpler. Just make sure your pipeline has a test stage defined and add the Dependency Scanning template to .gitlab-ci.yml:

```
stages:
  - test


include:
  - template: Security/Dependency-Scanning.gitlab-ci.yml
```

Like the other scanners, Dependency Scanning has several configurable options. Also, like the other scanners, these are controlled either by setting global variables in .gitlab-ci.yml or by overriding job definitions and setting job-scoped variables in that file.

For example, the following code sets a job-scoped variable that tells Dependency Scanning's Python analyzer to look for a dependency configuration file with a non-standard name instead of the traditional requirements.txt file:

```
gemnasium-python-dependency_scanning:
  variables:
    PIP_REQUIREMENTS_FILE: "hats-for-cats-requirements.txt"
```

Viewing Dependency Scanning's findings

The vulnerability report shows any potential security problems detected in your project's dependencies. For example, here are five critical and high-severity vulnerabilities stemming from Hats for Cats' dependency on an old version of the Django library, as specified in the sample requirements.txt file:

	Detected	Status	↓ Severity	Description	Identifier	Tool
☐	2022-06-17	Needs Triage	● Critical	Improper Neutralization of Special Elements used in an SQL Command ('SQL Injection') in Django requirements.txt	CVE-2022-28346 + 1 more	Dependency Scanning
☐	2022-06-17	Needs Triage	● Critical	Improper Neutralization of Special Elements used in an SQL Command ('SQL Injection') in Django requirements.txt	CVE-2022-28347 + 1 more	Dependency Scanning
☐	2022-06-17	Needs Triage	◆ High	Loop with Unreachable Exit Condition ('Infinite Loop') in Django requirements.txt	CVE-2022-23833 + 1 more	Dependency Scanning
☐	2022-06-17	Needs Triage	◆ High	Exposure of Resource to Wrong Sphere in Django requirements.txt	CVE-2021-45116 + 1 more	Dependency Scanning
☐	2022-06-17	Needs Triage	◆ High	Uncontrolled Resource Consumption in Django requirements.txt	CVE-2021-45115 + 1 more	Dependency Scanning

Figure 7.5 – Dependency Scanning findings

By now, you should have a firm grasp of what Dependency Scanning does and how to use it. Let's move on and look at a Docker-focused security scanner: Container Scanning.

Using Container Scanning to find vulnerabilities in Docker images

Container Scanning does for Docker images what Dependency Scanning does for your project's dependencies: it checks for known vulnerabilities in the particular versions of Linux distributions that your project uses as a base when it builds Docker images.

Understanding Container Scanning

If you package and deploy your application as a Docker image – or, technically, an Open Container Initiative-compliant image – you should use GitLab's Container Scanning feature to find known vulnerabilities in the base Linux distribution that your image is built on top of.

If you haven't worked with Docker images before, this might sound mysterious, but it's not complicated. Think of a Docker image as a little bit like a virtual machine. There's a special file called `Dockerfile` that serves as a "recipe" for creating that virtual machine. This `Dockerfile` file specifies which Linux distribution to use as the virtual machine's operating system, which additional software packages you should install on top of Linux to support your application, and ultimately what application you want to install on the virtual machine. This whole stack of the operating system and the dependencies and your application makes up a Docker image.

Container Scanning looks for vulnerabilities both in the software packages that come installed by default in that base Linux operating system and in any additional packages that you specified in your `Dockerfile`. As you would expect, the older the Linux distribution, and the more dependencies you install on it, the more problems Container Scanning is likely to find.

Although Container Scanning doesn't know how to find vulnerable packages in all versions of all Linux distributions, it does support the last two or three versions of the most commonly used distributions. Unless you use a truly exotic distribution to serve as the base of your application's Docker image, you should be able to use Container Scanning. The GitLab documentation has a list of all supported distributions if you'd like to make sure your images are scannable.

Container Scanning has an optional feature that is disabled by default: it can also look for vulnerabilities in "language packages," which are libraries that are added by a language's package manager. For example, you might use Ruby's `bundler` utility to install the `Ruby on Rails` gem, or Python's `pip` tool to install the `Flask` module. You might notice that this functionality covers the same ground as GitLab's Dependency Scanning – and as a result, often produces duplicate findings. Because of this, many GitLab users rely on Dependency Scanning instead of enabling this feature in Container Scanning.

Although Container Scanning can look for problems in any Docker image that it can access via the web, its default behavior is to scan any images it finds in your project's **Container Registry**. The Container Registry is a feature provided for all GitLab projects and lets you store Docker images in a safe, access-controlled location instead of storing them on a site such as Docker Hub, which is open to everyone, or in an instance of a tool such as Artifactory. To use Container Scanning to inspect an image in the Container Registry, you'll need your pipeline to build a Docker image and then push it to the registry. We'll discuss this process in the next chapter on deployment strategies.

Enabling and configuring Container Scanning

You can enable Container Scanning by manually editing `.gitlab-ci.yml` or by using the GitLab GUI. To enable it manually, make sure your pipeline contains a `test` stage and include the Container Scanning template:

```
stages:
  - test
```

```
include:
  - template: Security/Container-Scanning.gitlab-ci.yml
```

To configure Container Scanning with the GUI, you can use the same technique as for the other scanners discussed so far: click the **Security & Compliance** option in the left navigation pane, select **Configuration**, and find the control for enabling Container Scanning. This will produce an MR that adds the preceding template to your CI/CD configuration file. Merge this MR, and you're done.

If you're happy with having Container Scanning look for Docker images in your project's Container Registry, these manual or GUI-based techniques for enabling the scanner are the only steps you need to perform. But if you need to change its default behavior, you can use two of the same techniques you've used to configure other scanners: set a global variable or override a job definition and set a job-scoped variable. Some of the configuration options available for this scanner include aiming the scanner at a Docker image stored in a location other than your project's Container Registry, enabling language package scanning, or setting the minimum severity level that a vulnerability must have to be included in the Container Scanning's findings.

Viewing Container Scanning's findings

It's not unusual for Container Scanning to find dozens of vulnerabilities in a Docker image that you've built, especially if you're using a less-than-recent Linux distribution as your base image. When you consider the huge number of packages that are installed by default on every Linux distribution, and the speed with which vulnerabilities are found in open-source packages, this is not surprising.

For example, Alpine Linux is known as one of the smallest major distributions, meaning that it has fewer packages installed than other popular distributions, such as Ubuntu or Debian. This makes it a popular distribution to use as a base for Docker images. If you build a Docker image based on Alpine Linux version 3.14.1, which is only 10 months old at the time of writing, Container Scanning finds no fewer than 30 vulnerabilities among its default packages. You can see a handful of the highest severity vulnerabilities found in a Docker image built on this distribution, as displayed in the **Vulnerability Report** area:

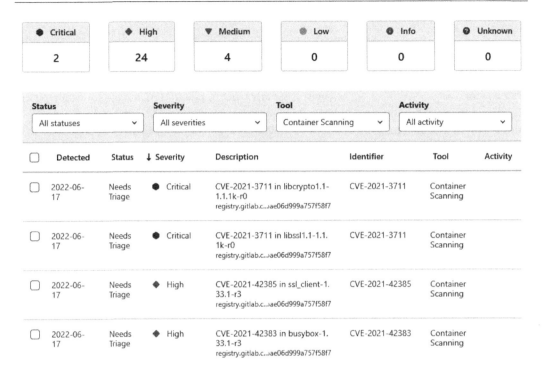

Figure 7.6 – Container Scanning findings

Now that we've covered the basics of Container Scanning, let's take a look at yet another security scanner: License Compliance.

Using License Compliance to manage licenses of dependencies

It can be easy to lose track of what software licenses are used by your project's various dependencies. It's also easy to forget which licenses are compatible with your project's overall license, and which licenses should be excluded for various reasons. This is where GitLab's License Compliance feature can help out.

Understanding License Compliance

Most open-source libraries are released under a software license. There are hundreds of licenses available – though only 20 or so are commonly used – and the legal details of each vary considerably. If you use a third-party library in your project, you must make sure that the library's license and the license under which you intend to release your software are compatible with each other. If they are incompatible, you must replace that dependency with an alternative library that uses a friendlier license.

What do we mean by "compatible" when talking about licenses? Most licenses are considered to be **permissive**, meaning that you can use software released under that license for almost any purpose. Two well-known examples of this type of license are the MIT license and the BSD license. You generally won't face any compatibility problems if you stick to dependencies that use permissive licenses. Other licenses are **protective** rather than permissive, meaning that they restrict how you can use software that's released under those licenses. Here are some examples of the restrictions imposed by protective licenses:

- Some open-source licenses such as GPL or AGPL fall under a category informally called **copyleft**. Software released under these licenses can be used as dependencies in other projects, but only if those other projects are themselves released under the same copyleft license. For example, if your Hats for Cats app uses an open-source Python sorting library that is released under the GPL license, then *the entire Hats for Cats project must also use the GPL license*. It's not hard to see how this would be a problem if you intended to sell your software rather than release it as open source.

  To use more controversial terms, copyleft licenses are sometimes called "viral" because they can be thought of as "infecting" parent projects. This disease metaphor is probably unfair, and many fine pieces of software have been released using copyleft licenses, but the fact remains that you need to be careful about using them.

- Some licenses explicitly *disallow use by certain industries*, such as the military. Code released under a military exclusion license can't be used as a dependency for missile guidance software, for example.

- A license could *exclude usage of the software by certain countries*. This isn't commonly seen, but it is legal for a license to include restrictions of this type.

As you can see, it's important to understand what licenses your project's dependencies use so that you're aware of any restrictions imposed by those licenses and you steer well clear of any dependencies that are released under licenses that will restrict your ability to use or sell your software in the ways that you intend.

GitLab's License Compliance feature has three phases:

- The scanner looks through your project's dependencies and generates a list of all licenses used.
- The software development team – or your company's legal department – creates **license policies** that explicitly allow or deny each license that's found in your project's dependencies. Alternatively, you can preemptively create license policies before any dependencies are added to the project if you already know which licenses are incompatible with your main project's overall license.
- If a developer introduces a new dependency on a branch, and that dependency uses a license that has been denied, the License Compliance feature blocks the merge request for that branch until the license is removed or the block is overridden.

From this workflow, you can tell that creating license policies is an important part of using the License Compliance feature. To view, create, delete, or edit license policies, click **Security & Compliance** in the left navigation pane and then click **License compliance**. Here's what that screen looks like when you've approved two licenses and denied two other licenses:

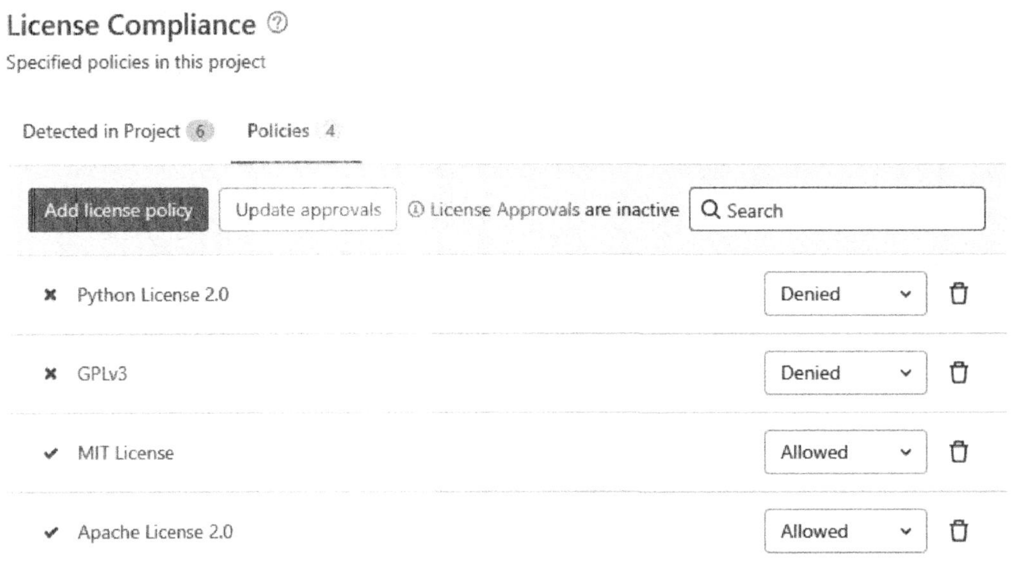

License Compliance

Specified policies in this project

	Status
✖ Python License 2.0	Denied
✖ GPLv3	Denied
✔ MIT License	Allowed
✔ Apache License 2.0	Allowed

Figure 7.7 – License policies

The workflow description mentions the power of License Compliance to block any merge request that introduces a dependency that uses a license that has been explicitly denied with a license policy. To block an MR, License Compliance deactivates or hides the **Merge** button so that it can't be clicked. Here's a blocked MR, which displays a list of licenses used by a new dependency (and its dependencies) that have been introduced on the MR's branch:

Using License Compliance to manage licenses of dependencies 191

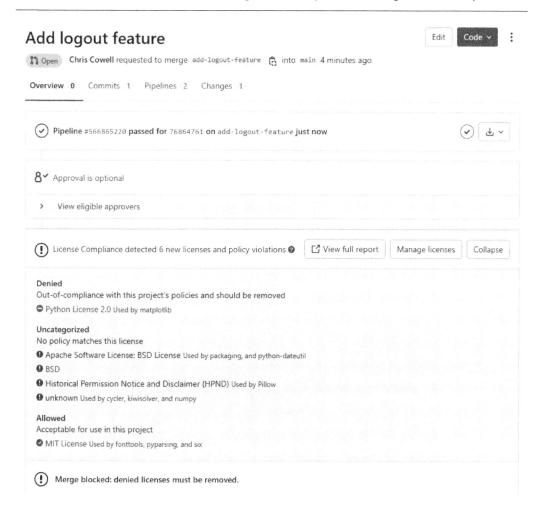

Figure 7.8 – Merge request blocked by a denied license

Using GitLab rulesets to unblock an MR

GitLab has several other triggers that cause an MR to become blocked until some sort of corrective action is taken, in addition to the case you've just seen. To take just one example, when a developer writes new product code without writing automated tests to cover that code, GitLab can be configured to notice that the "code coverage" figure on the developer's branch has dropped, and the MR for that branch will be blocked until the developer adds automated tests that test their new code.

Any MR that is automatically blocked can be unblocked with a GitLab feature called **approval rules**. These rules allow specific people to unblock an MR simply by **approving** that MR. Each of these approval rules has a name; the rule that lets you override blocks caused by denied licenses is called **License-Check**. We don't have room to go into configuring approval rules here, but they are quite straightforward to set up and use. The GitLab documentation can give you more details.

Enabling and configuring License Compliance

You can't use the GUI to enable License Compliance, but the manual technique of enabling it should seem very familiar by now. Just ensure that you have a `test` stage defined in your pipeline and include the License Compliance template:

```
stages:
  - test

include:
  - template: Security/License-Scanning.gitlab-ci.yml
```

Configuring License Compliance can be accomplished in the same way you configure the other scanners: edit `.gitlab-ci.yml` to either set a global variable or override a job definition and set a job-scoped variable.

As mentioned previously, an important part of configuring License Compliance is creating the license policies that stipulate which open-source licenses are allowed or denied for your project's dependencies. To create or edit these policies, navigate to the **Security & Compliance** option in the left navigation pane, click **License compliance**, and click the **Policies** tab. From there, you can add policies to either allow or deny any of the hundreds of licenses that GitLab recognizes. You can create policies for licenses, regardless of whether your project contains dependencies with those licenses. It might make sense for your legal team to create policies for any denied licenses before the development of your project begins so that MRs are blocked immediately if they introduce dependencies that use denied licenses.

> **Prerequisite for editing license policies**
> This is not well documented by GitLab, but to add, remove, or edit license policies, you must first run at least one instance of a pipeline that contains the License Scanning job. This "unlocks" the allowed and denied license lists and lets you edit policies.

Viewing License Compliance's findings

Unlike the other scanners we've looked at so far, License Compliance does not display its findings in the **Vulnerability Report** window. To see which licenses it has identified among the *dependencies on your project's default branch*, click the **Security & Compliance** option in the left navigation pane, and then click **License compliance**.

To see which licenses are used by *dependencies that are on a feature or bugfix branch*, navigate to the pipeline details page for a pipeline that ran against that branch and click the **Licenses** tab. This view also shows you which licenses are allowed, which are denied, and which are not yet categorized.

You're now equipped to put License Compliance to use in your projects. It's time to tackle the final security scanner provided by GitLab: Infrastructure as Code Scanning.

Using IaC Scanning to find problems in infrastructure configuration files

In the last decade or so, the phrase "treat hardware as cattle, not pets" has been used to describe a new approach to managing computers. By thinking of hardware as a fungible commodity rather than a collection of special snowflakes, development and operations teams are liberated from carefully configuring and maintaining the computers they use to host deployment environments, run databases, serve web applications, or do any of the countless other tasks involved with developing and deploying software. By using so-called IaC tools such as Ansible or Terraform to configure and maintain the configuration state on hardware (whether real or virtual, local or cloud-based), system administrators can adjust server capacity, create new environments, or experiment with hardware configurations without worrying about how difficult it will be to revert their systems if something goes wrong or an experiment fails. To get back to normal, they can simply wipe out the old machines and reconfigure them automatically with IaC tools, using settings that have already been proven to work. The time savings and freedom this grants development teams are enormous.

But with this new freedom comes a new kind of vulnerability. It's easy to create configuration files for IaC tools that introduce security vulnerabilities to machines that are configured with those files. GitLab's IaC scanner looks for exactly that sort of vulnerability. Once they are identified, a team can remediate them in the configuration file and then easily reconfigure their machines using the newer, safer setup.

Understanding IaC Scanning

GitLab's IaC Scanning is a specialized form of SAST. It looks through a project's repository to see whether it can find any configuration files from the supported IaC tools (the GitLab documentation can give you an up-to-date list of which IaC tools this scanner supports). It then identifies any vulnerabilities or poor programming practices in those configuration files.

Here's a trivial Terraform configuration file that creates an S3 bucket:

```
resource "aws_s3_bucket" "testBucket" {
    bucket = "myBucket"
    acl = "authenticatedRead"
}
```

This code looks simple enough, but it introduces several security vulnerabilities and fails to follow some best practices for Terraform configuration files, as you'll see in an IaC scanning report later in this chapter.

Enabling and configuring IaC scanning

As with many of the other scanners, you can enable IaC Scanning either with the GUI or by manually editing .gitlab-ci.yml. To enable it through the GitLab GUI, you can use the same technique you used to enable the other scanners: under the **Security & Compliance** option in the left navigation pane, click **Configuration**, tell the GUI to create a merge request, and merge the merge request.

To enable IaC Scanning manually, add a `test` stage to your project's pipeline if it doesn't already have one, and include the scanner's template:

```
stages:
  - test

include:
  - template: SAST-IaC.latest.gitlab-ci.yml
```

IaC Scanning doesn't currently offer any configuration options but may do so in the future.

Viewing IaC Scanning's findings

The Terraform configuration for creating an S3 bucket that was presented previously contains quite a few problems in just a few lines of code. There are some security vulnerabilities and some failures to follow best practices around creating S3 resources. The findings shown in the Vulnerability Report are invaluable in helping you understand where you need to tighten up your Terraform code to eliminate these problems:

Detected	Status	↓ Severity	Description	Identifier	Tool
2022-06-16	Needs Triage	● Critical	S3 bucket without MFA Delete Enabled. MFA delete cannot be enabled through Terraform, it can be done by adding a MFA device (https://docs.aws.amazon.com/IAM/latest/UserGuide/id_credentials_mfa_enable.html) and enabling versioning and MFA delete by usin... main.tf:1	S3 Bucket Without Enabled MFA Delete	SAST
2022-06-16	Needs Triage	● Critical	S3 Buckets should not be readable to any authenticated user main.tf:3	S3 Bucket ACL Allows Read to Any Authenticated User	SAST
2022-06-16	Needs Triage	● Critical	If algorithm is AES256 then the master key is null, empty or undefined, otherwise the master key is required main.tf:1	S3 Bucket SSE Disabled	SAST
2022-06-16	Needs Triage	▼ Medium	S3 bucket should have versioning enabled main.tf:1	S3 Bucket Without Versioning	SAST
2022-06-16	Needs Triage	● Unknown	All names should follow snake case pattern. main.tf:1	Name Is Not Snake Case	SAST
2022-06-16	Needs Triage	● Unknown	AWS services resource tags are an essential part of managing components main.tf:1	Resource Not Using Tags	SAST
2022-06-16	Needs Triage	● Info	IAM Access Analyzer should be enabled and configured to continuously monitor resource permissions main.tf:1	IAM Access Analyzer Not Enabled	SAST
2022-06-16	Needs Triage	● Info	Server Access Logging must be enabled on S3 Buckets so that all changes are logged and trackable main.tf:1	S3 Bucket Logging Disabled	SAST

Figure 7.9 – IaC Scanning findings

By looking at the **Tool** column of the findings in the vulnerability report, you'll see that the IaC Scanning findings are all listed as coming from SAST instead of the IaC scanner. That's because the IaC scanner is classified within GitLab as belonging to the SAST group of tools. To see only IaC findings in the vulnerability report, you'll need to pick **SAST** in the **Tool** dropdown – and even then, you'll still see findings from the SAST tool and any third-party scanners you've integrated into the SAST group of tools.

This concludes our survey of GitLab's seven security scanners. Let's move on to discuss two features that GitLab offers to make its security scanners easier to use and more powerful: reports and vulnerability management.

Understanding the different types of security reports

All GitLab security scanners display their results in three separate reports. Because each report shows results from all of the scanners, there's no need to bounce around the GitLab GUI, collecting information from all the different scanners. However, each of the three report locations presents a slightly different spin on the scanners' findings. It's important to understand how these three reports differ, so let's look at each one:

- The **vulnerability report** is the report that we've shown in screenshots throughout this chapter. It shows the findings of any scanner that ran during the last pipeline on your project's default branch (normally `main` or `master`). If you want to know how secure your stable code base is, look at the vulnerability report. It won't tell you anything about the state of security on any feature or bugfix branches – only the default branch.

- The **pipeline details page** for each pipeline that runs tells you about security problems that exist on whatever branch that pipeline ran on. So, if a pipeline ran against the default branch, its pipeline details page will contain the same information as the vulnerability report. But the pipeline details page for pipelines that run against feature or bugfix branches will alert you to whatever vulnerabilities exist on those branches, regardless of whether they also exist on the default branch. This page will reveal a tab called **Licenses** if License Compliance is enabled and has detected dependencies with licenses, and a tab called **Security** if it has findings from any of the other scanners to display. The types of information displayed on the pipeline details page are identical to what is displayed in the vulnerability report, albeit formatted slightly differently.

- Every **merge request** displays scanner results from the most recent pipeline that ran against the MR's source branch. However, the reports found in MRs are different from the vulnerability report and the pipeline details report in an important way: an MR report only displays the *differences* between vulnerabilities found by the last pipeline that ran on the MR's source branch and vulnerabilities found on the MR's target branch. In other words, it shows a delta view rather than a full list of all vulnerabilities on its branch.

Let's consider an example to illustrate the difference between these three reports:

1. Imagine that the `main` branch for Hats for Cats has one SAST vulnerability and one problem spotted by Secret Detection.
2. A developer makes a branch off of `main` called `make-hats-sortable`.
3. Following the best practices of GitLab Flow, the developer creates an MR with `make-hats-sortable` as the source branch and `main` as the target branch.
4. The developer commits code to the `make-hats-sortable` branch. Let's say that the commit fixes the SAST vulnerability but introduces a new DAST vulnerability.

Here's what each of the three reports will show at this point:

- The **vulnerability report** displays the SAST and Secret Detection problems since both of those issues exist on the `main` branch.
- The **pipeline details page report** for the most recent pipeline that ran against the `make-hats-sortable` branch (that is, the merge request's source branch) shows only the vulnerabilities found by Secret Detection and DAST since the SAST vulnerability has been fixed on that branch.
- The **merge request report** shows the delta view of the vulnerabilities on its source and target branches. In this case, it reports that the SAST vulnerability is fixed and the DAST vulnerability has appeared, but it doesn't list the Secret Detection vulnerability since that exists on both the `make-hats-sortable` and `main` branches.

That concludes our discussion of the different types of GitLab security reports. After you read these reports and understand where your security vulnerabilities lie, how do you track your progress in remediating those vulnerabilities? That's the topic of the next section.

Managing security vulnerabilities

Whenever any scanner except License Compliance finds a vulnerability, it grants that vulnerability the **Needs Triage** status. This status shows up in the vulnerability's entry in the vulnerability report and the pipeline details page report.

You should decide what you intend to do about each vulnerability that has that status and change its status accordingly. Here are the possible status values:

- **Dismissed** means that you do not intend to remediate this vulnerability. Maybe you've determined that it's a false positive, maybe you've decided it's a real problem but isn't worth fixing, or maybe you've realized that it doesn't apply to your product or your users.

- **Confirmed** means that it's a real problem, and you do intend to fix it. After setting a finding to this status, you would normally create an issue to track your progress as your team works to remediate this vulnerability. GitLab offers a few shortcuts in the report GUIs to do this, and even prepopulates the issue's title and description with information from the finding to make it as easy as possible to fix.
- **Resolved** means that you have fixed the problem, so it no longer exists in your project. This status has to be set manually. *GitLab will not automatically resolve vulnerabilities.* This is because it does not want to accidentally resolve problems that are still present, thereby giving you a false sense of security.

GitLab's vulnerability management feature just boils down to setting the status of a vulnerability and then optionally using a GitLab issue to track progress on fixing that vulnerability. A typical vulnerability management workflow might look like this:

1. A scanner reports a vulnerability, giving it the **Needs Triage** status.
2. The development team triages the vulnerability and decides not to fix it, in which case you set its status to **Dismissed** and stop the workflow.

    Alternatively, the team triages the vulnerability and decides that it does need to be fixed, in which case you can set its status to **Confirmed**.
3. Optionally, you can create an issue that contains information about the vulnerability and possibly instructions on how to fix it. This issue is discussed, added to a sprint, and assigned to a developer just like any other issue.
4. The developer assigned to the issue creates a branch, creates a merge request for that branch, and fixes the issue on that branch.
5. The "delta" security report for the merge request shows that the issue exists on the default branch but no longer exists on the developer's branch.
6. Your team merges the merge request. The vulnerability is now remediated in the default branch.
7. You close the issue.
8. On the vulnerability report, you must set the vulnerability's status to **Resolved**.

This process may feel cumbersome when you see it laid out like this, but most people quickly get used to the flow and come to appreciate the visibility it gives them into the state of security in their projects.

Now, you know how to track your team's efforts at fixing security vulnerabilities in your code. There's one final topic to tackle in this chapter: using security scanners other than the ones that are provided by GitLab.

Integrating outside security scanners

Many teams are committed to using one or more security scanners that are not part of GitLab's security offering. Never fear – it's usually possible to integrate outside scanners into your GitLab CI/CD pipelines.

Integration has two parts. First, you need to tell your pipeline to trigger the outside scanner. This is easy, so long as your scanner comes packaged in a Docker image and can be run from the command line:

1. Create a new pipeline job in the `test` stage (unless there's a reason to run it elsewhere).
2. Use the `images` keyword in the job definition to specify the location of the Docker image that contains the scanner you'd like to add to your pipeline.
3. In the `script` section of the job definition, trigger the scanner using whatever CLI command you use when you run it manually. You might need to pass some options to the CLI command to control where it generates its results file, and what format it uses for that file.
4. Add `allow_failure: true` to your job definition so that the pipeline will continue to run even if the outside scanner finds vulnerabilities.

The second part of integrating an outside scanner is to tell GitLab how to include the scanner's results in the three standard GitLab security reports that we've discussed in this chapter. GitLab can only incorporate these results if they are written to a JSON file that conforms to specific JSON schemas, where each scanner type (SAST, DAST, and so on) has a separate schema. The documentation for each scanner type provides more information about these schemas.

> **Integrating third-party scanners that generate non-standard results files**
>
> If your third-party scanner can't generate results files that validate against the appropriate schema, you'll need to write a short script to parse the results and create a new results file that does conform to the schema. You'll need to trigger this script somewhere in your pipeline after the scanner runs.

In the job definition you create for the third-party scanner, you must declare the scanner's results file to be an artifact, specifically an artifact that contains the results for a certain type of security report. For example, if you are integrating an additional SAST scanner that creates a results file called `my_scanner/results.json`, you would need to include this code in the job definition that runs that scanner:

```
artifacts:
  reports:
    sast: my_scanner/results.json
```

This high-level description may be all you need to integrate third-party scanners, but if you need more detailed configuration instructions – including guidance on results schemas, best practices for what to name your pipeline job and results files, and more – the official GitLab documentation has a very thorough page on exactly this topic.

Summary

Security is one of the biggest and most complicated topics covered in this book, so congratulations on making it through! Let's take stock of what we learned in this chapter.

First, we covered some common principles that underly all of GitLab's security scanners. We discussed the fact that all of the scanners are open-source tools developed outside of GitLab, and why that's a good thing. We saw that some scanners use different analyzers to support different computer languages, though all scanners support the most commonly used languages, and some scanners are completely language-agnostic. We learned about the implications of packaging the scanners as Docker images. We saw that scanners don't stop CI/CD pipelines when they find vulnerabilities, and we learned that it's usually possible to integrate outside scanners into your pipelines if the GitLab-provided scanners aren't sufficient for your needs.

Then, we marched through the list of GitLab security scanners, learning what kinds of problems each one looks for, how to enable them with the GUI or manually, how to configure their behavior, and how to view their findings. We saw the following:

- SAST looks for vulnerabilities in source code
- Secret Detection looks for sensitive information that should not be stored in Git repositories
- DAST finds vulnerabilities in running web apps or Web APIs
- Dependency Scanning spots known vulnerabilities in your project's third-party libraries
- Container Scanning finds known problems with Linux distributions that form the base of your Docker images
- License Compliance identifies dependencies with licenses that are incompatible with your overall project license
- IaC Scanning looks for infrastructure configuration files that could introduce vulnerabilities into computers that you manage

Finally, we investigated three topics adjacent to the scanners themselves: the differences between the three different security reports provided by GitLab, managing security vulnerabilities that are identified by the scanners, and integrating outside scanners into your pipeline for projects that need even more protection.

Unfortunately, security concerns have become such a large and important part of developing software. But as we've seen throughout this chapter, GitLab's suite of tools for detecting and fixing security vulnerabilities is one of its most powerful and valuable features. We can breathe a little easier knowing that many potential problems can now be identified early in the development process when there's still plenty of time to fix them before they result in embarrassing, expensive, or reputation-damaging security breaches in production.

At this point, your code has been written, verified, and secured. The next step in the software development life cycle is to package and deploy it. We'll tackle those tasks in the next chapter.

8
Packaging and Deploying Code

In the previous chapters, you learned how to use GitLab for source code management, as well as to set up CI/CD pipelines that build, test, and perform security scanning against the code you've checked in. You have hopefully now developed a confident understanding of both the infrastructure around GitLab CI/CD and the syntax used to author pipelines.

In this chapter, we will continue our journey through the stages of software development, focusing now on packaging and deploying code. We will use a combination of GitLab's built-in features and common industry tools to deploy our code to an endpoint or environment. The goal is to answer the question, *how do we make the application we have built and tested available to our users?*

This chapter will introduce new vocabulary, adding to our knowledge of GitLab CI/CD syntax. It will also mention, and the examples will use, third-party tools such as Docker, as well as cloud service providers such as Google Cloud Platform. Since this book's core focus is on GitLab's features and we don't have the space for a technical deep dive into every tool that could be used with GitLab, you may be unfamiliar with some of the technologies referenced in this chapter. We will therefore strive to use industry-standard language, focus on each tool's integration with GitLab, and provide examples that can be replicated without requiring further knowledge from the reader. After completing this chapter, you will be equipped with the skills needed to use GitLab's native package and container registry features for hosting completed builds. You will also extend your knowledge of GitLab CI/CD to include deploying to review and production environments, using traditional or cloud-native infrastructures.

Here is how we'll cover the topics in this chapter:

- Storing code in GitLab's package registry for later re-use
- Storing code in GitLab's container and package registries for later deployment
- Deploying to different environments using GitLab Flow
- Deploying to a review app for testing
- Deploying to real-world production environments
- Deploying to a Kubernetes cluster

Technical requirements

Like the previous chapters, you'll get the most out of this chapter if you have an account on a GitLab instance (SaaS or self-managed). Moreover, the topics and examples in this chapter will increasingly focus on deploying to environments that live outside GitLab. The infrastructure tools that are referenced include the following:

- A server hosting GitLab (or GitLab.com)
- Self-hosted runners (or SaaS runners hosted on GitLab.com)
- Docker (also available on SaaS runners hosted on Gitlab.com)
- Kubernetes
- Cloud platform services (such as Amazon Web Services, Google Cloud Platform, or Heroku)

If you wish to minimize the amount of tooling you need to install and maintain yourself, we recommend using GitLab.com with SaaS runners. We also recommend creating an account on a cloud service platform if you wish to practice deploying to live or complex infrastructure. Just be aware of the potential charges when using these services.

Storing code in GitLab's package registry for later re-use

As part of the goal of serving as a complete DevOps platform, GitLab includes the option to enable package and container registries in each project. The package registry supports hosting software packages and language packs in a variety of formats, and the container registry serves as a repository of purpose-built container images. These features allow teams to conveniently host, organize, and version-control completed builds alongside their source code. We will discuss the package and container registries in turn.

Locating GitLab's container and package registries

GitLab projects technically support three types of built-in registries. They are package, container, and infrastructure registries that can be used to store completed code, whether for use by end users or other software projects. This book will focus on the package and container registries; the infrastructure registry is a recent addition to GitLab that is specifically for hosting Terraform modules. GitLab also supports pushing artifacts to external or third-party registries, though that is beyond the scope of what we will cover here.

Figure 8.1 shows where GitLab's packages and container registries can be found at both the project and group level, under **Packages and registries** in the left navigation pane.

Storing code in GitLab's package registry for later re-use   203

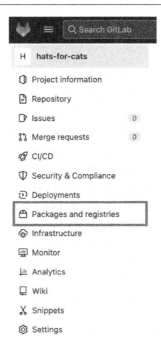

Figure 8.1 – Packages and registries in the left sidebar

When you hover over **Packages and registries**, you will see that each of the package, container, and infrastructure registries have a dedicated page to navigate to, as shown in *Figure 8.2*.

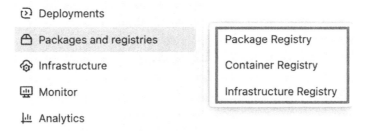

Figure 8.2 – Packages and registries sub-menu items

If we have not yet configured or pushed artifacts to any of the registries, we will see an appropriate message when we navigate to the registry page. *Figure 8.3* shows the message we see on the **Package Registry** page, along with a reference to the GitLab documentation for using the package registry.

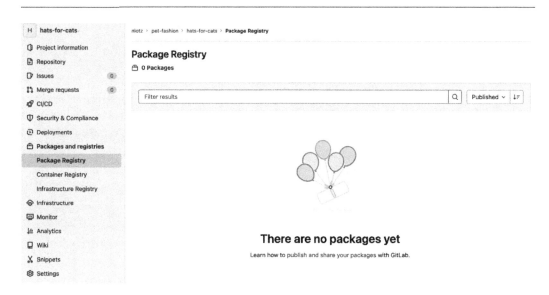

Figure 8.3 – Project package registry with no packages

Figure 8.4 shows us an unpopulated **Container Registry**. Here, GitLab suggests Docker commands we could use to build a containerized version of our application that we then push to the container registry.

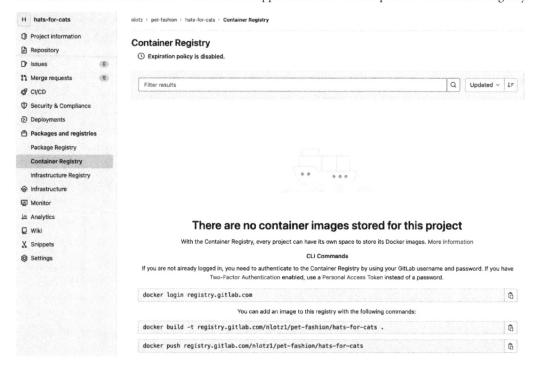

Figure 8.4 – Project container registry with no container images

We will soon see that a typical way to push to GitLab's registries is to configure CI/CD jobs that execute commands to build an artifact, authenticate it with the registry, and push the artifact to the registry, often using GitLab's API.

Getting started with the package registry

The package registry is enabled by default in GitLab, though it can be disabled by GitLab administrators at the instance level. In project settings, you can also choose to toggle the package registry feature on or off under **Settings | General | Visibility, project features, permissions**. If **Packages** is toggled off, the feature will not be available in the left sidebar. *Figure 8.5* shows where the package registry can be enabled or disabled in the project settings.

Figure 8.5 – Enabling the package registry in project settings

The question now arises, how do we use the package registry? That is, how do we populate it with our software? There are two primary steps to populate the package registry: authenticate to the registry, and build and upload packages using CI/CD jobs. But before diving into those steps, let's first list the package formats supported by GitLab.

Supported package formats

As of this writing, the following package manager formats are generally available and fully supported in GitLab's package registry:

- Generic packages
- Maven
- npm
- NuGet
- PyPI

The following package formats are either behind a feature flag or have known issues with their use:

- Composer
- Conan
- Debian
- Go
- Helm
- Ruby Gems

Each package manager has its own configuration format and syntax. To maintain consistency, as well as to keep our focus on the concepts underlying GitLab's package, we will show examples using generic package formats. We will start with authenticating to GitLab's package registry.

Authenticating to the registry

We mentioned earlier in this chapter that working with GitLab's registries takes place largely through CI/CD jobs. The actions of authenticating, uploading to, and using packages from the package registry should be represented by job tasks defined in GitLab CI/CD configurations. In general, you can authenticate to GitLab's package registry with one of the following four types of credentials:

- A personal access token, to authenticate with a user's permissions
- A project deploy token, for accessing all packages in a project
- A group deploy token, for accessing all packages in all projects in a group or its subgroups
- A job token, for accessing packages in the project for which the CI/CD job is defined

> **Deploy tokens and job tokens are not tied to users**
>
> Unlike personal access tokens, deploy tokens and job tokens are special kinds of GitLab credentials that are not tied to a particular user, but rather can serve as an alternative way to authenticate without specifying user credentials. Deploy tokens and job tokens are often used to programmatically access a repository, or in our case, read and write to the package registry.

In our example, we'll create a project-level deploy token in the Hats for Cats project. *Figure 8.6* shows where we can create a new deploy token under project **Settings | Repository | Deploy Tokens**. Here, we can give the token a human-readable name, an optional expiration date, and an optional username that's specific to the token (if we don't enter an optional username, GitLab will auto-generate one for us).

Finally, we select which permissions we want to grant the token. The permission names can appear slightly ambiguous, but `read_registry` and `write_registry` refer to reading and writing to the *container* registry only, while `read_package_registry` and `write_package_registry` refer to reading and writing to the package registry.

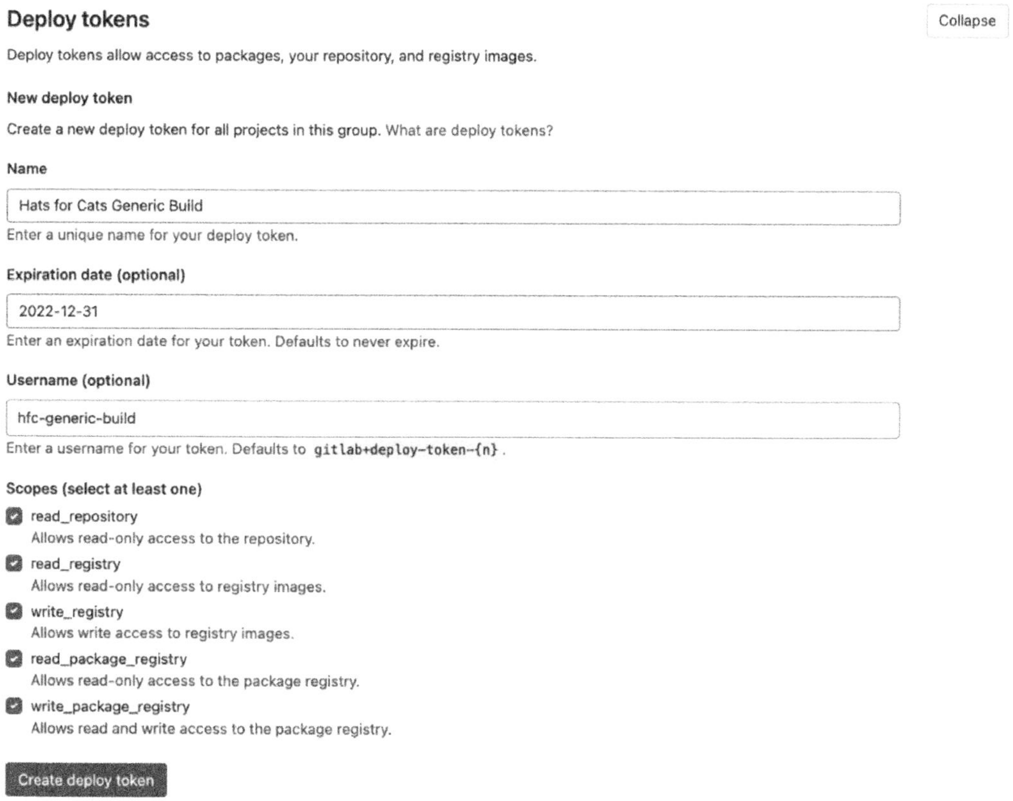

Figure 8.6 – Creating a new deploy token

Once we create a deploy token, GitLab will provide a password that we'll need to save somewhere safe (see *Figure 8.7*). We will use the deploy token password to authenticate our commands to the package or container registry.

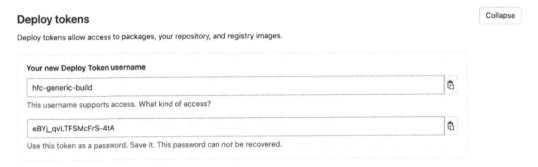

Figure 8.7 – Deploy token password

> **Don't forget to save your deploy token!**
>
> Be sure to save the password for the deploy token somewhere safe and secure! Once you leave the page, you will not be able to recover the password, as GitLab will not persistently store the credential.

After you finish creating the deploy token and saving the password, GitLab will show the token and its details under **Active Deploy Tokens**, as shown in *Figure 8.8*. A project maintainer or owner can choose to revoke the token if it should no longer be used.

Active Deploy Tokens (2)

Name	Username	Created	Expires	Scopes	
Hats for Cats Generic Build	hfc-generic-build	Sep 24, 2022	in 3 months	read_repository, read_registry, write_registry, read_package_registry, write_package_registry	Revoke

Figure 8.8 – Active deploy tokens

We can now use the token we created to authenticate to the registry. The exact syntax we'd use for authentication would depend on our package manager, that is, the type of package we are creating or using. In the simplest case, we may include our credentials in the header of a `curl` command, as shown here:

```
curl --user "hfc-generic-build:<deploy token password>" ${CI_
API_V4_URL}/projects/${CI_PROJECT_ID}/packages/generic/stable-
releases/0.0.1/my_app.tar.gz
```

When run in a CI/CD job, the preceding command authenticates to the project's package registry in which the pipeline is running. The authentication credentials are provided by the `--user` flag, where we provide the username and password (shown as a placeholder here) for our deploy key. The output of the command will be to download the `my_app.tar.gz` package.

Using a deploy key is a programmatic way to pull or download from the registry. Downloading package files can also be done via the UI. *Figure 8.9* shows an example of a `stable_releases` package, version 0.0.1, that has been added to the package registry.

Figure 8.9 – Entry in the package registry

If we click on **stable_releases**, we see downloadable application files under the **Assets** heading (see *Figure 8.10*). We see the filenames (and file types by their extensions), size, and creation date. Selecting the filename downloads the file to your local computer. Under **History**, we see when it was published to the registry, which pipeline build pushed the package, which commit launched the pipeline, and the package name and version.

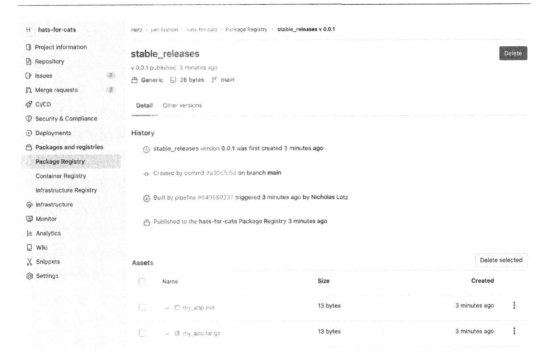

Figure 8.10 – Package files and build history

Now that we understand how to authenticate to and access packages in the package registry, we will now use CI/CD jobs to build, push, and update packages in the registry.

Building and pushing packages to the package registry

As we've mentioned several times already, GitLab recommends using CI/CD jobs to build and publish to the registry. Technically, writing to the registry can just take place via API calls, so GitLab CI/CD isn't strictly required. However, build and artifact management is well suited to GitLab Flow, and it is helpful to have the process standardized in a similar manner to your other software development workflows. For that reason, we will create a CI/CD pipeline to build and push to the registry.

The exact job syntax will be dependent on the programming languages and package managers you use to build software. The GitLab documentation has specific syntax examples for authenticating, reading, and writing to the registry using Python, Maven, and other tools. To keep things conceptual, and because we don't have the space to showcase every supported language or tool, we will use generic packages as our example, and our commands will be `curl`-style API calls.

A CI/CD configuration may look like the following:

```
stages:
  - build
  - publish
```

```
build_app:
  stage: build
  script:
    - make my_app
    - tar -czvf my_app.tar.gz .
  artifacts:
    paths:
      - my_app.tar.gz

publish_to_registry:
  stage: publish
  script:
    - $PACKAGE_FILE=$(ls | grep *.tar.gz)
    - curl --user "hfc-generic-build:<deploy token password>" --upload-file my_app.tar.gz "${CI_API_V4_URL}/projects/${CI_PROJECT_ID}/packages/generic/stable_releases/0.0.1/$PACKAGE_FILE"
  dependencies:
    - build_app
```

The preceding example .gitlab-ci.yml content contains two stages: a build stage that compiles a C-style application and a publish stage that pushes the build artifact to the package registry. The build stage contains one job that builds our code. We then create an archive file containing the completed build and supporting files. The archive file is specified as an artifact in the build job so that the downstream publish job will have access to it.

The publish_to_registry job authenticates to the registry and uploads the build artifact. Note the presence of some dynamic CI/CD variables in the curl command (that is, the terms beginning with CI_). These variables are a convenient way to reference the correct URL and path to the registry in your project. Note we also categorize the build as a generic package, part of "stable release" version 0.0.1.

We might also add a Unix timestamp to distinguish between different builds in the registry. We can modify the build job as follows to include a timestamp in the artifact filename:

```
build_app:
  stage: build
  script:
    - make my_app
    - TIMESTAMP=$(date +%s)
```

```
      - tar -czvf my_app_$TIMESTAMP.tar.gz .
  artifacts:
    paths:
      - ./*.tar.gz
```

Figure 8.11 shows the updated file asset in the registry. Note the timestamp in the filename in the `tar` command in the build script. The archive size and creation date are also shown. A developer can then click the filename to download the archive, which they can then unpack on their local system.

Assets			Delete selected
Name	Size	Created	
my_app_1664121721.tar.gz	2.54 KiB	4 minutes ago	

Figure 8.11 – File in the package registry with a timestamp

Building and pushing packages to the container registry

GitLab also has a container registry for storing Docker images. Like the package registry, Docker images can be created and pushed to the registry with CI/CD jobs. Authentication is conceptually similar to the package registry, but you'd use container platform tools such as Docker to authenticate, build, push, and pull container images.

The following Docker command can be used to authenticate to the container registry, using our deploy token from earlier. We will use similar Docker commands to also build a containerized version of our application and push it to the registry:

```
docker login --username "hfc-generic-build" --password "eBYj_qvLTFSMcFrS-4tA" $CI_REGISTRY
```

Our CI/CD job for "containerizing" our application and pushing it to the registry might look like the following:

```
publish_to_container_registry:
  stage: publish
  image: docker:stable
  services:
    - docker:dind
  variables:
    IMAGE: $CI_REGISTRY_IMAGE/my_app/0.0.1
  script:
```

```
    - docker login -u "hfc-generic-build" -p "<deploy token
password>" $CI_REGISTRY
    - docker build -t $IMAGE .
    - docker push $IMAGE
```

Let's explain what is happening in the preceding CI/CD job, step by step:

1. We name the job `publish_to_container_registry` as part of the **publish** stage.

2. We then include two containers in the CI/CD job runtime environment: a container with the official Docker tooling (`image: docker:stable`) and a service container with "Docker-in-Docker" tooling (`docker:dind`). The latter container type allows us to build containers inside our already-containerized CI/CD job environment (hence the Docker-*in*-Docker moniker).

3. Next, we define a variable called `IMAGE` that will specify the name of our container image, as well as its destination endpoint in the container registry. The `IMAGE` variable will be referenced as arguments to the `docker` command.

4. Finally, the script section of our CI/CD job contains three commands:

   - The first command, `docker login`, authenticates to the container registry using our deploy token
   - The second command, `docker build`, builds a containerized version of our application
   - The final command, `docker push`, then pushes the newly built container image to the container registry

> **Be careful when building containers with Docker-in-Docker**
>
> While it's simple and straightforward, Docker-in-Docker uses the `--docker-privileged` flag by default, which can give the service running the containers root access to the host machine. If this is a security concern, GitLab also provides instructions for using a build tool called **kaniko** to build container images from a Dockerfile. See the GitLab documentation for more details.

It turns out that if we just add the preceding job to our CI/CD pipeline configuration and then run the pipeline, the job will fail. That is because we are missing another required component of building a container image. A file in our repository called `Dockerfile` is required to act as a "recipe" for how our container image will be built and what it should contain. Normally, a Dockerfile will contain instructions such as dependencies that should be installed, services that should be started, or ports that should be open. In this example, we will keep the Dockerfile extremely simple. A very minimal Dockerfile might contain the following:

```
FROM alpine:latest

# copy all of the files in this project into the Docker image
```

```
RUN mkdir public-app/
ADD . public-app/

WORKDIR public-app
```

The preceding Dockerfile does the following:

- It uses a minimal Linux distribution called Alpine Linux as the base operating system for the container we are building
- It creates a directory in the container called `public-app/`
- It puts all our repository files in the `public-app/` directory
- It makes `public-app/` the working directory when the container is launched

Figure 8.12 shows how our project repository might look after we update our `.gitlab-ci.yml` file and create the Dockerfile.

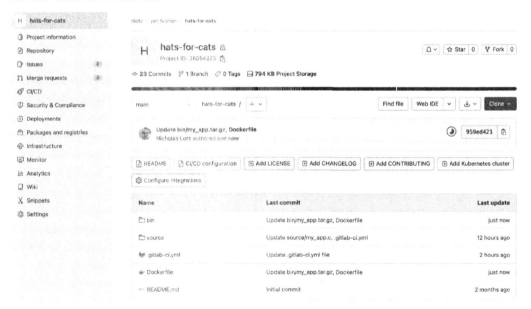

Figure 8.12 – Our repository with the Dockerfile

Now, when we run a CI/CD pipeline, we can see the Docker commands represented in the `publish_to_container_registry` job log, as shown in the following screenshot (*Figure 8.13*). Notice how the output of the `docker build` command shows it following the recipe we specified in `Dockerfile`. The job script ends with confirmation that the container image was pushed to the project's container registry.

Figure 8.13 – Job log for publishing to the container registry

Checking the container registry, we in fact see a reference to the container name as we specified in the CI/CD job (*Figure 8.14*).

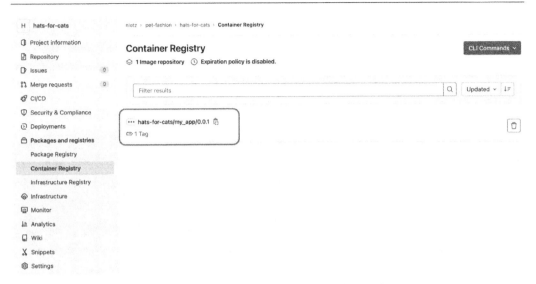

Figure 8.14 – Image repository in the container registry

If we click on the container name, we can see the builds themselves (*Figure 8.15*).

Figure 8.15 – Latest artifact in the project container registry

So far, everything we have discussed covers finding, authenticating to, and writing to GitLab's package and container registries. In the next section of this chapter, we will actually use and deploy the assets we have created and uploaded.

Storing code in GitLab's container and package registries for later deployment

GitLab's package and container registries are useful not only for making software available for users to download but also for storing packages and libraries for use in CI/CD pipelines, or for deployment to an environment. In this section, we will discuss how to programmatically interact with the registries via CI/CD jobs.

Using images from the container registry

In the previous section, we built a containerized version of our app and pushed the image to GitLab's container registry. Recall that the CI/CD jobs we used to build the container image themselves run in containers, hence the reference to terms such as `docker:stable` and `docker:dnd`. In this example, we are pulling from a public container registry, that is, Docker Hub.

However, we can also pull container images we have pushed to GitLab's container registry and use them as the basis for running our CI/CD jobs. We can use them in our pipelines just as we did with public container images, using the `image` keyword, like in the following snippet:

```
use_container_from_registry:
  stage: run
  image: registry.gitlab.com/nlotz1/pet-fashion/hats-for-cats/my_app/0.0.1:latest
  script:
    - ls -al     # Show the current directory as our container's working directory
```

Figure 8.16 shows our job output when we pull our container from the local registry to run our job.

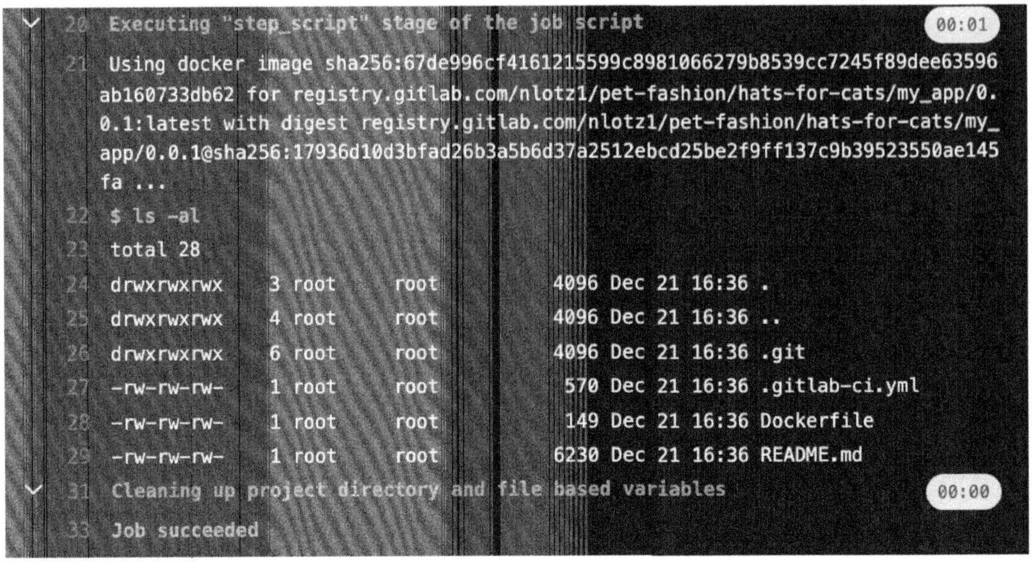

Figure 8.16 – Using a local container in a CI/CD job

Note that the job log shows GitLab pulling the image from the container registry, as well as the contents of the container's filesystem (that is, the files we included when we built the container in the first place).

Using packages from the package registry

Using packages in the package registry follows a similar theme as publishing packages to the registry. The exact step and syntax for pulling from the registry will depend on the package type. In general, you'll be required to specify the group and project where the package lives (i.e., the namespace in GitLab), the package name, and the package version. Consistent with the example from earlier, we might use a CI/CD job to pull down and run a generic package from our registry:

```
use_package_from_registry:
  stage: run_package
  script:
    - 'wget --header="JOB-TOKEN: $CI_JOB_TOKEN" ${CI_API_V4_URL}/projects/${CI_PROJECT_ID}/packages/generic/stable_releases/0.0.1/my_app_1665515895.tar.gz'
    - tar -xvf my_app_1665515895.tar.gz
    - ./my_app
```

The job log in *Figure 8.17* shows the output of authenticating and pulling down the package file via GitLab's API. In this example, the package is then extracted from its archive file and run.

Figure 8.17 – Using the package from the registry in a CI/CD job

GitLab's documentation shows different steps to authenticate and download packages for different package managers, but the principles remain the same.

Now that we understand how we can publish download packages in the context of CI/CD jobs, we will next incorporate these steps into a typical GitLab development workflow.

Deploying to different environments using GitLab Flow

We have so far discussed how to store and use our completed code by publishing to and pulling from GitLab's package and container registries. Now, we will learn about some of GitLab's features for organizing deployments of code to particular environments.

GitLab has two terms, **environments** and **deployments**, that are used to describe and categorize the location and version of a deployed application. An environment is represented by a name and a URL, which serve as organizational labels inside GitLab. Whenever an application is deployed to that environment via CI/CD, GitLab creates and categorizes it as a new deployment.

Environments are created via the **environment** keyword in a CI/CD job. That prompts GitLab CI/CD to associate the job and resulting deployment with that environment, along with the specified name and URL. In the following example, we've modified two of our previously created jobs to deploy our app to testing and production environments, respectively. The container version of the app is deployed to an environment called `testing`, and the generic app to an environment called `production`:

```
use_package_from_registry:
  stage: run_package
  script:
    - 'wget --header="JOB-TOKEN: $CI_JOB_TOKEN" ${CI_API_V4_URL}/projects/${CI_PROJECT_ID}/packages/generic/stable_releases/0.0.1/my_app_1665515895.tar.gz'
    - tar -xvf my_app_1665515895.tar.gz
    - ./my_app
  environment:
    name: testing
    url: https://test.example.com

use_container_from_registry:
  stage: run_container
  image: registry.gitlab.com/nlotz1/pet-fashion/hats-for-cats/my_app/0.0.1:latest
  script:
    - ls -la
  environment:
    name: production
    url: https://prod.example.com
```

Figure 8.18 shows that environments are represented in the GitLab UI under **Deployments | Environments**.

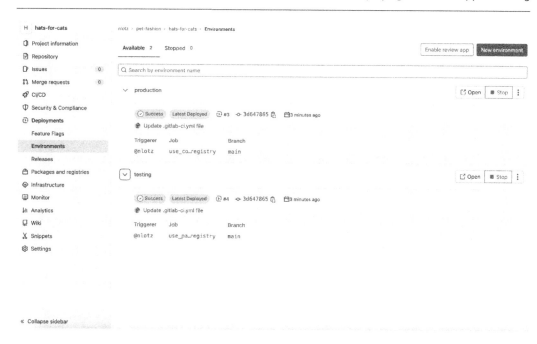

Figure 8.18 – Environments in the GitLab UI

Each environment is updated when a new commit creates a pipeline with a CI/CD job deploying to that environment. The GitLab UI shows the commit SHA for the latest deployment, the GitLab user who triggered the commit, the branch it was triggered on, and the CI/CD job deploying to that environment. The **Open** button on the top right serves as a link to the URL specified when the environment was defined (e.g., `https://prod.example.com`).

We can see that by integrating environments into GitLab CI/CD, we can set up more advanced workflows, such as using CI/CD keywords like **rules** to ensure certain environments are only updated when code changes on certain branches. The next section in this chapter will show such an example.

Deploying to a review app for testing

GitLab has a feature called a **review app** that allows developers to preview their changes directly within a merge request. Review apps use a special kind of environment called **dynamic environments**, whose names and URLs are set and changed based on the value of CI/CD variables. If you look back at *Figure 8.18*, you will notice a button that says **Enable review app** on the top right of the **Environments** page. *Figure 8.19* shows that selecting the button provides a block of code you can paste into your `.gitlab-ci.yml` file that creates a job that deploys to a review app environment.

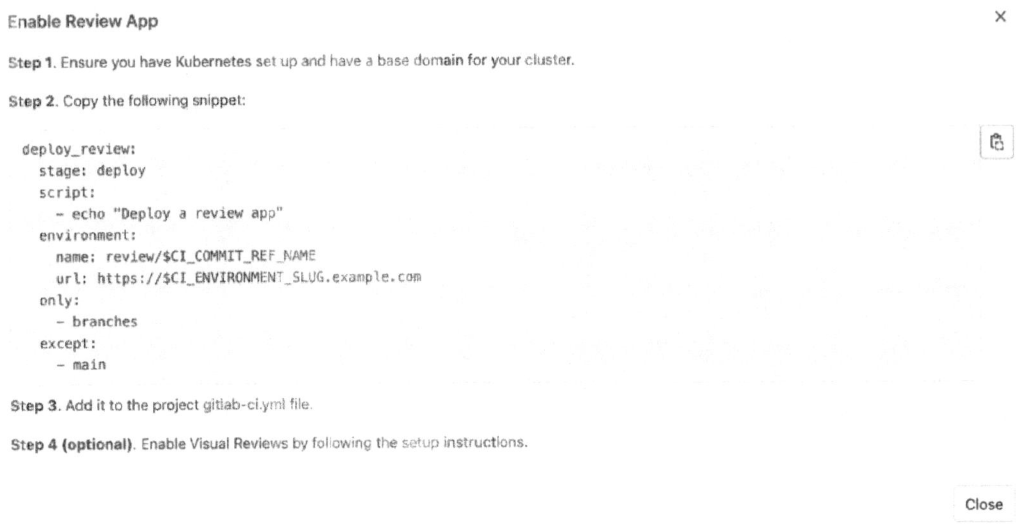

Enable Review App
Step 1. Ensure you have Kubernetes set up and have a base domain for your cluster.
Step 2. Copy the following snippet:
deploy_review:
stage: deploy
script:
- echo "Deploy a review app"
environment:
name: review/$CI_COMMIT_REF_NAME
url: https://$CI_ENVIRONMENT_SLUG.example.com
only:
- branches
except:
- main
Step 3. Add it to the project gitlab-ci.yml file.
Step 4 (optional). Enable Visual Reviews by following the setup instructions.
Close

Figure 8.19 – Enable Review App

There are two key items to note in the job content. The first is the use of predefined CI/CD variables to specify the environment name and URL. The name of the review environment will be dynamically updated based on the triggering branch, and the URL will be updated based on the dynamic environment name. This is useful for spinning up temporary ad hoc environments during the development process.

The second item to note in the review app CI/CD job is its `only/except` keywords. The review app environment will *only* be deployed when a pipeline is triggered on a Git branch, *except* the main branch. The logic is that a branch represents a development line, but the main branch might be a more stable staging or production environment that is static rather than dynamic.

One other useful element of review apps is their easy accessibility from a merge request. If a merge request pipeline has a review app job defined for the triggering branch, a link to the review app's URL will be accessible from the merge request page (see *Figure 8.20*).

Pipeline #668196806 passed for 133648b3 on new-feature just now
Deployed to review/new-feature just now
View app

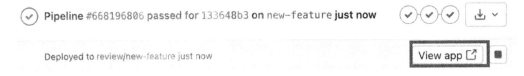

Figure 8.20 – View review app from a merge request

The link to the review environment can also be seen on the CI/CD job log (see *Figure 8.21*).

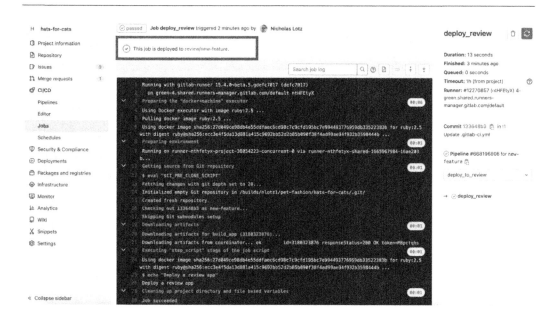

Figure 8.21 – Review app CI/CD job log

To summarize, review apps simply extend our understanding of environments to include dynamic creation and updates. They are best used to represent rapidly changing development environments and are easily accessible for developers and reviewers to preview the latest version of their applications.

Now that we have learned about previewing changes with review apps, let's finally turn to how we might deploy into production.

Deploying to real-world production environments

In the examples presented so far, we have shown that environments are simply organizational categories in GitLab with associated names and URLs. In the real world, however, environments represent actual infrastructure, be it your computer's or someone else's. That means recognizing the constraints on the available resources and the importance of proper security and access control.

In this day and age, it is increasingly common to use cloud service providers such as AWS, Microsoft Azure, and Google Cloud Platform for application hosting. These services not only outsource the need for infrastructure management but they also provide programmatic interfaces for managing your environments.

Moreover, suites of developer tools for managing these resources have accompanied the rise of cloud service providers, apart from the cloud vendor-provided tools. Software such as Terraform, Ansible, and Chef is available to declaratively manage cloud resources. That is, they let you store descriptions of infrastructure as text in a Git repository. Thus, similar workflows for infrastructure change management can be used as those for managing application development.

There is more to cloud service utilization than we could possibly cover within this one chapter. However, it is worth pointing out how GitLab can assist with one of the most important aspects of application environment administration: secret management. We've already explained the concept of CI/CD variables and how they can be used in CI/CD configurations and exported to the environments where jobs run. For variables of a sensitive nature, such as deploy keys, GitLab provides a special place in group- or project-level settings so that their values are not exposed in the project's repository.

Say, for example, you wish to deploy to an environment hosted in AWS. You will be required to provide credentials to authenticate to AWS, generally in the form of an AWS access key and a secret key. However, you would not want to directly enter those values into your CI/CD deployment scripts, as that leaks your credentials into the code base and its version history.

You can instead navigate to your project's **Settings | CI/CD** and expand the **Variables** section, as shown in *Figure 8.22*. Here, you can create variables that you can reference in your `.gitlab-ci.yml` file, just like any other variable, without having to hardcode their values into the configuration.

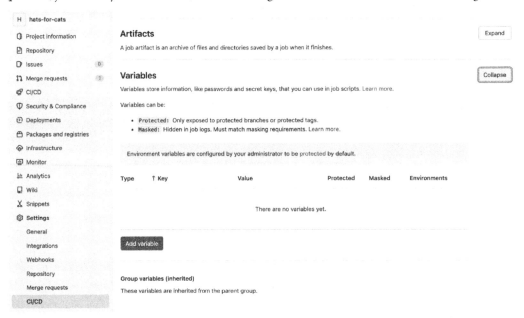

Figure 8.22 – Project-level CI/CD variables

Importantly, creating a variable in this way provides some additional gatekeeping on its use and exposure. Aside from setting the variable's name and value, you can limit the environments in which it can be used. You can also choose to limit the variable to protected branches and tags (that is, branches and tags with restrictions on who can contribute to or modify them). And *Figure 8.23* shows you can also mask the variable, meaning that job logs would only display asterisks or **[MASKED]** if there were an attempt to leak its value.

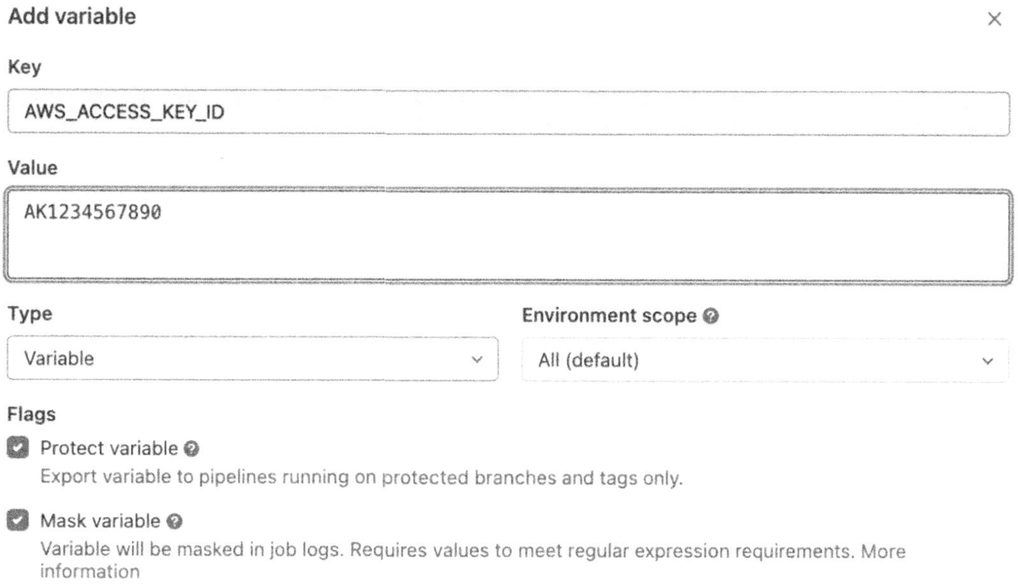

Figure 8.23 – Project-level CI/CD variable settings

These explanations only scratch the surface of deployment considerations in real-world environments. However, in these security-conscious times, we found it best to focus on the key area of secret management to demonstrate how GitLab can make the deployment process seamless and secure. In the next and final section, we'll learn about GitLab's integration with Kubernetes for cloud-native deployments.

Deploying to a Kubernetes cluster

We previously discussed the ubiquity of cloud services as alternatives to self-hosted infrastructure. In a similar vein, container orchestration systems such as Kubernetes have become increasingly popular as alternatives to the manual management of bare-metal servers or container hosts.

Deploying to Kubernetes with GitLab CI/CD can be conceptually similar to the workflows we have covered thus far. You can set up a GitLab runner with a Kubernetes executor, which communicates to the clusters using the Kubernetes API. Alternatively, GitLab optionally offers an additional approach called the **GitOps workflow**, which is not wholly reliant on CI/CD pipelines. We will summarize each of them in turn.

The CI/CD workflow

Using the concepts so far, you can use a normal CI/CD setup to deploy containerized applications to Kubernetes. This requires a runner registered with the Kubernetes executor. During runner registration, information such as cluster host and authentication information is provided. The CI/CD script will then include direct API calls in the cluster, specifying commands to build, test, or deploy your code.

Because this workflow involves runners sending imperative commands to a Kubernetes cluster, we call this a **push-based** workflow. It's convenient in that there are no additional dependencies required to interact with Kubernetes. However, we can run into issues if the cluster or deployments have changed in any way outside the CI/CD workflow, causing potential problems if the cluster is in a state other than what the CI/CD jobs expect.

For this reason, GitLab increasingly recommends a different approach to working with Kubernetes called a GitOps workflow.

A GitOps workflow

GitLab provides an alternative method of Kubernetes integration that does not use CI/CD directly. Rather, it uses an agent installed on a Kubernetes cluster that communicates back to the GitLab instance. These steps can be performed by navigating to **Infrastructure | Kubernetes clusters** in your project and then selecting **Connect a cluster** to follow the provided instructions for creating and registering a new agent (see *Figure 8.24*).

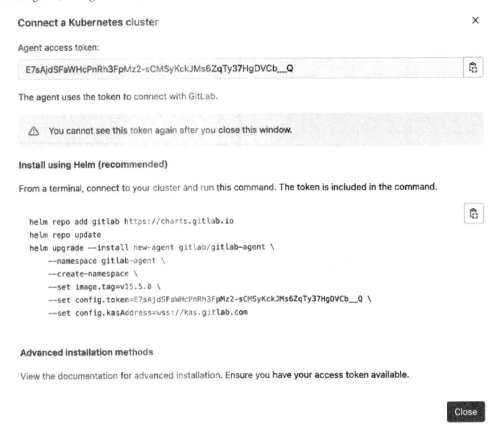

Figure 8.24 – Connecting a Kubernetes cluster to GitLab

Once a connection is established, the agent will automatically detect changes when configuration and deployment files are updated in the repository and will change the cluster state accordingly. This is due to the bidirectional streaming between the cluster agent and GitLab server. Essentially, the agent initiates all communication to work around any networking restrictions that obstruct the Kubernetes cluster (see *Figure 8.25*).

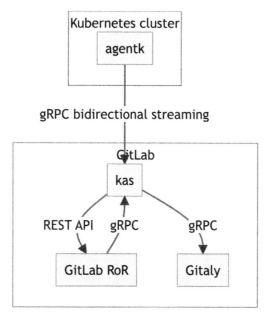

Figure 8.25 – GitLab agent for Kubernetes architecture

GitLab therefore refers to the GitOps workflow as a **pull-based approach**, one that is increasingly favored over traditional pushes by CI/CD pipelines.

Summary

In this chapter, we described various ways of packaging and deploying our code. This included making use of GitLab's package and container registries, CI/CD environments, and methods for interacting with cloud-native infrastructure.

Even if you may not use all of the discussed features or services in your day-to-day work, we hope this chapter provided a useful bridge to more practical, real-world use cases of GitLab's features.

The next chapter will build upon what we've learned already. It will also introduce advanced features for improving CI/CD speed and performance, increasing developer productivity, and optimizing your ability to quickly build and ship software.

Part 3
Next Steps for Improving Your Applications with GitLab

This part of the book leads you through advanced CI/CD pipeline topics. These include speeding up pipelines using directed acyclic graphs, integrating third-party tools into pipelines, using pipelines to spot performance problems in your code, and many other topics. You will also get a chance to review everything you've learned so far with an end-to-end example demonstrating how to use GitLab to take a realistic software project through the entire software development life cycle. Finally, you'll learn how to fix common problems with GitLab pipelines and get a peek at where GitLab might be going in the future.

This section comprises the following chapters:

- *Chapter 9, Enhancing the Speed and Maintainability of CI/CD Pipelines*
- *Chapter 10, Extending the Reach of CI/CD Pipelines*
- *Chapter 11, End-to-End Example*
- *Chapter 12, Troubleshooting and the Road Ahead with GitLab*

9
Enhancing the Speed and Maintainability of CI/CD Pipelines

In this chapter, we're going to cover the different tools and methods you can leverage to enhance the speed and maintainability of your CI/CD pipelines. Our goal in this chapter is to cover three main methods for how to speed up your pipelines. We don't plan on covering every method to speed up a CI pipeline in GitLab, but rather the most impactful methods on pipeline speed.

We will cover the following topics in this chapter:

- Accelerating pipelines with directed acyclic graphs and parent-child architecture
- Building code for multiple architectures
- When and how to leverage caching or artifacts
- Reducing repeated configuration code with anchors and extensions
- Improving maintainability by combining multiple pipelines and leveraging parent-child pipelines
- Securing and accelerating jobs with purpose-built containers

Accelerating pipelines with directed acyclic graphs and parent-child architecture

GitLab supports the usage of the **directed acyclic graph** (**DAG**) pattern for building CI pipelines. Under normal usage with GitLab, each stage represents a series of jobs that need to be completed. Each stage is comprised of multiple jobs that are executed in parallel. Once a stage completes, then the next stage begins, until the pipeline completes. This is the typical processing loop that GitLab utilizes to complete a CI pipeline.

However, it is possible to create an internal loop of CI jobs that are directed to execute in a specific order that does not loop. This pattern is called a **DAG** or directed acyclic graph. *Directed* refers to the ordering of operations, *acyclic* refers to the fact it only happens once, and *graph* indicates the ordering of steps.

When leveraged properly, the DAG pattern can dramatically decrease the time it takes a pipeline to complete. This occurs because you are creating processing loops inside of the CI pipeline and are explicitly defining the order of operations for CI jobs outside of stages. A good example of this is if one job's execution is dependent on another job's execution, you can leverage the `needs:` keyword to ensure they're run one after another outside of a Stage ordering. This creates a simple DAG process.

How to create a DAG in GitLab CI

The following is an example of a normal GitLab CI pipeline. The following is a YAML implementation of the example we described in the introduction:

```
Job1:
   stage: A

Job2:
   stage: A
Job3:
   stage: B

Job4:
   stage: B
```

In a traditional pipeline, as shown here, jobs defined in `stage: B` will only begin execution after all jobs in `stage: A` have finished. The following is an example of this same pipeline set up to leverage DAG:

```
Job1:
   stage: A

Job2:
   stage: A
Job3:
   stage: B
   needs: ["Job1"]
```

```
Job4:
    stage: B
```

By adding the `needs` keyword to `Job3`, we have created a relationship between `Job1` and `Job3`. So, as soon as `Job1` is completed, `Job3` will begin execution. This occurs outside of regular stage ordering. In the event `needs` is not defined, stage ordering will be respected. As we can see with `Job4`, for `Job4` to begin execution, `stage: A` has to complete properly. However, if `needs: []` is defined but blank, then GitLab will execute that job the moment a pipeline starts and not assign it to any stage for execution.

Building code for multiple architectures

GitLab CI enables you to build artifacts for multiple architectures at once. This can easily speed up software builds by two or three times since, with multiple architectures, you typically have to build the software multiple times for each architecture. Here, we're going to use CI jobs and pipelines to execute a software build for multiple architectures at the same time.

When building software for multiple architectures, there are some special requirements. The first requirement is that you must have GitLab Runners installed and configured on a machine running each architecture. For this section, we're going to use three platforms as an example: `x86_64`, `arch64`, and `powerpc`. In this case, the expectation would be that you have a machine for each of the three architectures, with a GitLab Runner installed on it. That GitLab Runner also needs to have a tag assigned to it for which architecture it is running on.

The second requirement is that the toolchain you use to build your software must be able to support a multi-architecture build. For this demo, we're going to use GCC and a multi-architecture Docker image. We're also going to be using the `parallel:` and `matrix:` keywords for GitLab CI.

The `parallel:` keyword is designed to allow a CI job to run multiple times in parallel. So, for example, if you set `parallel: 5` in a CI job, that CI job will run 5 times inside of that pipeline, in parallel.

The `matrix:` keyword is designed to work with the `parallel:` keyword to spin up multiple CI jobs at a time, with different variables assigned to them. The following is an example of what this looks like when used in a pipeline for multi-architecture builds:

```
my-multiarch-ci-job:
    stage: build
    image: multiarch/crossbuild
    script:
        - make helloworld
    parallel:
        matrix:
```

```
        - ARCH: x86
          CROSS_TRIPLE: " "
        - ARCH: arch64
          CROSS_TRIPLE: "arch64-linux-gnu"
        - ARCH: powerpc
          CROSS_TRIPLE: "powerpcle-linux-gnu"
    tags:
      - $ARCH
```

The preceding example is going to do three key operations:

- First, with the use of parallel: and matrix:, GitLab is going to spin up three separate jobs – one for each of the variable pairs I've defined with ARCH and CROSS_TRIPLE.
- Second, each of those jobs will have a tag assigned to them, reflecting whatever value is defined in ARCH:. This will cause that job to be assigned to the appropriate runner for that tag.
- Third, GitLab will expose the CROSS_TRIPLE: environment variable to the multiarch/crossbuild container. This environment variable is used by the container to properly configure the GCC toolchain so that it's ready to build for that architecture.

When the container spins up, and the CI job executes, the make helloworld command will be run. This command will invoke the preconfigured GCC toolchain and cause it to begin building our application binaries. The resulting binaries will be built to support the specified architecture.

By building multi-architecture binaries this way, we take the complexity out of a multi-architecture build. We make those multi-architecture builds repeatable and easily understandable. We also run those builds in parallel so that they're not waiting on each other, and we can see the results built from each architecture quickly.

> **Important note**
> The parallel: and matrix: keywords can be used in any circumstance where you need multiple CI jobs with the same configurations, but with different injected variables. The matrix: keyword can also accept an array as the environment variable value. The environment variable key, however, *cannot* be an array.

When and how to leverage caching or artifacts

With GitLab, there is often confusion about the usage of caching or artifacts. Many users are curious as to which functionality to leverage and when. We aim to demystify both in this chapter and give you the tools to implement either approach while explaining the benefits and pitfalls of each pattern.

Caching should be thought of as a method to save items that are commonly used in CI jobs or stages. It shouldn't be thought of as a means to pass items between stages or jobs – that's what artifacts are for. The difference is important because of the implementation and configuration of each. A cache is not built or designed to be a method to move items between CI jobs. Because of this, in the future, any features or changes that are made to it will be tailored toward that functionality.

Artifacts are the main way to support storing items created by your CI job indefinitely, as well as passing them as a dependency to other CI jobs. With artifacts, you get insight into what was stored, and you can link CI jobs with hard dependencies on each other to ensure that the artifacts are shared. With caching, there is only a soft link. A job using a cache will still work if a cache doesn't exist; however, a job with an artifact will not.

The next consideration between caching and artifacts is how they're stored, and the networking calls involved. Cache bundles are processed by the GitLab Runner, and the GitLab Runner's configuration determines where it is stored. Under default configuration parameters, the cache is stored on the machine where the runner is operating. In terms of containers, the cache is destroyed. By adding an S3 configuration to the GitLab Runner, the Runner will push all cache bundles to S3 storage. Any further CI jobs that use that cache will pull it from S3 storage before the CI job begins.

In the case of artifacts, the Runner doesn't play a role in its processing. Every artifact bundle is uploaded to the GitLab instance directly. GitLab's configuration then determines when and where that artifact is stored. The most common configuration is also an S3 storage provider. Any future CI jobs that require this artifact also download it before the start of the CI job. Like cache bundles, the artifact bundle is then uncompressed into the working directory for usage.

> **Important note**
> In this chapter, we will talk about two types of dependencies. The first is CI job dependencies, which should be handled with artifacts. CI job dependencies essentially link the result from one CI job to another. The second dependency type is toolchain dependencies, which are the dependencies of your application – usually, third-party libraries. These are used by multiple CI jobs or multiple CI pipelines, so they should leverage caching.

Caching characteristics

These are the things that separate caching from artifacts:

- You can define a cache per job by using the `cache` keyword. Otherwise, it is disabled.
- Subsequent pipelines can use the cache.
- Subsequent jobs in the same pipeline can use the cache if the dependencies are identical.
- Different projects cannot share the cache.
- By default, protected and non-protected branches do not share the cache. However, you can change this behavior.

Artifact characteristics

These are the things that separate artifacts from caching:

- You can define artifacts per job.
- Subsequent jobs in later stages of the same pipeline can use artifacts.
- Different projects cannot share artifacts.
- Artifacts expire after 30 days by default. You can define a custom expiration time.
- The latest artifacts do not expire if **Keep latest artifacts** is enabled.
- You can use dependencies to control which jobs fetch the artifacts.

Using caching

The first step in leveraging the usage of caching is adding the configuration to your GitLab CI file. The following is a code sample of how this is done. If you look at this sample, you'll see we've defined a CI job labeled `MyCIJob`. From there, we've defined a `cache` block and added a `path` parameter with a list of the directories and files we want to cache. This is the minimum viable code necessary to cache items as part of your CI job:

```
MyCIJob:
  cache:
    paths:
      - theDirectoryToSave/*
      - myFileToSave.js
```

Now, every time this CI job spins up, it will use the same cache bundle every single time. This is very useful when you have dependencies that are downloaded every time a CI job runs. By placing these dependencies inside a cache, they won't need to be downloaded every time. Instead, GitLab will insert these dependencies at the beginning of the job. This cuts down time on CI jobs significantly, ultimately reducing the CI pipeline time to completion.

Now, we're going to take this a step further. Let's assume you have four separate CI jobs, and two of each of the CI jobs want to share a cache. In the previous example, we created a generic cache that could be used for all jobs. But in this example, we want to link a cache between two CI jobs. This can be done with the addition of the `key` value:

```
MyCIJob:
  cache:
    key: cache1
    paths:
```

```
      - theDirectoryToSave/*
      - myFileToSave.js
```

With the addition of the `key` value, GitLab will have an identifier with which to determine when and which cache bundle to download. This key value can obtain a string, a variable, or any combination of both. Many users will end up using a GitLab predefined variable as a key so that GitLab can manage the cache more effectively. For example, if you use the `$CI_PIPELINE_ID` variable, then that cache bundle will only be leveraged inside of a pipeline with an ID matching `$CI_PIPELINE_ID`. This means that every pipeline will have its own brand-new cache bundle.

A final configuration you can leverage with caching is the ability to change when and how the cached bundle gets uploaded and downloaded:

```
MyCIJob:
  cache:
    key: cache1
    policy: pull
    paths:
      - theDirectoryToSave/*
      - myFileToSave.js
```

As you can see, the cache GitLab CI object has a value called `policy`. By default, this is set to a value of `push-pull`, which means the cached bundle is pulled down when the job starts and pushed up when the job ends. However, you can also configure this to push or pull. By setting it to push, it will push the cache object but never pull it, while by setting it to pull, it will pull a cache but not push updates to the bundle.

Using artifacts

In the previous section, we discussed caching. Much of the same concepts of caching are going to apply to artifacts, but artifacts have a richer feature set. Because artifacts are used for things such as reporting, passing artifacts between jobs, and job dependency management, they require a deeper feature set. Let's start with a basic artifact object and build a more intricate one from that:

```
MyArtifactJob:
  artifacts:
    paths:
      - theDirectoryToSave/*
      - myFileToSave.js
```

From the preceding example, you can see it's very similar to caching at its core. We've added an artifact job, assigned an `artifacts:` object to it, added a `paths:` object to that, and listed the files we want to be artifacted. From here, when `MyArtifactJob` executes, at the end of the pipeline run, it will send everything listed in `paths:` to GitLab and store it.

Similar to the cache's `policy` option, which defines what to do with the cache, artifacts have a `when` object that allows you to specify what happens to the artifact when an artifact is created. Its options are `on_success`, `on_failure`, and `always`. The first option, `on_success`, will upload an artifact only on a job's successful execution. The second, `on_failure`, will only upload when the job fails. Finally, `always` will always upload an artifact no matter the outcome. When applied to our job, the resulting job will look as follows:

```
MyArtifactJob:
  artifacts:
    when: 'on_success'
    paths:
      - theDirectoryToSave/*
      - myFileToSave.js
```

In conclusion, the preceding job will only execute when other CI jobs are successful. It will then store the objects in the `theDirectoryToSave/` folder, in the `myFileToSave.js` file.

Leveraging artifacts as job dependencies

Now that we've covered the basics of artifacts, let's use them in a real-world scenario by chaining jobs together with artifacts. By leveraging the `dependencies` keyword in a CI job block, we can pull artifacts from another job and make an intrinsic connection between two separate CI jobs.

Our application will be built by the `MyBuildJob` job, which will be defined shortly. You may recognize much of the syntax from earlier chapters. This first job is an example of how to build a Node.js-based application. First, we leverage the `npm install` command to pull down any dependencies used to build this application. To keep this example simple, we're not leveraging a cache for dependencies, but we should be in production.

Secondly, we're running the `npm build` command to build the Node.js application. The common standard of all Node.js projects is that their built files are produced in a folder named `dist`. The Node.js dependencies are commonly stored in `node_modules`.

Lastly, we have an artifact definition that lists both the folders of `node_modules` and `dist` as needing to be archived. Now, when this job is executed and completed, GitLab will store all of the items in the two folders listed:

```
MyBuildJob:
  image: nodejs:latest
  script:
```

```
    - npm install
    - npm build
  artifacts:
    when: 'on_success'
    paths:
      - node_modules/*
      - dist/*
```

The following CI job, defined as `MyDependentJob`, has been built to pull the artifacts from our previous job. Then, it leverages those artifacts in the build of a Dockerfile. The `dependencies` keyword is the glue that connects these two jobs:

```
MyDependentJob:
  image: docker:latest
  dependencies:
    - MyBuildJob
  script:
    - docker build
```

As we can see, by using the `dependencies` keyword, we are instructing GitLab to make sure that `MyDependentJob` has everything it needs to run. Without this functionality, `MyDependentJob` would be required to pull down these artifacts itself, which will take additional time and configuration.

Reducing repeated configuration code with anchors and extensions

All GitLab CI pipeline files must be valid YAML. This also means they support various templates and repeatable code patterns that the YAML language supports. Writing multiple CI job definitions for each CI job in a pipeline can be time-consuming and lead to serious maintainability concerns. If you leverage the same variable in multiple places in a pipeline, it's better to have it defined once, and then referenced multiple times. This way, when you need to change the variable, you do it in one place as opposed to many. Not only is this easier to do, but it's also safer as with large pipelines, multiple variable replacements can lead to errors.

The three methods GitLab and YAML offer for creating reusable CI pipelines are **anchors**, the **extends** (`extends:`) keyword, and a **reference** (`!reference`) tag. In the following sections, we're going to explain the benefits and usage of each of these three methods. Each method comes with pros and cons in terms of functionality.

Anchors

The first method we're going to review is **anchors**. YAML anchors allow you to duplicate or inherit properties of one CI job to another. With anchors, you can define an entire GitLab CI job or a few attributes and then repeat them.

Here, we're going to utilize a basic YAML anchor. As you can see, `&job_definition` is the anchor we're going to set. Then, we're going to use it in `jobOne` and `jobTwo` to pull in the content from `&job_definition`:

```yaml
.job_definition: &job_definition
  image: node:latest
  services:
    - postgres

jobOne:
  <<: *job_definition
  script:
    - npm build

jobTwo:
  <<: *job_definition
  script:
    - npm test
```

Once GitLab has processed the CI file, the result will look something like this. Here, the contents of `&job_definition` has been merged into our two CI jobs:

```yaml
jobOne:
  image: node:latest
  services:
    - postgres
  script:
    - npm build

jobTwo:
  image: node:latest
  services:
    - postgres
```

```
script:
  - npm test
```

In the preceding example, we defined a job with a dot (.) at the beginning of it. This dot means the CI job will not be executed as a CI job and merely exists as a reference. This was defined as `.job_definition:`. After this definition, we added a YAML anchor. This is the `&job_definition` statement that you can see. Everything after the `&` symbol defines the name of the anchor. Then, we define what a normal job should look like.

After, we define two CI jobs, each with different `script:` blocks. However, we use the `<<:` keyword to tell the YAML processor that we want to merge the `.job_definition:` attributes and keywords with this job. The `*` character followed by the name of the anchor references the anchor we defined with the `&` symbol.

The result is the two jobs inside of the merged result code block.

> **Important note**
> YAML anchors can only be used in the same GitLab CI file in which they were defined. This means that if you are leveraging the `includes:` keyword to break your CI files into multiple files, you must use `extends:` or `!reference` instead of YAML anchors.

The extends: keyword

The second way of reusing CI jobs and configuration inside GitLab CI files is via the `extends:` keyword. The `extends:` keyword and YAML anchors are very similar in the way they operate. One major difference is that YAML anchors are mostly used for duplicating a single value or attribute across your CI pipeline file, whereas `extends:` is more often used to reuse entire configuration blocks inside your CI pipeline file. In the preceding anchor example, `extends:` is a better fit for usage.

In the following example, we're defining a `.rules_definition` block. Then, we're including it in the `.job_definition` block and using the `.job_definition` block in `jobOne` and `jobTwo`. Any job definitions that begin with a dot (.) are not processed by GitLab as an actual job. Instead, they are treated like templates:

```
.rule_definition:
  rules:
    - if: $CI_PIPELINE_SOURCE =="push"

.job_definition:
  extends: .rule_definition
  image: node:latest
```

```
    services:
      - postgres

jobOne:
  extends: .job_definition
  script:
    - npm build

jobTwo:
  extends: .job_definition
  script:
    - npm test
```

After GitLab processes the preceding CI file, the final merged result will look as follows. Here, the contents of .rule_definition and .job_definition, which were defined once, are now included in both jobOne and jobTwo:

```
jobOne:
  image: node:latest
  services:
    - postgres
  script:
    - npm build
  rules:
    - if: $CI_PIPELINE_SOURCE =="push"

jobTwo:
  image: node:latest
  services:
    - postgres
  script:
    - npm test
  rules:
    - if: $CI_PIPELINE_SOURCE =="push"
```

As you can see, this example is slightly different than the one we used for anchors. That's because another key difference between anchors and extends: is that extends: can inherit configuration from multiple CI job definitions.

Because of this, you can see the resulting merged job definitions have an added `rules:` attribute assigned to them. This is inherited through the `.job_definition` CI job, from the `.rules_definition` CI job.

Reference tags

The third method of reusing configuration inside CI files is by using `!reference` tags. `!reference` tags are custom YAML tags that are used to select keyword configurations from other CI job sections and reuse them in the current section. They're very similar in usage to YAML anchors, but you can use reference tags in multiple CI files. On the other hand, YAML anchors can only be used in the same file in which they were defined. Let's look at an example.

Create a `Build.gitlab-ci.yml` file that looks like this:

```
.build-node:
  stage: deploy
  before_script:
    - npm install
  script:
    - npm build
```

Create a `.gitlab-ci.yml` file that looks like this:

```
include:
  - local: Build.gitlab-ci.yml

Build-My-App:
  stage: build
  script:
    - !reference [.build-node, script]
    - echo "Application is Built"
```

The result after GitLab processes these two files should look like this:

```
Build-My-App:
  stage: build
  script:
    - npm build
    - echo "Application is Built"
```

In the preceding example, a job definition was created in `Build.gitlab-ci.yml`. Then, we included that `Build` CI file in our main `.gitlab-ci.yml` file. After, we used the `!reference` keyword to pull the script block straight from the `.build-node` job definition. By leveraging `!reference` instead of `extends:`, we can only pull the configuration we want from that job definition, as opposed to the whole job definition. If we had used `extends:`, we would have brought over the `stage:` and `before_script:` attributes of that CI job definition as well.

Improving maintainability by combining multiple pipelines and leveraging parent-child pipelines

Most GitLab users simply utilize a single `.gitlab-ci.yml` file for their pipelines. This approach is perfectly acceptable, but in many cases, the amount of code inside this file can become very large and difficult to maintain. GitLab has introduced the ability to include multiple gitlab-ci files together as one. In this section, we're going to cover how to break up a `.gitlab-ci.yml` file into multiple sections. Later, we're going to cover how to take a second `.gitlab-ci.yml` file and execute a second child pipeline, and then discuss the reasons why you may want to do this.

Leveraging includes for maintainability

Create a `.gitlab-ci.yml` file that looks like this:

```
  "Build Application":
    stage: build
    script:
      - code here


  "Build Container":
    stage: build
    script:
      - code here
  "Deploy Container":
    stage: deploy
    script:
      - code here


  "Deploy Production":
    stage: deploy
    script:
      - code here
```

This preceding code shows an example of what a traditional `.gitlab-ci.yml` file looks like. For this example, we've included four jobs – two build jobs and two deploy jobs. In a normal `.gitlab-ci.yml` file, this would be tens of jobs with tons of logic between them, likely spanning hundreds of lines of code. This is a perfectly acceptable practice, but it is difficult to maintain and manage. As with all forms of source code, we want to ensure that the code we write is legible and understandable at a glance to ensure maintainability.

To break this code up, and make it more maintainable, we can leverage the `include:` keyword in the GitLab CI's syntax. This keyword is used to tell GitLab's YAML processor when to combine multiple YAML files into a single context. Let's use this tool to break up our CI file into separate CI files for reusability.

Create a `Build.gitlab-ci.yml` file that looks like this:

```
"Build Application":
  stage: build
  script:
    - code here

"Build Container":
  stage: build
  script:
    - code here
```

Create a `Deploy.gitlab-ci.yml` file that looks like this:

```
"Deploy Container":
  stage: deploy
  script:
    - code here

"Deploy Production":
  stage: deploy
  script:
    - code here
```

Create a `.gitlab-ci.yml` file that looks like this:

```
include: "Build.gitlab-ci.yml"
include: "Deploy.gitlab-ci.yml"
```

Here, we split the individual jobs into files based on stages. Then, we included those files in our `.gitlab-ci.yml` file. When GitLab's CI processor goes through our `.gitlab-ci.yml` file, it will merge each YAML file into a single context from top to bottom. This means that if I write the same job in `Build.gitlab-ci.yml` and `Deploy.gitlab-ci.yml` because `Deploy.gitlab-ci.yml` is included last, it will overwrite whatever was in the Build CI file. This is a simple example and method of separating your CI files for more maintainability. Next, we're going to focus on combining an example from earlier with this method.

Leveraging includes for reusability

Earlier, you learned how to use includes to help with maintainability. In this section, we will combine the usage of `include:` and the knowledge we learned earlier in this chapter around anchors and extensions to show you how to create reusable pipelines. We'll start with an example.

Create a `Templates.gitlab-ci.yml` file that looks like this:

```
.npm-build:
  stage: build
  variables:
    NPM_CLI_OPTS: ""
  before_script:
    - npm install
  script:
    - npm rebuild $NPM_CLI_OPTS
```

In the preceding GitLab CI file, we've created a very simple CI job definition. Because this CI job's name begins with a `.`, this job will not run on its own. We've included a `variables:` block and inserted an empty `NPM_CLI_OPTS` variable as a placeholder. Then, we used that variable in our `script:` block when we executed the `rebuild` command. The reason for this default variable is that we want to have a sane default when this job is used.

We've named this CI file `Templates.gitlab-ci.yml` to indicate that it houses our CI job templates and not actual CI job definitions. However, we want to leverage this in a CI pipeline. The following example shows how to achieve this.

Create a `.gitlab-ci.yml` file that looks like this:

```
include: Templates.gitlab-ci.yml
My-NPM-Job:
  extends: .npm-build
  variables:
    NPM_CLI_OPTS: '--global'
```

Here, we're including all job definitions from the `Templates.gitlab-ci.yml` file, and we're starting our own job based on those definitions. However, in the `variables:` block, we're adding our own variables to control how the template CI job definition will run.

This method of templating a CI job and then using variables to expose configuration options for it is similar to how componentization occurs in traditional software development. It follows the same purpose, rules, and goals, even though the syntax is different.

Includes from remote areas

The `include:` keyword is not delegated to a single project or repository. You can include GitLab CI files from the open internet as well. Some examples of remote includes are listed here:

- Including from a separate project and branch:

    ```
    include:
      - project: "my-group/my-project"
        ref: my-branch
        file: 'Templates.gitlab-ci.yml'
    ```

- Including from a remote location:

    ```
    include:
      - remote: 'https://www.google.com/Templates.gitlab-ci.yml'
    ```

- Include from a template on the GitLab instance (`lib/gitlab/ci/templates`):

    ```
    include:
      - template: 'Templates.gitlab-ci.yml'
    ```

> **Important note**
> You can include a CI file from anywhere the starter of a CI pipeline has access. Provided that the person who starts the CI pipeline has read access to the included file, the pipeline will succeed. However, if the person does not have access, the pipeline will fail.

Leveraging parent-child pipelines

Now that we've spoken about including multiple YAML files and how you can templatize them for reusability, let's talk about how we can leverage them with the `trigger:` keyword to create child pipelines.

A **child pipeline** is a pipeline that is triggered by another pipeline. The triggering pipeline is referred to as the **parent pipeline**. Once a parent pipeline triggers a child pipeline, the parent's pipeline execution waits for the new child pipeline to complete before it resumes. This is a powerful tool for building multiple pipelines to support a monorepo, or for breaking one large complex pipeline into smaller, more manageable pipelines.

To invoke a child pipeline, simply add the `trigger:` keyword as the parent to an `include:` statement. The following example will execute the `build.gitlab-ci.yml` file as a child pipeline:

```
My-Child-CI-Job:
    stage: build
    trigger:
      include:
        - project: "my-group/my-project"
          ref: my-branch
          file: 'Build.gitlab-ci.yml'
```

With the preceding example, in a CI pipeline view, you will see a CI job that states `My-Child-CI-Job`. This CI job will have another pipeline attached to it labeled `Downstream Pipeline`. In that view, you will be able to see all of the jobs from the child pipeline and their execution status.

> **Important note**
> An invoked child pipeline accepts all normal CI job attributes and keywords. Keywords such as `rules:` can determine when a child pipeline is invoked. The `environment:` keyword can also tie the invocation of a child pipeline to approval rules or environment tracking.

Securing and accelerating jobs with purpose-built containers

GitLab, when set up properly, runs all the CI jobs of a pipeline in a container. This means that the entire build operation happens in a container. Because of this, container stewardship is exceptionally important. If a CI job happens in an insecure container, then that means the entire CI job and pipeline are insecure. If a CI job uses a non-performant container, that CI job and pipeline will take much longer to complete, resulting in a much slower time to show results. In every measurable way, the container used for your CI jobs is the most important part of your pipeline.

> **Important note**
>
> To quickly set or identify which container a specific CI job is using, look for the `image:` attribute in a CI job. This attribute will define the source of the container image, and the exact container image being used.
>
> A second area to look for this container image is at the top of the CI job log. There will be a message indicating which container image is being used.

We aim to resolve these concerns with a practice we call *purpose-built containers*. These are containers whose entire design is to be used in a CI pipeline. Here, we will outline some attributes of these containers and explain how to build them. When building containers for a CI pipeline, try to follow as much of this guidance as possible. Even if you're not able to achieve every item mentioned here, following them as much as possible will result in a much more secure, performant, and maintainable container for your CI pipeline.

The first item to consider is the file size of the container. A container for use in GitLab CI should contain only the minimum number of components necessary to run and perform its tasks. This container should also only perform one set of tasks. This means you would have a separate container for each toolchain – that is, one for Java and one for Node.js. You do not want to mix multiple toolchains because it will explode your container's file size. There is rarely a scenario where you would need multiple toolchains in the same container as they are usually executed in separate CI jobs. A good rule to follow is that if a CI job does not need something, that something should not be included in the container.

The second item to consider is ensuring your containers are multi-use. You still want to keep your toolchains in separate containers; however, you should avoid embedding configuration inside of a container that will prevent it from being used in multiple CI jobs or multiple pipelines. A good example of what to include would be encryption certificates so that the container can communicate with any resources it needs. An example of what not to include would be any configuration or settings that are related only to a single CI job or pipeline. The difference between these two items is that the first example (certificate) is used to enable the container to work properly, whereas the second example (configuration or setting) will restrict which CI jobs and pipelines the container can run in.

The third item to consider is preventing the container from being run under normal use. A purpose-built container for GitLab CI should effectively be a zombie or a shell. There should be no circumstance where the container executes anything other than what the CI job instructs it to. This can be performed by ensuring the container's entry point is empty. If a Docker container executes anything as it starts in a GitLab CI, it can cause conflicts and will also take more time to start.

The fourth item to consider is to avoid adding needless layers inside of a Docker container. With every RUN or ADD command in a Dockerfile, Docker will create a new layer. Needless layers can balloon the size of the Docker container significantly and thus violate the first concern. When you run commands in a Dockerfile, you should use the & operator liberally to chain together run commands. We have provided an example of this usage in our Dockerfile example.

The final item to consider is privilege. A Docker container running in GitLab CI does not typically need elevated permissions to run and perform operations. On OpenShift and some Kubernetes platforms, any Docker container with elevated privileges may not be allowed to run and execute. Setting a random user ID when creating the container will help prevent these platforms from giving the container any form of privilege. If you need to provide permissions to a file or folder, they should be granted to a group as opposed to individual users.

A purpose-built container example

Here, we have provided an example of a purpose-built container. This example follows all the considerations we listed previously. This is a Docker image that has been built upon the `alpine:3.12.0` base container. From there, we have a RUN command that combines multiple commands in one line. It makes use of the & operator to chain together multiple APK package manager commands. This reduces the number of layers in the Docker file. At the end of that command line, we assign a folder to the group of the running user. In doing so, we reserve the ability to manipulate that folder, but we prevent it from gaining any privilege from a bad group assignment:

```
FROM alpine:3.12.0
RUN apk update && apk add -no-cache nodejs npm && mkdir ~/.npm
&& chmod -R g=u ~/.npm


USER 1001


CMD ["echo", "This is a purpose built container. It is meant to
be used in a pipeline and not executed."]
```

For the first consideration, you can see it is being met with `apk add -no-cache nodejs npm`. Node.js is the only toolchain that is installed in this container.

For the second consideration, you can see no configuration is embedded in the Dockerfile. This means the container will pull all of its configurations from the CI job's configuration.

For the third consideration, you can look at the line starting with `CMD ["echo"`. This line prevents the container from running outside of a CI job. It presents an error message and kills the container.

For the fourth consideration, look at the line starting with `RUN apk`. This line has multiple commands strung together with &. Each RUN command in a container creates a second layer. Here, we are using as few RUN commands as possible.

For the fifth consideration, we close the container with `USER 1001`. This line forces all commands in the container to be run as a random user ID. This means no commands will run with any form of escalated privilege.

Summary

In this chapter, we learned about many tools we can use with GitLab CI to create fast and reusable pipelines. We started with DAGs, which allow us to make pipelines execute faster. Then, we learned how to build code for multiple architectures. With the introduction of mainstream ARM platforms, this is going to gain importance over time. Later, we learned when to leverage caching or artifacts in pipelines for dependency management.

The last two topics we covered are likely the most important. We learned three different methods to build reusable pipeline definitions so that you don't have to write the same logic in multiple places. Finally, we learned about a concept called *purpose-built pipelines*, which enables you to build fast, secure, and stable containers to execute your CI workloads in.

In the next chapter, you're going to learn how to expand the reach of your CI/CD pipelines.

10
Extending the Reach of CI/CD Pipelines

In this chapter, we aim to extend the reach of CI/CD pipelines into common automation use cases. By the end of this chapter, you should have an idea of what's possible with CI/CD pipelines. You'll see that they are not necessarily just for build and deployment tasks, but also automation tasks, which make the job of an engineer easier, repeatable, and more reliable. CI/CD pipelines are always meant to ease the burden of work on an engineer so that they can focus on more novel and important tasks.

The following topics will be covered in this chapter:

- Using CI/CD pipelines to spot performance problems
- Integrating third-party tools into your CI/CD pipelines
- Using CI/CD pipelines for developing mobile apps

Using CI/CD pipelines to spot performance problems

There is no better time to do performance testing than during an automated CI/CD pipeline. With performance tests, you want them to be routine and against a stable unchanging environment or deployment. If you run performance tests against an environment or deployment that constantly changes, you will not have reliable results. Without reliable results, the entire notion of performance tests goes out the window. You want to understand how your changes affect your performance; without stable results, you can't infer that understanding.

With GitLab, there are multiple ways to run performance tests. For web or API-based deployments, GitLab includes a native performance tool that will cover in this chapter and go over its integration. However, you, the end user, can take this a step further and cover more metrics such as CPU/memory/storage usage in a CI/CD pipeline. We will not be covering how to collect these metrics in this chapter since that is unique to every user's environment. However, we strongly recommend that you capture these metrics as part of your CI/CD pipeline.

GitLab's native integrated performance testing tool for API and web-based deployments will check numerous metrics for active deployment. Some of those metrics include page load time, first page paint time, and total blocking time. In a merge request (pictured in the following screenshot) you can see how your code changes will impact the performance of the web/API deployment:

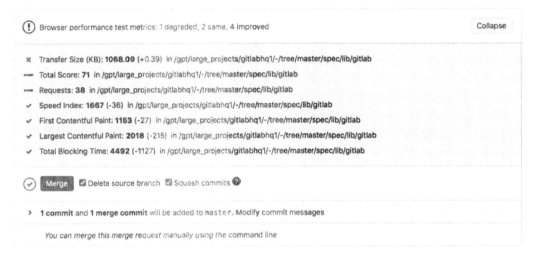

Figure 10.1: Performance metrics view in a merge request

> **Always double-check your testing criteria**
>
> Your testing results are going to be directly dependent on your testing criteria, test settings, and environments. You should always question if your testing criteria, settings, and environments are accurate. You should never assume they are accurate. If they are not accurate, your test results will never be accurate.

How to integrate browser performance testing

Integrating browser performance testing is quite easy – you just need to include the GitLab templates as part of your CI/CD pipeline and then instruct GitLab where your API or web deployment can be accessed. See the following example.

```
include:
  - template: Verify/Browser-Performance.gitlab-ci.yml
browser_performance:
  variables:
    URL: https://myWebOrApiURL.local/
```

With the preceding job template, we're invoking the `browser_performance:` templates from GitLab. Then, we're overwriting the `URL` variable of the job. This URL is what tells the Performance Testing Suite where to reach out and scan our application for performance. With this configuration, GitLab will check our application and report the results back to our merge request.

How to integrate load performance testing with k6

The second type of testing that is used in GitLab CI/CD by default is load testing with a tool named k6, provided by the company Grafana. GitLab provides a template for running this tool as part of your CI/CD pipeline as well. However, there is an additional step of creating and specifying a k6 configuration file to run a proper k6 load test.

We're going to go over this process here. Before we do, note that you should never run these load tests in production. Production load tests should run on an identical non-production environment. To get accurate load testing results, the load testing tool should be the only item communicating with your environment. Without further ado, let's integrate load testing. Add the following code to your `.gitlab-ci.yml` file:

```
include:
  - template: Verify/Load-Performance-Testing.gitlab-ci.yml
load_performance:
  variables:
    K6_TEST_FILE: '<PATH TO FILE>' #.gitlab/tests/k6.js
```

The preceding code will execute k6 as part of our pipeline. However, now, we need to inform k6 how to test our application and provide GitLab with a test file to run. We're going to assume that this file lives at the `.gitlab/test/k6.js` path. We're going to walk through how to build this file.

The following code is going to load the libraries and functions that will affect our load test. Without these, the remainder of our load test file will fail. Next, we're going to add our settings:

```
import { check, group, sleep } from 'k6';
import http from 'k6/http';
```

The following code is going to define the options for our test. For 5 minutes, we're going to ramp up to 100 users accessing the website. Then, we're going to hold at 100 users for 10 minutes. Finally, over 5 minutes, we're going to ramp down to 0 users. That means this test will run for 20 minutes in total:

```
export const options = {
  stages: [
    { duration: '5m', target: 100 },
    { duration: '10m', target: 100 },
```

```
      { duration: '5m', target: 0 },
    ],
    thresholds: {
      'http_req_duration': ['p(99)<1500']
    },
};
```

Then, we must set the threshold for failure. We want to see 99% of all requests respond within 1,500 milliseconds. Anything outside that will fail. Next, we're going to execute the actual load test.

The following code will execute our performance tests using k6 against our website. With this file now being successfully built, we can execute our pipeline and have repeatable load tests:

```
export default() => {
  const myResponse = http.get('<MY URL or ENV VAR>').json();
  check(myResponse, { 'retrieved url: (obj) => obj.length > 0
});
  sleep(1);
};
```

With the performance testing set up, we're going to shift our focus to how to utilize feature flags to enable and disable parts of our application after deployment.

Using feature flags to allow business-driven release decisions

GitLab comes with the ability to set up feature flags in the UI. It is based on the *third-party* unleash library. Once you set up the feature flags in the GitLab UI, you will need to set up your application to communicate with GitLab to check for feature flags. We'll cover examples of both of these steps, but GitLab does not do this for you: it is up to your application developers to do this work.

Once the feature flags have been configured in the UI, an API call from the application is necessary to check the flag and change the logic of the application accordingly. Let's walk through how to set up the feature flags in the UI:

1. In a project, open the navigation pane on the left-hand side. Click **Deployments | Feature Flags**. This will take you to the main feature flag section. In the top right, click **New feature flag**. This will take you to a new view:

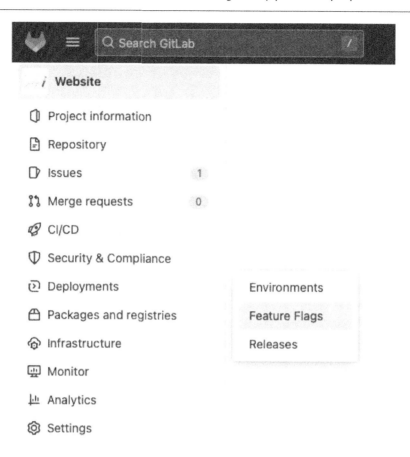

Figure 10.2: Feature Flags in GitLab's navigation pane

2. You will be presented with a form. Fill it out and plan your strategies accordingly. You can set multiple strategies based on environments, user lists, and user IDs, and assign percentages to different groups. Once submitted, it will look like this:

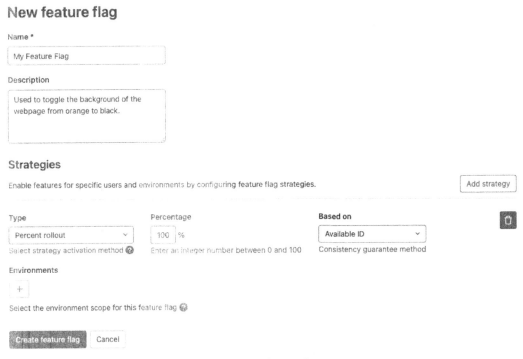

Figure 10.3: Main feature flag view

3. Feature flags are exceptionally powerful when launching new features. By placing a new feature behind a feature flag, you can turn off part of your application by toggling a flag. This can help prevent a rollback of a release or an emergency support ticket:

Figure 10.4: Feature Flags detail view

In *Figure 10.4*, you can see the presence of our newly created feature flag. On the left-hand side, under **Status**, you can see a checkbox, which is used to enable or disable this flag.

How to configure your application for feature flags

In this section, we're going to cover a single use case for checking feature flags in an application. The following is a Ruby code sample that will check for feature flags and toggle a code path based on the flag that is set. Your team's application developers will need to set up their applications based on their toolchains and language usage:

```
require 'unleash'
require 'unleash/context'
unleash = Unleash::Client.new({
  url: 'http://gitlab.com/api/v4/feature_flags/unleash/42',
  app_name: 'production',
  instance_id: '29QmjsW6KngPR5JNPMWx'
})

unleash_context = Unleash::Context.new
unleash_context.user_id = "123"

if unleash.is_enabled?("my_feature_name", unleash_context)
  puts "Feature enabled"
else
  puts "Feature disabled!"
end
```

In this Ruby example, you begin by setting the GitLab information, including the URL of the GitLab instance, the app's name (corresponding to the environment in GitLab), and the instance ID (the numeric ID of your GitLab project).

The `user_id` parameter is an example of passing information to GitLab. In this example, we're passing a user ID that GitLab will match with your feature flag strategy if configured. The next step is invoking `unclear.is_enabled`, which accepts a feature name as a variable, then reaches out to GitLab to determine if you are in the group that has the flag enabled. Then, the code path that is enabled will be executed.

Now that we've covered the usage and purpose of feature flags, we're going to work on how to integrate third-party tools into your CI/CD pipelines.

Integrating third-party tools into your CI/CD pipelines

In this section, we're going to cover how to integrate third-party tools into a CI/CD pipeline. The preferred method to integrate a third-party tool into a CI/CD pipeline is to containerize it, create a CI/CD job that uses that container, and then invoke our tool as part of that job. In many cases, this is a requirement and is the first step in setting up an integration.

> **Tool format expectations**
>
> This section is based on the belief that the tool you want to integrate is already compiled and ready to be integrated into your pipeline. In the event it is not, you can add CI jobs before those mentioned here to compile or assemble the tool. Then, you can invoke the CI jobs and steps in this section.

Creating our tool container's Dockerfile

In the previous chapter, we discussed how to build purpose-built containers. We're going to use that method here to integrate your tool. If you haven't read the *Securing and accelerating jobs with purpose-built containers* section of the previous chapter yet, we highly recommend that you read it first and then come back.

The first step in this process is to set up a new GitLab project for your tool and container. Once you have this set up, commit the binaries, configuration, and other files you wish to be placed in the container. The next step is building the container and placing those items inside of it. Create a Dockerfile in your repository and add the following sample code. `$mybinary` is a placeholder for your binary's filename; `myTool` will be your tool's name.

As shown in the following code, we have created a new container derived from `alpine:3.13.0`. We updated the container, then created a directory for our tool. After that directory was created, we added all the files in our repository to that folder, permissioned them with a wide permission, and set our binary as executable:

```
FROM alpine:3.13.0
RUN apk update && mkdir /opt/myTool
ADD . /opt/myTool

RUN chmod 777 -R /opt/myTool && chmod +x /opt/myTool/$mybinary

USER 1001

CMD ["echo", "This is a purpose-built container. It is meant to be used in a pipeline and not executed."]
```

This is a simplified example of how to integrate a third-party tool. You should always customize the permission's values to the least privilege necessary to run your tool. You should also only put the files required for your tool to run in the container. For this example, we're casting a wide net and including everything, as well as wide permissions.

Automating our container's build

Now that we have a Dockerfile, we want to build the container. As a bonus, we're also going to turn on container scanning. Create a `.gitlab-ci.yml` file in your repository if you haven't already. We're going to populate that `.gitlab-ci.yml` file with the following code:

```
Container_Build:
  stage: build
  image: docker:20.10:16
  services:
    - docker:20.10:16-dind
  variables:
    DOCKER_HOST: tcp://docker:2376
    DOCKER_TLS_VERIFY: 0
  script:
    - docker login -u $CI_REGISTRY_USER -p $CI_REGISTRY_PASSWORD $CI_REGISTRY
    - docker build -t $CI_REGISTRY_IMAGE:latest .
    - docker push $CI_REGISTRY_IMAGE:latest
```

> **Avoiding a pipeline run on every commit**
>
> When making multiple pipeline changes, you may not want to kick off a pipeline run every time you make a change. If you start your commit message with `[CI SKIP]`, GitLab will not start a pipeline for that commit.

The preceding code is the most basic example of a Docker-in-Docker build. First, we utilize `image: docker:20.10.16` to define the version of Docker we want to build against. Then, we define the Docker service we want to build with – that is, the `dind` container. Next, we set the `DOCKER_HOST` and `DOCKER_TLS_VERIFY` variables so that the Docker and `dind` containers can talk to each other. Finally, we invoke the `docker build` command to build our container, and the `docker push` command to upload it to GitLab's container registry.

> **GitLab Runner requirements for Docker**
>
> Building a Docker container typically requires the usage of a GitLab Runner capable of doing Docker-in-Docker container builds. GitLab.com shared Runners come with this capability preconfigured. If you're using a self-hosted Runner, you may need to reconfigure it. Refer to the GitLab documentation for how to achieve this.

Container scanning

GitLab offers container scanning as part of the container-building process. We want to take advantage of this to identify any dependency or other vulnerabilities with our container. Enabling this is simple: you need to have a test stage defined in your `.gitlab-ci.yml` file. Then, simply add the following code block to the top of your `.gitlab-ci.yml` file:

```
include:
  - template: Jobs/Container-Scanning.gitlab-ci.yml
```

Invoking the third-party tool

At this point, we should have a container with our third-party tool built, scanned, and placed inside the GitLab container registry. All that is left now is to invoke our tool. We can do this by creating a CI/CD job that's pointing to our container and calling our executable in the container:

```
Test_Job:
  stage: test
  image: path/to/my/container
  script:
    - /opt/myTool/$myBinary
```

So far, we've walked through how to build a container with tools, how to scan a container, and how to invoke that tool via a CI/CD job. This is a basic example to show you the art of what is possible. With this process, you can clone third-party tools, custom scripts, custom configurations, or whatever else you want to include as part of your CI/CD pipeline.

There are major benefits to doing this. For example, any container that runs as part of a CI/CD pipeline has access to the GitLab API and GitLab repository. This means you can run a CI/CD job as part of your pipeline for something such as metrics collection or configuration verification as well. CI/CD jobs built in this way can automate almost anything.

If you build and containerize a custom tool, be sure to share it with the community.

In the next section, we're going to discuss how to build mobile applications using GitLab CI/CD and Fastlane.

Using CI/CD pipelines for developing mobile apps

In this section, we're going to discuss how to set up CI/CD pipelines in GitLab for mobile application development. There are many benefits to automating the mobile development process at the packaging stage, most notably the fact that packaging a mobile application involves multiple certificates, entitlements, and configuration files, which take a substantial amount of time to assemble when packaging an application. In addition to that, the testing process around mobile applications can be manual and tedious. By automating things such as screenshots across multiple devices, we can shave hours off a developer's workload.

This section assumes you have all the requirements listed next configured and working already. We're not going to cover how to do mobile development, but rather how to automate your mobile development practices using Fastlane and GitLab.

Requirements

For this section, you will need the following:

- A macOS device or VM running the latest version of OS X, with Fastlane installed
- GitLab Runner installed on your macOS device
- An Apple developer account
- A Google developer account
- An application that can be built successfully on your macOS device

> **Read this before proceeding**
>
> If you can't meet these requirements, you should stop here until you can. This guide assumes you have a working, provisioned macOS device. It also assumes you can build a mobile application on the device.

Fastlane

In this chapter, we're going to be utilizing the Fastlane CLI tool to automate our tests, builds, and deployments. Fastlane is a tool that works with both Android and iOS build processes. It is an opensource tool that can be installed for free on macOS and Windows platforms. You can read more about it in the Fastlane documentation located at https://docs.fastlane.tools/getting-started/ios/setup/.

We're going to assume you have Fastlane installed on your machine. If not, please refer to the Fastlane documentation linked previously for your platform. The first step in this process is to open your mobile application project and create a Fastlane configuration file named Fastfile. Fastfile is the primary configuration file used by Fastlane. We're going to make our Fastfile look like this:

```
lane :beta do
  build_app(Scheme: "MyApp") # For iOS
  gradle( task: 'assemble', build_type: 'Release') # For Android
end
```

To build our mobile application for both iOS and Android, we simply need to run the `fastlane beta` command. Assuming your iOS and Android applications can already be built on the macOS device, this command should automate their building. We can put this into a GitLab CI file like this:

```
"Build Mobile Applications":
  stage: build
  tags:
    - my-osx-runner
  script:
    - fastlane beta
```

This GitLab CI job will automate the Fastlane process via GitLab pipelines. We are leveraging the `tags:` keyword to ensure that this build happens on a specific macOS device. Without this keyword, the build could happen on any GitLab Runner.

Fastlane – deployment

You can deploy your mobile application to the Android and Apple stores. However, you will need to set up all mobile certificates for production use before setting up Fastlane. When those certificates expire, someone will need to update them on the macOS device. Nevertheless, if they have been set up, you can modify your `Fastfile` like this:

```
lane :appstore do
  sync_code_signing(type: "appstore")
  build_app(scheme: "MyApp")
  upload_to_app_store
end

lane :playstore do
  gradle(task: 'assemble', build_type: 'Release')
  upload_to_play_store
end
```

The preceding additions to your Fastfile will build your application and release it to the respective app stores. You simply need to run the `Fastlane appstore` and `Fastlane playstore` commands. A corresponding GitLab CI/CD configuration file would look like this:

```
"Deliver Mobile Applications":
  stage: release
  tags:
```

```
      - my-osx-runner
    script:
      - fastlane appstore
      - fastlane playstore
```

Fastlane – automated testing

Assuming you have unit tests set up for your projects already, Fastlane can automate those as well. It does not automatically set up the tests, but if you have them built as part of your project's configuration, Fastlane can invoke them. This process is similar to every step before – we begin with Fastfile modifications, as seen in the following example:

```
lane :iosTest do
  run_tests( devices: ["iPhone 6s", "iPad Air"], scheme: "MyAppTests")
end
lane :androidTests do
  gradle(task: "test")
end
```

Just like before, we can amend our GitLab CI/CD configuration file to add automated testing as well:

```
"Test Mobile Applications":
  stage: test
  tags:
    - my-osx-runner
  script:
    - fastlane iOSTests
    - fastlane androidTests
```

At times, using Fastlane may feel like you're cheating. Once you have an established mobile project on a device, Fastlane can take it from there. Mobile development before Fastlane was a tedious and manual process. CI/CD pipelines were filled with a large amount of code and logic to make a build happen and then be deployed.

In this section, we discussed how to build a Fastfile to configure Fastlane, how to run Fastlane commands, and, most importantly, how to add them to a GitLab CI/CD configuration file. We've said it before, but in closing, it's worth repeating: Fastlane and automating mobile development with GitLab CI/CD pipelines is best suited for a macOS device that is already provisioned and set up to build a mobile application. Start there, and then use GitLab CI and Fastlane to handle the rest.

Summary

In this chapter, we covered the benefits of including performance checks inside your CI/CD pipeline. We also covered how to include GitLab's native performance testing tools. Following that, we covered the benefits of feature flags and how they can protect your deployments and prevent time-consuming rollbacks. Then, we moved on to integrating third-party tools as part of your CI/CD pipeline and how to containerize them for use. Finally, we walked through how to automate the creation and deployment of mobile applications using Fastlane.

In the next chapter, we're going to cover an end-to-end example that leverages everything you've learned about in this book.

11
End-to-End Example

By now, you've seen how the different parts of GitLab help you write, review, verify, secure, package, and deploy software. These features have been presented one at a time, so let's put them all together in a single end-to-end example so you can see the whole process in one fell swoop. There won't be any new material in this chapter, so it will be a great chance to review what you've learned in earlier chapters and see it all consolidated in one extended workflow.

This chapter is broken into many subsections, each showing how to use GitLab to help with a different part of the software development life cycle:

- Setting up your environment
- Writing code
- Establishing the pipeline infrastructure
- Verifying your code
- Securing your code
- Improving your pipeline
- Delivering your code to the right environment

Technical requirements

If you'd like to follow along as we develop a piece of software with GitLab, all you need is an account on a GitLab instance, whether Software-as-a-Service (SaaS) or self-hosted.

Setting up your environment

Before you start writing any code, you need to organize a few preliminary things. Specifically, you need to make a GitLab project for storing your code and running your pipelines, you need to make some GitLab issues to help plan and track your work, and you need to clone the project's repository to your local computer so that you can write code using your favorite IDE instead of entirely within the GitLab GUI.

Making a GitLab project

Let's rewind to the beginning of our journey with the Hats for Cats web app. We know we want to make a web app for our online feline accessories store, so let's start by making a GitLab project to hold not only our web app's code but also the additional GitLab components that we'll be using as we build the app.

> **A note about the GUI**
>
> Throughout this chapter, we'll continue our practice of showing you code snippets but generally not showing the steps for using the GitLab GUI. This is because we want to avoid having the screenshots drift away from reality as the GitLab GUI changes in future releases.

We could make a Hats for Cats project directly within the top-level namespace of our GitLab account, but it seems likely that we'll want to make more projects in the future—perhaps for other web apps, perhaps for other versions of the web app aimed at different platforms—so first, let's make a GitLab group to hold all of our projects. Let's pretend that our company is called Acme Software, so we'll start with a group called, unsurprisingly, Acme Software:

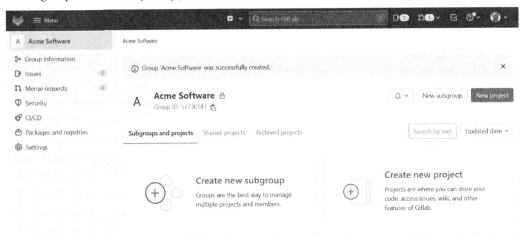

Figure 11.1 – The Acme Software group

Within this group, we can add a new project that holds the Hats for Cats web app. Let's call it `Hats for Cats`, and let's choose the **Create blank project** option rather than creating it from a project template. This means that it will begin its life with a boilerplate `README.md` file in its Git repository, but nothing else. Here's what the new project looks like immediately after creation:

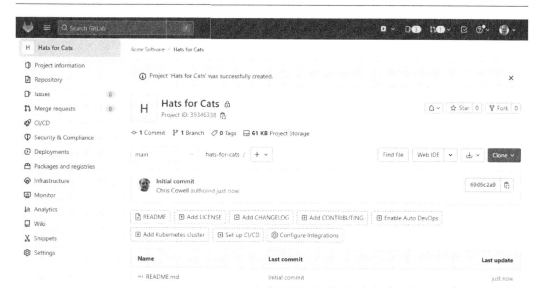

Figure 11.2 – The Hats for Cats project

As you already know, this project will hold not only the code for our web app but also the configuration file for our CI/CD pipeline, branches and **Merge Requests** (**MRs**) related to our code, packaged bits of code ready for deployment, and issues to help us plan and track our work. That leads nicely into the next step of our workflow: creating GitLab issues.

> **Placing all projects within a group**
>
> For technical reasons, the screenshots in the rest of this chapter show the **Hats for Cats** project directly under the user's account instead of within the **Acme Software** group. However, the best practice is to create all of your company or organization's projects within a single master group.

Planning work with GitLab issues

Using GitLab issues to plan and track your work is an optional but highly recommended part of writing software with GitLab. You can, of course, use other tools such as Jira or Trello to map out your work, but many developers find that GitLab issues give them all the power they need for standard project management tasks.

GitLab projects for non-trivial pieces of software might contain tens, hundreds, or, in extreme cases, thousands of issues—for instructional purposes, let's create just four issues for our project. To build the **minimum viable product** (**MVP**) for our web app, let's make issues with these titles:

- `Allow user to log in`
- `Allow user to search inventory`

- `Allow user to buy a hat`
- `Allow user to log out`

Once those are in place, let's think about GitLab labels. Some teams use multiple labels on each issue to indicate ownership, assign priority, or perform other administrative functions. Let's create and assign an unscoped **security** label to show that the login and log-out issues need extra scrutiny from our security team. Let's also make scoped **priority::high** and **priority::low** labels to indicate which features should be worked on first and which came come later. For now, just assign **priority::high** to the login issue—we'll decide as a team later what priority labels to give to the rest of the issues.

Next, let's tackle the metadata for the login issue, which is the feature we want to develop first. We open that issue, assign it to a developer, set the **Weight** field to **5** (which, after some discussion, we decide is a reasonable weight for a medium-sized task), use a quick action to estimate that it will take 15 hours of work to complete, and set a due date. Setting metadata at the same time that the issue is created is a practice that you often see among teams that use the Kanban workflow; if we were using the Scrum workflow, we might have saved assigning a due date, weight, or estimated hours until the next backlog grooming ceremony.

After creating these four issues, creating and assigning appropriate labels, and filling in metadata for one issue, clicking **Issues | List** in the left-hand navigation pane should show something like this. Notice that the metadata is displayed right in the issue list, which is handy:

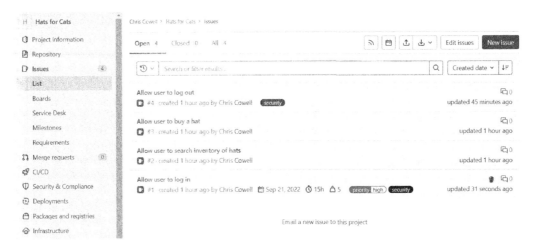

Figure 11.3 – Hats for Cats issues and issue metadata

You're done with getting your GitLab environment set up: you've created a GitLab group, made a GitLab project inside it, and made some issues to work against. Now, you're ready to start writing code and storing it in that project.

Setting up a local Git repository

Although we *could* do all of our development work within the GitLab instance, that would make writing code difficult and testing impossible. Instead, let's clone the repository to a local computer so that we can develop using whatever desktop IDEs or other tools we're most comfortable with.

First, we need to make sure that we've generated a public/private key pair on our workstation and uploaded the public key to our GitLab account. This only needs to be done once for any GitLab instance we're working with, so let's assume that we've already taken care of this. The GitLab documentation has more information about this process.

Next, we need to grab the address that we'll use to clone the **Hats for Cats** project's repository. Since we're using key-based security instead of manually entering authentication credentials with every Git command, we copy the project's SSH address using the GUI, and then clone it by running this command on our local machine (if you're following along at home, you'll see a slightly different address based on your GitLab account name):

```
git clone git@gitlab.com:acme-software/hats-for-cats.git
```

We can then move into the directory created by the clone operation and look around. If everything has worked as expected, we should see local copies of the same files that exist in the GitLab-hosted copy of the repository—which at this point is just one README.md file:

```
~$ cd hats-for-cats
~/hats-for-cats$ ls
README.md
```

Now, we're all set to do local development, push any changes we make up to the copy of the repository on GitLab, and pull down any changes that coworkers have pushed up.

Writing code

You're almost at the point where you can start coding. First, you'll need a Git branch to commit the code to. Then, you'll need a MR so that you can see the results of pipeline tasks that run against that code, and also so that you can eventually merge the code into the `main` branch. Let's go over those steps, and then make and push your first commit.

Creating a Git branch to work on

Now that we're ready to add the login feature requested by our first assigned issue, we need a Git branch to commit to. We might as well name our branch after the title of the issue we're working on:

```
git branch add-login-feature
```

Switch onto the new branch so any new commits end up on that branch and not on the `main` branch:

```
git checkout add-login-feature
```

At this point, we might as well push this branch up to the GitLab-hosted copy of the repository so that it exists in both places. For the first push, we need to use a slightly longer command:

```
git push --set-upstream origin add-login-feature
```

For subsequent pushes, after we've added some commits, we can rely on a simpler command:

```
git push
```

If we look at the project's repository in GitLab, we can see that it now lists **add-login-feature** within the dropdown of the project's branches.

Creating an MR

Let's follow GitLab best practices and immediately make an MR associated with the branch we just created. Navigate to **Ns** in the left-hand navigation pane and click on **New merge request**. Select **add-login-feature** as the source branch and **main** as the target branch, and click **Compare branches and continue**.

Title the MR `Draft: add login feature` and add `Closes #X` in the description field, where X is replaced by the number of the **Allow user to log in** issue (tip: as soon as you type # in the description, the GUI will present you with a dropdown showing all the issues you've created, so you don't need to look up the issue number manually). Now, we've created the "three amigos" of issue, branch, and MR, so we're ready to get to work developing our feature.

Committing and pushing code

It's time to write some code! Instead of writing an actual login page with real GUI elements and logic, let's use our local computer to make a file called `login.py` in the root of the **add-login-feature** branch of our project's Git repository. Populate that file with placeholder code, such as `print("Welcome to Hats for Cats!")`. Since we're doing this on our local computer rather than on GitLab, we need to use Git terminal commands or a GUI tool for Git (such as **Sourcetree** or **Tower**, or the Git tools built into IDEs such as **IntelliJ IDEA** or **Visual Studio Code**) to add our new file to the Git staging area and then commit it with an appropriate message. Perform these operations on the command line like this:

```
git add login.py
git commit -m "add initial version of log in page"
```

It's important to reiterate at this point that the local commit will *not* trigger a CI/CD pipeline. The GitLab instance doesn't know that the commit exists, and even if it did, it doesn't have any way of seeing the code included in that commit. However, as soon as we push any local commits up to GitLab, it will detect those commits in its own copy of the repository and run a pipeline against whatever commits we pushed up.

Let's push the **add-login-feature** branch now:

```
git push
```

> **Pushing frequently is important!**
> We could have waited to push this branch until we had made several local commits to it, but since much of the power of GitLab's CI/CD pipelines comes from having them run frequently against small code changes, it's usually wisest to push after every local commit.

This was such a simple edit—adding a single file that contains a single line of code—that you might be wondering why we didn't just make the edit and commit the change within the GitLab GUI instead of going through the hassle of editing and committing locally and then pushing that edit up to GitLab. Honestly, with a change this small, we could easily have gotten away with performing the edit right on GitLab. If this were a real-world project, that's exactly what we would advise you to do, but since most development work is quite a bit more complicated than the placeholder code included here, we thought it would be helpful to show you the typical *edit-and-commit-locally-and-then-push* workflow that you'll be using for most of your development work.

Establishing the pipeline infrastructure

You've stored some code in the repository, so now it's time to set up a pipeline to run a variety of tasks to build, verify, and secure your code. In some cases, you might also want to set up a GitLab Runner to execute those pipeline tasks, although that task is usually taken care of for you by your GitLab administrator or the GitLab SaaS platform.

Creating a pipeline

Pushing commits to GitLab so that it can run CI/CD pipelines on our new code won't work unless we define what tasks we'd like our pipeline to perform. We'll add several tasks to our **Hats for Cats** project's pipeline as we go through the rest of this chapter, but for now, let's get a bare-bones pipeline in place.

Just as we did with our initial file, we could create the `.gitlab-ci.yml` pipeline configuration file locally, commit it, and push it up to GitLab, but since the GitLab GUI offers a handy editor dedicated to writing and debugging pipeline configuration files, it often makes more sense to edit it on GitLab. Having a local copy of `.gitlab-ci.yml` isn't important since we can't use it to run pipelines on our local machine anyway.

In the left-hand navigation pane, select **CI/CD | Editor** to fire up the dedicated pipeline editor, select the **add-login-feature** branch from the dropdown, and create a new `.gitlab-ci.yml`. At this point, we're not sure what stages we're going to end up needing in our pipeline. It could be reasonably argued that there's no point defining stages until you actually need them, but we're fairly confident that we'll need the basic trio of `build`, `test`, and `deploy`, so in the interest of fleshing out this example, let's add all three right now:

```
stages:
    - build
    - test
    - deploy
```

Since Python is an interpreted rather than compiled language, we don't have any jobs to define within the `build` stage yet. We also haven't written any automated tests yet, so there's no point in adding jobs to execute tests. We'll want to run some security scans and do other verification tasks, but we'll define those jobs later. We're also going to need to deploy our code to various environments, but that too will be tackled down the road. For now, let's just add a dummy job so that GitLab doesn't complain about the lack of any job definitions in our pipeline (if we didn't, GitLab would actually consider the pipeline configuration file to be malformed, and the linter that appears at the top of the dedicated editor would squawk at us). Paste this below the `stages:` section:

```
# temporary job that we'll delete later
job1:
    stage: build
    script:
        - echo "in job1"
```

After committing this change, we navigate to **CI/CD | Pipelines** in the GitLab GUI to confirm that the pipeline ran—it should have triggered automatically when we committed the changes to `.gitlab-ci.yml`—and that it executed `job1` on a shared runner without any problems. Of course, if you're working on a GitLab instance that doesn't offer any shared runners, you'll need to create your own runners for this project before the pipeline will run. Fortunately, that's the very next step in our workflow.

Creating a runner

As you know, users of the SaaS version of GitLab can run their pipelines on the GitLab Runners provided as part of their software subscription, but if you're using a self-hosted version of GitLab, or if you want to run some pipelines on your own hardware to avoid exhausting your subscription's GitLab Runner minutes, you'll want to set up one or more of your own GitLab Runners. Let's create some specific runners that are dedicated to our **Hats for Cats** project.

We decide to create runners on a spare Linux box that's lying around. Remembering that the versions of the GitLab Runner binary that's included in major Linux distribution repositories are often a few versions old, we consult the GitLab documentation to find out how to add the official GitLab repository to our Linux box's package management system, download the latest GitLab Runner binary, install it as a service, and make sure it's running. Since the exact process for this varies by the operating system and Linux distribution, we won't include explicit instructions here.

> **GitLab Runner versions**
>
> Although GitLab Runners usually work even when they are a few minor versions away from the version of the GitLab instance (15.0 vs. 15.3, for example), they will operate most reliably if you keep the two versions in sync.

Once the `gitlab-runner` binary is installed on the computer that will host the runners, we need to create runners by registering them. Before doing so, we need to collect some information. We've already decided that the runners will be specific to the **Hats for Cats** project, so we navigate to **Settings | CI/CD | Runners** and make note of both the GitLab instance's URL and the project's registration token, as displayed on that screen. Let's say that we're using a self-hosted GitLab instance at `https://gitlab.hats-for-cats.com`, and that the registration token for the **Hats for Cats** project is `abc123`.

We decide to register two runners. We could call them anything we want, but we settle on the most obvious naming scheme: **Hats for Cats 1** and **Hats for Cats 2**.

Next, we choose to use the Docker executor with both runners since that gives them the most flexibility: they can handle any CI/CD pipeline job because they can execute jobs within a Docker image that has all of the required tools already installed. We decide to specify `alpine:latest` as the default Docker image that the runners will use for jobs that don't specify an image since that's the smallest full-featured Linux distribution and therefore the quickest to download. Finally, we decide not to add any tags to the runners since we don't intend either runner to be special-purpose in any way.

Of course, we can't register runners with the Docker executor unless Docker is installed and running on the machine that's hosting the runners. Installation instructions for Docker change occasionally and vary according to the operating system, so the official Docker documentation is your best source of information for this step.

Once Docker is up and running on the same host machine as the runners we could register a single runner interactively with `gitlab-runner register`, but in this case, let's register the runners non-interactively by passing in all the details as options to a single terminal command. We register the first runner using this command on the Linux box that will host the runners (changing the `--url` and `--registration-token` values as appropriate):

```
sudo gitlab-runner register \
  --non-interactive \
```

```
--url "https://gitlab.hats-for-cats.com/" \
--registration-token "abc123" \
--executor "docker" \
--docker-image "alpine:latest" \
--description "Hats for Cats 1"
```

> **Do I need to use sudo?**
> Check the GitLab documentation to find out whether the `gitlab-runner` binary requires `sudo` or administrator permissions on your operating system; the command behaves differently on different platforms.

We can run the same command, changing the value of the `--description` option, to create the second runner.

Now that both runners have been registered, let's double-check that they're both up and running:

```
~$ sudo gitlab-runner verify

Runtime platform                   arch=amd64 os=linux pid=6365
revision=bbcb5aba version=15.3.0
Running in system-mode.

Verifying runner... is alive      runner=LuKAFv53
Verifying runner... is alive      runner=Rtq7yC5e
```

Finally, let's refresh the GitLab page that we reached via **Settings | CI/CD | Runners** and make sure both runners were able to check in with our GitLab instance and declare themselves ready to accept jobs from the **Hats for Cats** project. Here's the relevant portion of that screen:

Figure 11.4 – Specific runners for the Hats for Cats project

Before proceeding, you might want to review the GitLab documentation to learn more about the `concurrent` and `check_interval` options in the master configuration file for your registered runners. Sometimes, adjusting the values of these two options can help runners pick up jobs more quickly. This configuration file is `/etc/gitlab-runner/config.toml` on Linux systems that run the `gitlab-runner` binary as root, but might exist in other locations when `gitlab-runner` is not run as root or is run on other operating systems. Running `gitlab-runner list` (with or without `sudo`, depending on how you registered your runners) should reveal the location of this file on your system.

> **Optional: disabling shared runners**
>
> If you're following along in your own GitLab account, you might want to go to **Settings | CI/CD | Runners** and disable all the shared runners for the **Hats for Cats** project. This ensures that all of the project's CI/CD pipeline jobs will be assigned to one of the two runners we just registered.

With a basic CI/CD pipeline configuration file in place and two runners registered, we've completed the setup of the basic pipeline infrastructure for our project. Now, we need to start filling the pipeline with jobs so that it can run all the tests and scans that make GitLab pipelines such a powerful software development tool.

Verifying your code

Let's configure your pipeline so that it can verify your code by running functional tests, Code Quality scanning, and fuzz tests.

Adding functional tests to the pipeline

Many teams start populating their pipelines by adding tasks to run automated functional tests to make sure their code is behaving the way it was designed to. You learned in previous chapters that there are many different sorts of functional tests. In this example, we'll add some basic automated unit tests written with the `pytest` framework. Our project's code is not yet complicated enough to require real unit tests, but for the sake of this example, we can add dummy tests so that GitLab can run them and display their results.

Before adding any tests, let's make our login code *slightly* more complicated by adding a function that our tests can exercise, and a "to-do" comment that not only reminds us to flesh out this placeholder function later but also gives the Code Quality scanner something to detect when we add it to our pipeline down the road. Either locally (in which case you need to follow up with a commit and a push) or in the GitLab GUI, add this simple code to the **add-login-feature** branch's copy of the `login.py` file:

```
def log_user_in(username, password):
    return (username == "Dana") and (password == "p@ssw0rd")
```

```
# TODO: replace this placeholder code with real logic
```

We also need to declare a dependency on the `pytest` framework so that GitLab can install it before running the automated tests. Since this is a Python project, we declare this dependency in a new `requirements.txt` file at the top level of the project repository (still on the **add-login-feature** branch) with a single line of content:

```
pytest==7.1.3
```

There are different ways to group automated unit tests in files and directories, but let's keep things simple by adding a single `test_login.py` file at the root level of the repository, in the same **add-login-feature** branch that we've been working in.

We'll put three tests in that file: one to check our login feature with good credentials, one to test logging in with a bad username, and one to test logging in with a bad password. We also need to import the function being tested so that it can be called by the unit tests. Add this code to `test_login.py`:

```
from login import log_user_in

def test_login_good_credentials():
    assert log_user_in("Dana", "p@ssw0rd")

def test_login_bad_username():
    assert not log_user_in("foo", "p@ssw0rd")

def test_login_bad_password():
    assert not log_user_in("Dana", "foo")
```

> **Expanding your automated tests**
>
> These unit test examples are simpler than what you would typically use in a real project. Most unit test frameworks—regardless of which language they test—offer a wide variety of options and additional features to make your tests more comprehensive and powerful. We advise you to get to know your chosen test framework thoroughly since automated tests are such an important part of writing high-quality code.

Let's add a job to the `test` stage of our pipeline to install the `pytest` library (as listed in `requirements.txt`) and run the tests. The job should ask the runner to execute its commands in a Docker container that has a recent version of Python. The `pytest` test framework automatically identifies any files that contain tests, so we don't need to specify which test file to execute. We do need to tell `pytest` to generate an output file in the `junit` format, which is a test results format that

GitLab knows how to ingest and display. Add this job definition to your existing .gitlab-ci.yml file on the **add-login-feature** branch:

```
unit-tests:
    stage: test
    image: python:3.10
    script:
        - pip install -r requirements.txt
        - pytest --junit-xml=unit_test_results.xml
```

Now that we have defined a real job in our CI/CD pipeline, you can delete the definition for the temporary job1 job if you want to declutter the pipeline configuration file.

After the pipeline triggered by this commit completes, you'll notice that even though the unit-tests job ran successfully, the pipeline details page doesn't show any test results. That's because we didn't tell GitLab to preserve the results as an artifact. Let's fix that by adding this code to the end of the unit-tests job definition, making sure all lines are indented correctly so that this code is understood by GitLab as part of the existing job definition:

```
    artifacts:
        reports:
            junit: unit_test_results.xml
        when: always
```

This should get us to a state where our unit tests are running and passing, which is a huge step forward in ensuring that our code lives up to its design specifications. If you've been following along, you should see output similar to this on the **Tests** tab of the most recent pipeline details page, showing that all three of our unit tests are running and passing:

Pipeline	Needs	Jobs 1	**Tests 3**

Summary

3 tests	0 failures	0 errors	100% success rate	0.00ms

Jobs

Job	Duration	Failed	Errors	Skipped	Passed	Total
unit_tests	0.00ms	0	0	0	3	3

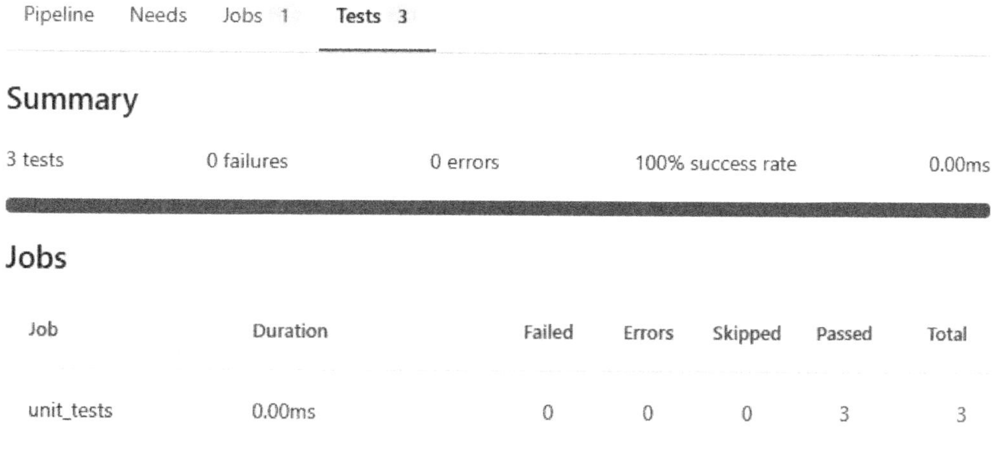

Figure 11.5 – Test results on a pipeline details page

Once your automated tests pass, you can be confident that your code is doing what it was designed to do. However, just behaving correctly isn't good enough: your code also needs to be written well. This helps to ensure that your code is readable and maintainable and will be less likely to develop bugs when you extend it with new features in the future, so now, let's look at how to make sure your code is of high quality.

Adding Code Quality scanning to the pipeline

Let's add a task to our pipeline called Code Quality scanning, which will help us assess the quality of our code. As with all of GitLab's scanners, Code Quality only works with certain computer languages. However—as described in the GitLab documentation for this feature—it supports all of the usual suspects, including Python.

We enable the scanner by including its template at the end of our project's CI/CD configuration file, on the same **add-login-feature** branch where we've done all of our work:

```
include:
    - template: Code-Quality.gitlab-ci.yml
```

If you inspect the pipeline that was triggered by committing this change to `.gitlab-ci.yml`, you'll notice that the Code Quality scanning job failed. Don't panic! This failure stems from Code Quality being something of an odd duck among GitLab's scanners. It uses a technique called **Docker-in-Docker**, which requires that the runner assigned to the Code Quality job must be configured in a certain way. Although all shared runners provided by GitLab for SaaS customers are capable of running Code Quality jobs, the runners we registered earlier are not, so let's create a new runner just to handle Code Quality. The GitLab documentation has more information about why the special configuration is necessary for this one type of scanning, but the details are not important for most GitLab users to understand. For the purposes of this demonstration, you just need to know that we can register a new runner called `runner for code quality` by typing this command on the same machine that's hosting our other runners. Just like when we registered those runners, you'll need to replace the `--url` and `--registration-token` values with the appropriate values for your system:

```
sudo gitlab-runner register \
  --non-interactive \
  --url "https://gitlab.hats-for-cats.com/" \
  --registration-token "abc123" \
  --executor "docker" \
  --docker-image "docker:stable" \
  --description "runner for code quality" \
  --tag-list "code-quality-capable " \
  --builds-dir "/tmp/builds" \
```

```
--docker-volumes "/cache"\
--docker-volumes "/tmp/builds:/tmp/builds" \
--docker-volumes "/var/run/docker.sock:/var/run/docker.sock"
```

We configured this new runner with a `code-quality-capable` tag, which indicates that it can handle running Code Quality jobs. In order to make sure that our job is assigned to this specific runner, we need to override the Code Quality scanner's job definition and assign it the same tag. While we tinker with the pipeline configuration file, let's also disable a service that's used by some runners to handle this job but that isn't required by our runner. Add this job definition override to the end of your `.gitlab-ci.yml` file:

```
code_quality:
    tags:
        - code-quality-capable
    services: []      # disable all services
```

As soon as we commit this last change, GitLab kicks off a pipeline run and presents the Code Quality results in a new **Code Quality** tab on the pipeline details page:

Figure 11.6 – Code Quality results on a pipeline details page

The Code Quality scanner reminds us to take care of the "to-do" comment we added to `login.py` earlier. Good advice, but let's ignore it for now so we can move on to fuzz testing.

Adding a fuzz test to the pipeline

Let's set up a fuzz test to see whether the `log_user_in` function has any bugs that weren't caught by our automated unit tests. *Chapter 6* has a thorough description of the architectural elements involved in fuzz testing, so please refer back to that chapter if you need a refresher on what role each piece of code plays.

> **Reminder**
> Fuzz testing, like several other features discussed throughout the book, is only available with a GitLab Ultimate license. The GitLab documentation for each feature tells you which license tier that feature requires. The reason that this book doesn't mention which licenses are required for which features is that GitLab frequently makes features available at lower tiers after they've been tested in higher tiers for a while.

The fuzz test will test the `log_user_in` function that lives in the `login.py` file. If you remember from *Chapter 6*, this code is called the **code under test**. As it's written right now, this function is simple enough that we can tell just by looking at it that fuzz testing won't find any problems. In other words, fuzz testing is overkill for such a simple function, but we can imagine that the function might become more complicated in the future, and as it becomes more complicated, it will be more likely to have bugs. Therefore, it's a good idea to create a fuzz test for this simple code under test now so that it can find new bugs if we rewrite the function using more complicated and error-prone code in the future.

Let's put the **fuzz target** code in a file called `log_in_user_fuzz_target.py` in the root of the repository's **add-login-feature** branch. The file should contain this Python code:

```python
from login import log_user_in
from pythonfuzz.main import PythonFuzz

@PythonFuzz
def fuzz(bytes):
    try:
        string = str(bytes, 'UTF-8')
        divider = int(len(string) / 2)
        username = string[:divider]
        password = string[divider:]
        log_user_in(username, password)
    except UnicodeDecodeError:
        pass

if __name__ == '__main__':
    fuzz()
```

Most of this is boilerplate code copied from sample fuzz targets in the GitLab documentation. The section that requires some programming creativity on our part is the logic in the `fuzz()` method. This code converts the random bytes sent by the fuzz engine into a random string, uses the first half of the string as the username and the second half as the password, and passes the username and password to the code under test.

Next, we need to include the GitLab fuzz testing template in the `.gitlab-ci.yml` file in the `add-login-feature` branch. Add the `Coverage-Fuzzing.gitlab-ci.yml` template within the existing `include:` section after the Code Quality template that we've already added. The complete `include:` section should end up looking like this:

```
include:
    - template: Code-Quality.gitlab-ci.yml
    - template: Coverage-Fuzzing.gitlab-ci.yml
```

Because this template declares that fuzz test jobs run in their own `fuzz` stage, we must add that stage under the `stages:` keyword at the top of `.gitlab-ci.yml` in the `add-login-feature` branch. When you're done, the complete stage definition section should look like this:

```
stages:
    - build
    - test
    - deploy
    - fuzz
```

Finally, let's create a pipeline job to trigger the fuzz test against our code under test. Add this job definition to the end of `.gitlab-ci.yml` on the `add-login-feature` branch:

```
fuzz-test-for-log-user-in:
    image: python:3.10
    extends: .fuzz_base
    script:
        - pip install --extra-index-url https://gitlab.com/api/v4/projects/19904939/packages/pypi/simple pythonfuzz
        - ./gitlab-cov-fuzz run --engine pythonfuzz -- log_user_in_fuzz_target.py
```

If you check the pipeline details page for the pipeline that was triggered by this commit, you should see jobs for unit tests, Code Quality, and now fuzz testing. If you click into the fuzz testing job to see its output, you'll notice that it's sending a seemingly infinite number of sets of random data to the code under test, with no signs of stopping. However, we know from *Chapter 6* that it will stop as soon as it either finds a bug or times out. Because this pipeline is running on a non-default branch, the timeout is set to a hefty 60 minutes (default branches have 10-minute timeouts). While that might be a reasonable amount of time to uncover deep bugs in complicated code, it's overkill for our dead-simple login code.

Let's speed up our pipeline by configuring the job to send 1,000 sets of random bytes to the function being tested, and then stop if it hasn't found any bugs. Of course, we can bump up the maximum number of random data sets later if we think more complicated login code would benefit from more thorough fuzz testing.

To limit the number of runs performed by the fuzz test, cancel the currently running pipeline (there's no need to wait for it to time out after 60 minutes), and add these lines anywhere within the `fuzz-test-for-log-user-in` job definition. Make sure they're indented correctly so that you're defining a job-scoped variable and not a global variable:

```
variables:
    COVFUZZ_ARGS: '--runs=1000'
```

Also in the `fuzz-test-for-log-user-in` job definition, replace the second line in the `script:` section with the following (note that this is all a single long line of code):

```
- ./gitlab-cov-fuzz run --engine pythonfuzz --additional-args $COVFUZZ_ARGS -- log_user_in_fuzz_target.py
```

If you look at the output of a fuzz test job that runs after these changes, you'll see that it stops after the first 1,000 unsuccessful attempts to find a bug. You'll also notice that no **Security** tab shows up on the pipeline details page because the fuzz test has no findings to report (fuzz testing is considered by GitLab to be a type of security scanner rather than a type of code quality scanner, despite its aim of finding bugs rather than security vulnerabilities).

Our pipeline is really coming along! Let's keep the momentum going by adding some security scanners.

Securing your code

For this sample use case, you're going to add four scanners to your pipeline: **Static Application Security Testing** (**SAST**), Secret Detection, Dependency Scanning, and License Compliance. You'll also review how to add a third-party scanner.

Adding SAST to the pipeline

In general, adding a GitLab-provided security scanner to a pipeline is a trivial process. To enable SAST and make sure our Hats for Cats source code doesn't contain security vulnerabilities, we simply need to include a new template in `.gitlab-ci.yml` on the `add-login-feature` branch. Add this line anywhere within the existing `include:` section, making sure that it's indented correctly:

```
- template: Security/SAST.gitlab-ci.yml
```

This enables SAST, but we also want to configure it so that it doesn't scan our automated test file or our fuzz target file. The GitLab documentation tells us which variable to set to accomplish this. Add a new section to the end of `.gitlab-ci.yml` in order to set the correct global variable:

```
variables:
    SAST_EXCLUDED_PATHS: "test_login.py,log_user_in_fuzz_target.py"
```

> **Note**
> There are only two lines in this code: the second line is long enough that it wraps in a possibly confusing way.

Wait for the pipeline to finish and check out its details page. Under the **Security** tab, you'll see that SAST has reported a vulnerability about a hardcoded password in `login.py`. We will ignore this vulnerability for the sake of keeping the demo moving along, but it's comforting to see that SAST is up and running:

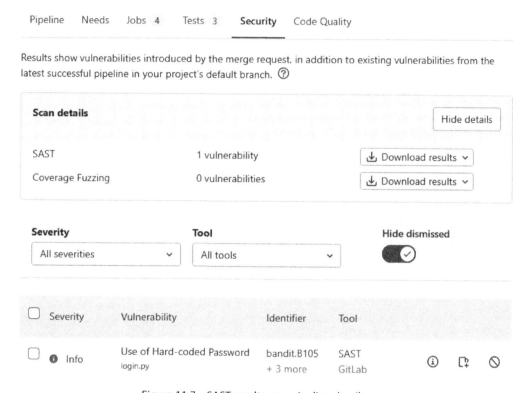

Figure 11.7 – SAST results on a pipeline details page

Adding Secret Detection to the pipeline

Let's add SAST's cousin, Secret Detection, to our CI/CD pipeline. On the `add-login-feature` branch, include a new template in the existing `include:` section of `.gitlab-ci.yml`. Double-check your indentation and we should be good to go:

```
    - template: Security/Secret-Detection.gitlab-ci.yml
```

We should consider some of the configuration options for Secret Detection. There's no need to enable "historic" mode since our repository only has a few commits and we're confident that we haven't added any secrets to it so far. However, it makes sense to tell Secret Detection not to scan our test files since any secrets kept in them will be made-up secrets for testing purposes only. In the future, we might group all of our test-related code into a `tests/` directory, but since we don't have that directory yet, we'll explicitly exclude individual files. Do this by overriding the appropriate job definition and setting a job-scoped variable:

```
secret_detection:
    variables:
        SECRET_DETECTION_EXCLUDED_PATHS: "login_test.py,log_user_in_fuzz_target.py"
```

> **Note**
> The last line in this code snippet is actually one line that wraps awkwardly, so be sure to paste it in as a single line.

Finally, let's give Secret Detection a secret to detect. Let's pretend that our intern Carl accidentally pastes an AWS access token into `login.py`. Add this line to the end of that file on the `add-login-feature` branch:

```
AWS_access_token = 'AKIAABCDEFGH12345678'
```

When the resulting pipeline finishes, check that the **Security** tab on its pipeline details page reports a security vulnerability from Secret Detection:

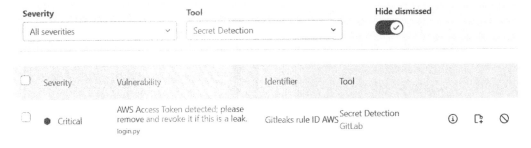

Figure 11.8 – Secret Detection results on a pipeline details page

Adding Dependency Scanning to the pipeline

So far, the only dependency that our project has declared is the `pytest` automated testing framework. Since that dependency won't be used in production, we probably don't care if it has security vulnerabilities, but it's smart to add Dependency Scanning to our pipeline so that we'll be alerted to any security problems in dependencies that we might add in the future.

On the **add-login-feature** branch, add this new line to the existing `include:` section:

```
- template: Security/Dependency-Scanning.gitlab-ci.yml
```

Now that Dependency Scanning is up and running, let's give it something to find. Let's say that the Hats for Cats web app will be built on the Django web app framework for Python and that we decide to use an older version of Django that we're already comfortable with. Add this new line to the end of the existing `requirements.txt` file on the `add-login-feature` branch, noting that it should be flush-left rather than indented:

```
django==3.2
```

Since this version is significantly behind the current version of 4.1.1, we might expect Dependency Scanning to find security vulnerabilities in it. Lo and behold, if we trigger a pipeline and then look at the **Security** tab on the pipeline details page, we see at least 15 potential problems with our dependency! You might find it helpful to use the **Severity** and **Tool** filters above the results table to reduce clutter and focus on the most important vulnerabilities:

Severity	Vulnerability	Identifier	Tool			
● Critical	Improper Neutralization of Special Elements used in an SQL Command ('SQL Injection') in Django requirements.txt	CVE-2022-28346 + 1 more	Dependency Scanning GitLab	ⓘ	⇱	⊘
● Critical	SQL Injection in Django in Django requirements.txt	CVE-2022-34265 + 2 more	Dependency Scanning GitLab	ⓘ	⇱	⊘
● Critical	Improper Neutralization of Special Elements used in an SQL Command ('SQL Injection') in Django requirements.txt	CVE-2022-28347 + 1 more	Dependency Scanning GitLab	ⓘ	⇱	⊘
● Critical	SQL Injection in Django requirements.txt	CVE-2021-35042 + 1 more	Dependency Scanning GitLab	ⓘ	⇱	⊘

Figure 11.9 – Critical severity Dependency Scanning results on a pipeline details page

Adding License Compliance to the pipeline

Since we've declared a few software dependencies for the **Hats for Cats** project, it's a good idea to add License Compliance scanning to the pipeline so that we don't run afoul of problems with incompatible licenses. On the `add-login-feature` branch, add a new template to the `include:` section, double-checking your indentation:

```
- template: Security/License-Scanning.gitlab-ci.yml
```

On the details page for the pipeline that was triggered by this edit, click on the new **Licenses** tab to see the different software licenses used by the Django and `pytest` libraries, and also by their dependencies. Interestingly, the License Compliance scanner was unable to figure out what license Django itself uses, so it's listed as **unknown**. Normally, you would consult with your legal team to decide whether to explicitly allow or deny each of these licenses by clicking on the **Manage licenses** button on this page, but in order to keep the demo moving along, we'll skip that step.

Figure 11.10 – Licenses used by project dependencies

> **Some scanners are excluded from this demo**
>
> You may have noticed that we didn't add DAST, Container Scanning, or Infrastructure as Code Scanning to our pipeline. We've excluded them partly because the Hats for Cats demo web app doesn't include enough functioning code to package into a Docker image and interact with as a normal user would, and because we don't need to use infrastructure-as-code tools to configure any new machines as part of the **Hats for Cats** project. Equally, we also want to show that not all scanners are relevant to all projects. You should enable and configure only the scanners that make sense for your particular project; adding unnecessary scanners complicates your CI/CD pipeline configuration file and bogs down your pipeline without adding any value.

Integrating a third-party security scanner into the pipeline

Imagine that there's a third-party security scanner that we've used in the past and want to add to our **Hats for Cats** project pipeline. It's called `gui-proofreader` and is a form of SAST scanning that checks for typos in user-facing text. Let's say that it's available as a Docker image on Docker Hub and that you can run the scanner against all the code in your repository by cloning the repository to a `gui-proofreader` Docker container and running the `proofread-my-gui.sh` shell script within that container.

Let's add a job to our CI/CD pipeline that does exactly that. Add this job definition at the end of `.gitlab-ci.yml` on the `add-login-feature` branch:

```
proofread:
    stage: test
    image: gui-proofreader:latest
    script:
        - ./proofread-my-gui.sh
```

That's enough to trigger the third-party scanner, but we still need to integrate its output into the GitLab security reports. This step is simple: declare the scanner's output as an artifact that contains a SAST report (there are several report types we could assign it to, but this particular scanner feels like a flavor of SAST, so let's use that). Add this code to the bottom of the definition of the `proofread` job:

```
    artifacts:
        reports:
            sast: gui-proofreader-report.json
```

Of course, we would need to adjust the name of the results file specified in the job definition to match whatever file name the `gui-proofreader` scanner actually generates. Also, GitLab will only be able to parse and display those results if the file conforms to GitLab's official JSON schema for SAST scanners (the details of the various security scanner results schemas are given in the GitLab documentation for each type of scanner). If the `gui-proofreader` scanner can't generate output using that schema, we will need to write a small script that converts the scanner's output into a JSON file with the appropriate schema, run that script in a separate job in a later pipeline stage, and move the artifact declaration from the `proofread` job into the new script's job.

Since this job won't work as written—as there's no Docker image called `gui-proofeader` on Docker Hub—it's best to either exclude this job definition from your `.gitlab-ci.yml` file or to comment it out. However, if you ever do want to integrate a third-party scanner, this is a model you can follow.

Improving your pipeline

You've set up a pipeline to make sure your code is of high quality and doesn't have security vulnerabilities. In many cases, you can stop there. However, for this sample use case, you'll go a step further and look into using a DAG to speed up the pipeline. You'll also see whether it's worth splitting the pipeline's configuration code into multiple files to improve readability and maintainability.

Using a DAG to speed up the pipeline

Our pipeline isn't complicated enough to justify converting it into a DAG quite yet, but if we continue to add more jobs, we'll eventually want to use DAGs for some or all of it for performance reasons. Let's preview this by using the `needs` keyword now to add some DAG elements to our pipeline.

First, let's say that we want the `code_quality` job to run only after the `unit-tests` job passes. After all, we might think that our code needs to work correctly before we worry about making it pretty and maintainable. We could accomplish that by putting `code_quality` in a later stage than `unit-tests`, but since they both feel like they conceptually belong to the **test** stage, let's keep them in that stage and instead set up a DAG to enforce the job order we want. Add this code to the end of the `code_quality` job definition:

```
needs: ["unit-tests"]
```

Now that one mini-DAG is set up, let's make another. Perhaps we're unhappy with the job that runs our fuzz test running after all of the other scanners are complete. This happens because the fuzz test job is in its own **fuzz** stage, which runs after the **test** stage. We could override its job definition and move it to the **test** stage, but in this case, we decide to use the DAG feature to allow it to run as soon as the pipeline starts instead of waiting around for its pipeline stage to be called. Add this code to the end of the job definition for `fuzz-test-for-log-user-in`:

```
needs: []
```

When we run a pipeline that contains these edits, we see exactly the behavior we'd hoped for: `fuzz-test-for-log-user-in` runs immediately and `code_quality` is paused until `unit-tests` completes:

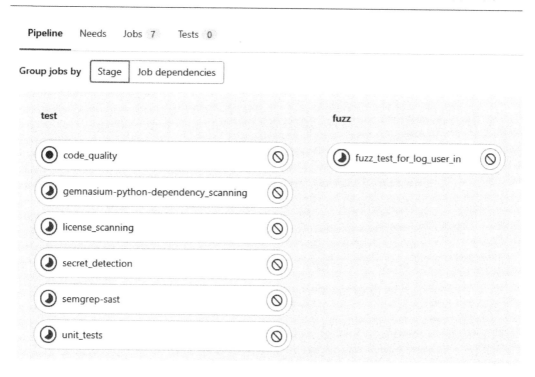

Figure 11.11 – DAG causing jobs to run not according to stage order

We can double-check our understanding of the pipeline's flow by clicking on **Job dependencies** in the pipeline details page and toggling **Show dependencies** on. After the pipeline finishes, we can see which jobs ran in what order, due to "needs" relationships:

292   End-to-End Example

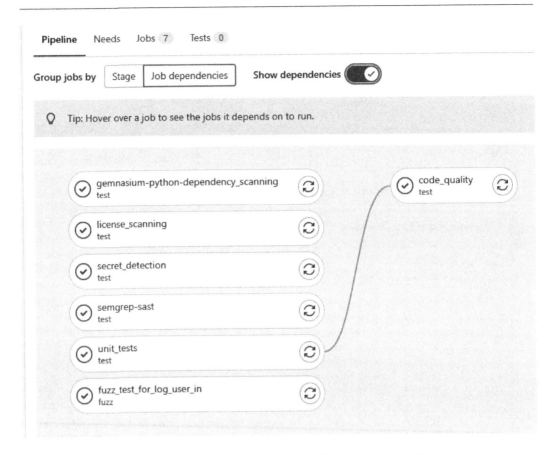

Figure 11.12 – Job dependencies view of the completed pipeline

Breaking the pipeline into several files

Now that we've set up our project's CI/CD pipeline to verify and secure our code, let's see whether we can keep our pipeline configuration well organized and easy to read. As the file stands right now, it's much simpler than .gitlab-ci.yml files for real-world projects tend to be, and normally we would suggest that our configuration file is clean enough as is and doesn't warrant any refactoring. However, in order to demonstrate how we might maintain it as it becomes more complicated, let's separate it into two files anyway.

Say we decide to standardize our security scanning process across all of our team's projects. A good way to do this is to separate our security-related job definitions into a different CI/CD pipeline configuration file, and then include it in each project's CI/CD configuration file.

Create a new file called `security-jobs.yml` in the root of the **Hats for Cats** project's repository, on the `add-login-feature` branch. Add this line to the new file:

```
include:
```

Cut these lines from the `include:` section of `.gitlab-ci.yml` and paste them into the `include:` section of `security-jobs.yml`:

```
  - template: Security/SAST.gitlab-ci.yml
  - template: Security/Secret-Detection.gitlab-ci.yml
  - template: Security/Dependency-Scanning.gitlab-ci.yml
  - template: Security/License-Scanning.gitlab-ci.yml
```

Finally, include the new configuration file in the original configuration file by adding this line anywhere within the `include:` section of `.gitlab-ci.yml`:

```
  - local: security-jobs.yml
```

When the pipeline runs after you make these changes, you'll see that it behaves exactly like it did before we refactored its configuration files. This demonstrates how you can break a long, complicated CI/CD pipeline configuration file into two or more subfiles, each of which can be reused in multiple projects if desired.

Note that because `security-jobs.yml` is in the same project as `.gitlab-ci.yml`, we used the `include:` keyword and `local:` sub-keyword to point to it. If we were including it from a different project, we'd need to use the `include:` and `file:` keywords instead. The GitLab documentation has more information on how to use different forms of `include:` in different situations, and is well worth reviewing.

Delivering your code to the right environment

Your code is written, verified, and secured. The only step left is to deploy it.

Deploying the code

The final task of our pipeline is to deploy the **Hats for Cats** code to the right environment. Normally, we'd define separate jobs to deploy code to a review environment, the pre-production environment, or the production environment. Then, we would use GitLab's `rules:` and `if:` keywords to control which one of those three jobs should run, depending on which Git branch the pipeline was running on.

To keep things simple in this example, let's just walk through how to deploy it to the production environment. We'll imagine that we want this to happen whenever we run the pipeline on the **production** branch.

As you learned in *Chapter 8*, there are countless techniques you can use to deploy code. Which technique you choose depends largely on what sort of environment you're deploying to: an AWS EC2 VM, a Kubernetes cluster, a bare-metal machine, or something else. For this example, let's imagine that we're deploying our code to a machine with an IP address of 192.168.0.1, which is running an Apache web server that hosts the Hats for Cats site. Furthermore, let's say that to deploy a new version of our web app, we simply need to copy our files to the right directory on the Apache host machine and issue a command to restart Apache.

This deployment process is very straightforward. Add this job definition to .gitlab-ci.yml on the add-login-feature branch:

```
deploy-to-production:
    stage: deploy
    image: registry.hats-for-cats.com/ubuntu-with-deploy-key:latest
    rules:
        - if: $CI_COMMIT_REF_NAME == "production"
    script:
        - scp -r . root@192.168.0.1:/home/hats-for-cats/production
        - ssh root@192.168.0.1 service apache2 restart
```

You might wonder about the image specified in this job definition. There are several ways we could set up the public/private SSH key pair that the scp command relies on, but one way to accomplish this involves making our own Docker image, which we store in an internal Docker container registry. Of course, we could also store this image within the container registry of this project or a different project, but for now, let's assume we have a separate, company-wide Docker container registry set up. The image contains a Linux distribution with the OpenSSH library (which provides the scp command) and also has a public/private key pair that was generated in advance. We then configure the Apache host computer to accept the private key from that Docker image. With that infrastructure in place, the GitLab Runner can execute scp from within the special Docker image, and the key pair takes care of authenticating to the Apache host.

The rules: and if: keywords in this job definition prevent the job from running unless the pipeline runs on the **production** branch. As mentioned previously, we'd normally create additional definitions for the deploy-to-review and deploy-to-staging jobs, which would each use different logic to specify which branches they should run on.

Since our `deploy-to-production` job won't run on the `add-login-feature` branch to which we're committing the edited `.gitlab-ci.yml` file, we won't see it run when the commit triggers a new pipeline. However, we do want to make sure it deploys code correctly, so how can we test this job?

First, we need to merge the `add-login-feature` branch into the **main** branch. We're done adding our code and configuring our pipeline, so now's a perfect time to merge anyway. Navigate to our **add login feature** MR, removing `Draft:` from the beginning of its title to make it mergeable, and click on the **Merge** button. Since we linked this MR to the **Allow user to log in** issue, merging the MR will automatically close the issue as well.

This merge adds all of our pipeline configuration details to the **main** branch. It runs a pipeline on that branch, but we still won't see the `deploy-to-production` job run since the pipeline isn't running on the **production** branch. Navigate to **Repository | Branches** in the left-hand navigation pane and create a new branch called **production**. Creating this branch triggers a new pipeline. Finally, we'll be able to see the `deploy-to-production` job running in that pipeline. Of course, we shouldn't expect it to actually pass because we haven't created the Docker image specified in the job definition, and we don't have an actual production environment living at `192.168.0.1`, but at least we can see that the job runs, which is all that we can realistically test at this point. Declare victory and crack open an iced beverage of your choice. This concludes the example workflow for the **Hats for Cats** project.

Summary

In this chapter, we made a group and project to hold our code and other related components and made issues to plan and track our work. Then, we cloned the project's repository to a local workstation so that we could write code using our favorite desktop tools. Then, we made a branch to commit our work to and an MR for that branch, linked it to an associated issue, and committed and pushed code for a new software feature. We set up a bare-bones CI/CD pipeline to which we can add a variety of tasks and registered specific runners for the project's pipeline. We added automated unit tests to the pipeline to make sure the code satisfies its design specifications, as well as Code Quality scanning, and registered a special runner just for that scanner. We also added a fuzz test to the pipeline to find bugs in critical functions, and SAST to the pipeline to find security vulnerabilities in our code. We added Secret Detection to the pipeline to find any secrets that were inadvertently committed to the repository and added Dependency Scanning to the pipeline to learn about any security problems in the third-party libraries that our project relies on. Then, we added License Compliance to the pipeline to exclude third-party libraries that use software licenses that are incompatible with our project's own license and integrated a third-party scanner into the pipeline, which is triggered automatically and integrates its results into existing GitLab dashboards and reports. We rewrote parts of the pipeline as a DAG to improve its performance and separated the pipeline configuration code into multiple files to improve its readability and maintainability and added logic so that code on the correct branch is automatically deployed to the production environment.

Although we covered a lot of ground, it's important to remember that this was just one example workflow. We used only a portion of the countless features offered by GitLab CI/CD pipelines, and we barely investigated any of the different configuration options for those features. There are often multiple ways of accomplishing the same tasks in a pipeline, and there are limitless ways you can organize those tasks into stages and jobs, so don't feel like this example is the *One True Way* to use GitLab CI/CD pipelines. Be creative, experiment, have fun figuring out what pipeline features are most useful for your projects, and enjoy discovering which configuration settings for those features make the most sense for you and your team.

In the next chapter, we will learn about troubleshooting and the road ahead with GitLab.

12
Troubleshooting and the Road Ahead with GitLab

By now, we have covered the end-to-end use of GitLab CI/CD for planning, building, testing, and shipping software. You should hopefully be familiar with the vocabulary of GitLab CI/CD pipelines and Runner infrastructure, and you should also have the confidence to develop and deploy basic applications with GitLab.

CI/CD occupies a constantly shifting space in the software industry. The best practices and tools of the trade today may very well be obsolete five years from now, if not earlier. We have made a conscious effort in this book to maintain a balanced focus between concepts and tooling. The goal is to preserve relevance by emphasizing CI/CD and DevOps fundamentals, while still offering you a chance to practice and follow along, even if the syntax and some of the tools change over the next several years.

The purpose of this final chapter is to synthesize what we've learned and guide you toward the next steps in your DevOps journey. We will first discuss some common troubleshooting scenarios and "gotchas" that you might encounter when working with CI/CD. Next, we'll discuss using GitLab CI/CD in an operations capacity, applying software development workflows and version control to your infrastructure. Finally, we will discuss how the industry is likely to change going forward, and summarize key takeaways from this book.

Here is how we'll cover the topics in this chapter:

- Troubleshooting and best practices for common pipeline problems
- Managing your operational infrastructure using GitOps
- Future industry trends
- Conclusion and next steps

Technical requirements

As in previous chapters, an account on a GitLab instance (SaaS or self-managed) is recommended. Some of the content in this chapter is more conceptual than example-based, but access to **Infrastructure-as-Code (IaC)** tooling such as Terraform and Ansible is recommended if you wish to practice the concepts discussed in the *Managing your operational infrastructure using GitOps* section. In that case, an account in a cloud service provider (such as AWS or Microsoft Azure) would be recommended for infrastructure provisioning and configuration management using your chosen IaC tool.

We will now turn to identifying and troubleshooting common issues when working with GitLab CI/CD.

Troubleshooting and best practices for common pipeline problems

Problems encountered in GitLab CI/CD pipelines tend to fall into two broad categories. The first category is errors or unexpected behavior caused by the syntax and logic in `.gitlab-ci.yml`, the primary CI/CD configuration file. The second category involves limitations or misconfigurations in the runner infrastructure used to run CI/CD jobs. We will address each of these categories in turn.

Troubleshooting CI/CD syntax and logic

When errors in GitLab CI/CD can be narrowed down to the content of `.gitlab-ci.yml`, the first step in troubleshooting is to identify whether the issue is faulty or unsupported syntax, or misconfiguration (or misunderstanding) of an otherwise valid YAML file.

Syntax errors in .gitlab-ci.yml

One of the easiest cases to troubleshoot (and therefore a good place to check for problems first) is syntax or formatting errors in `.gitlab-ci.yml`. A typical example is errors caused by omitting required keywords. GitLab CI/CD at minimum requires at least one stage (defined using the `stages` keyword), each job must be assigned to a stage, and then each job must do something (generally defined using the `script` or `trigger` keywords). The example that follows shows a very basic configuration that defines two stages and two jobs. However, the `compile_assets` job lacks a stage assignment. And the `build` stage, therefore, does not have at least one job assigned to it:

```
stages:
  - build
  - deploy

compile_assets:
  script:
    - echo "Run build scripts here"
```

```
publish_application:
  stage: deploy
  script:
    - echo "Run deployment scripts here"
```

Figure 12.1 shows the pipeline error that we see if we navigate to **CI/CD** | **Pipelines**:

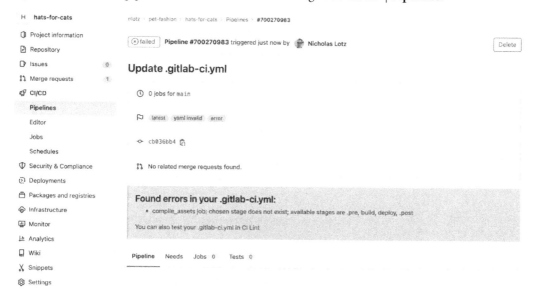

Figure 12.1 – Configuration error message shown on the pipelines page

Notice that GitLab does not even attempt to run the pipeline (that is, assign jobs to runners) when there is a YAML syntax error. We see the error mentions that the stage for the `compile_assets` job does not exist.

> **Default Stage Assignments for Jobs**
>
> The error shown in *Figure 12.1* is actually a bit nuanced. Technically, if a CI/CD job is not explicitly assigned to a stage in the config, GitLab will automatically assign it to the `test` stage. However, we did not define a `test` stage in this example. Therefore, GitLab is reporting that the "chosen" stage (to which GitLab would otherwise assign the `compile_assets` job) does not exist, as we only defined `build` and `deploy` stages.

GitLab will also produce an error if the configuration does not follow the correct YAML formatting. Let's attempt to fix the previous error by adding the `compile_assets` job to the `build` stage:

```
stages:
  - build
```

```
    - deploy

compile_assets:
stage: build
  script:
    - echo "Run build scripts here"

publish_application:
  stage: deploy
  script:
    - echo "Run deployment scripts here"
```

When we look at the pipeline graph again, we see another error, more generic this time, saying that the configuration does not have valid YAML syntax (see *Figure 12.2*). Despite the vagueness of the error, GitLab does include a link to a CI linter that can help identify where the problem might be:

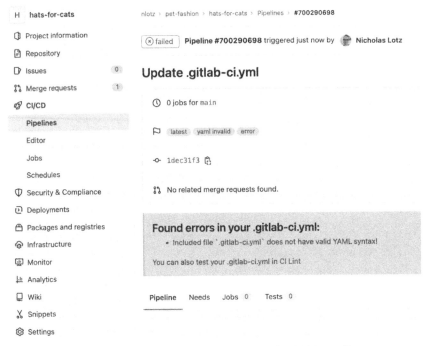

Figure 12.2 – Generic syntax error message for CI/CD pipeline

Following the link takes us to a tool called **Pipeline Editor**, which will inform us of the validity of the `.gitlab-ci.yml` file. In this case, *Figure 12.3* shows an error description referencing an unknown mapping value. Ultimately, the issue lies in the indentation requirements for YAML. The `stage` keyword must be indented at least two spaces so that it is a valid element in the `compile_assets` job definition.

Figure 12.3 – Pipeline Editor showing an invalid CI/CD configuration

After proper indentation, *Figure 12.4* now shows the Pipeline Editor describing valid CI/CD syntax. GitLab will now create a functioning pipeline from this configuration:

Figure 12.4 – Pipeline Editor showing a valid CI/CD configuration

Thus, a primary takeaway for CI/CD syntax issues is to take advantage of the Pipeline Editor so that you can check for logical and stylistic errors in your CI/CD configuration in real time. The editor is valuable for identifying typos, omitted required keywords, and YAML formatting issues.

CI/CD configuration logic and job order

Another key area of CI/CD troubleshooting is understanding the logic of your job definitions and order. As your pipelines get advanced, your `.gitlab-ci.yml` file might start to be filled with the `rules` keyword governing how jobs run, and your primary configuration might call other configurations as templates or downstream pipelines.

Consider the following CI/CD configuration:

```yaml
stages:
    - build
    - test
    - deploy

build_app:
  stage: build
  script:
    - echo "Run build on all branches"

static_tests:
  stage: test
  script:
    - echo "Run static tests only on feature branches"
  rules:
    - if: '$CI_COMMIT_REF_NAME == "main"'
      when: never
    - when: always
  needs: []

deploy_app:
  stage: deploy
  script:
    - echo "Run deploy only on main branch"
  only:
    - main
```

```
needs:
  build_app
```

Here, we have a mix of logical keywords and job ordering in the configuration. The `test_app` job uses the `rules` keyword so that it never runs on the `main` branch; otherwise, it runs on all other branches. Meanwhile, the `deploy_app` job uses the `only` keyword to specify it only runs on the `main` branch (and no other branches). Finally, the `deploy_app` job needs the `build_app` job to pass before it runs on the `main` branch, and the `static_tests` job runs independently on feature branches without waiting for any other jobs (such as `build_app`).

As your pipelines grow, the mix of logic and different CI/CD variables can be difficult to parse. There are some features in the GitLab UI that can help you keep your job logic and order straight. The **Job dependencies** (see *Figure 12.5*) and **Needs** tabs in **CI/CD** | **Pipelines** | **Pipeline ID** allow you to show which jobs are dependent on other jobs:

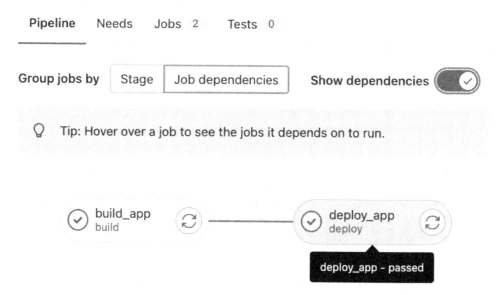

Figure 12.5 – Pipeline Editor showing a valid CI/CD configuration

The Pipeline Editor also has a **Validate** tab that allows you to simulate which jobs will run given the configuration's defined logic and job order. *Figure 12.6* shows a simulated pipeline that would result from a commit pushed to the default (`main`) branch:

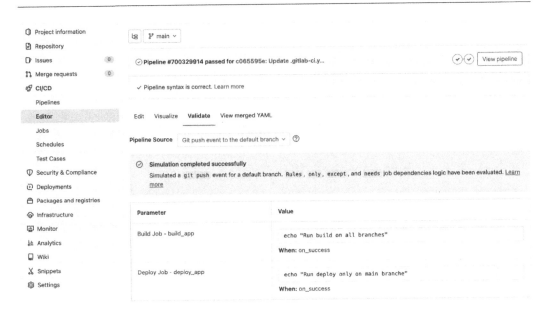

Figure 12.6 – Pipeline validation in Pipeline Editor

We heavily encourage you to make use of these features to organize and visualize your pipelines during development and deployment.

Troubleshooting pipeline operation and runner assignment

Aside from syntax and logic errors, it is also important to take note of the runners used for CI/CD execution, and ensure your pipeline configurations can be supported by your runner infrastructure. Examples of potential problems that can arise include mismanagement of runner tags and lack of or misconfigured container support.

Properly managing runner tags

The `tags` CI/CD keyword (not to be confused with tagged Git commits) tells GitLab to only assign jobs to runners that include the same tags. There are a couple of considerations needed to ensure that CI/CD job tags are properly understood and used.

When multiple tags are specified in a CI/CD job, that means GitLab will only assign a job to a runner that features all of those tags. For example, the following job will only be assigned to a runner that has the `ubuntu` tag, the `python3` tag, and the `amd64` tag:

```
deploy_to_linux:
  stage: deploy
  script:
```

```
    - ./deploy_script.py
  tags:
    - ubuntu
    - python3
    - amd64
```

On the other hand, the runner picking up the job can also have other descriptive tags associated with it, as long as those include at minimum the `ubuntu`, `python3`, and `amd64` tags. Check the runner's assigned tags under **Settings | CI/CD | Runners** if the job is not being picked up by the expected runner. Remember that different runners may be configured in different parts of GitLab – that is, at the project, group, or instance level.

Managing containerized CI/CD pipelines

Container-based environments such as Docker and Kubernetes are ever more frequently used by software teams for development, testing, and deployment. The `image` keyword is a critical keyword in a CI/CD job for specifying the type of Docker container in which a job must run. However, much is dependent on the proper execution of container-based CI/CD jobs, correct configuration syntax aside. Consider the following job definition:

```
launch_web_services:
  stage: deploy
  image: node:19
  services:
    - postgres:latest
  script:
    - npm start
```

The job's instructions are to start web services inside a container launched from a Node.js Docker image with a supporting Postgres database running alongside. Let's think about what the job requires in order to successfully execute:

- Runners in the environment that support Docker containers.
- Non-container runners won't inadvertently pick up the job.
- The runner has network connectivity to a container registry such as Docker Hub to pull down the base images.

This is just one simple example that requires developers to think about the infrastructure their jobs use for execution. One way to solve the second listed point, non-container runners picking up jobs, is to define a CI/CD tag specifically for container-based runners and include that tag in any jobs that use the `image` keyword.

Needing to manage operational infrastructure alongside application logic can be intimidating for developers. In the next section, we will introduce the concept of GitOps to help unify development and operations under a best-practice workflow.

Managing your operational infrastructure using GitOps

Development cannot be divorced from the infrastructure executing the code. We've seen this clearly as we've journeyed from using GitLab as a source code management tool to defining CI/CD pipelines to define how our source code is built and deployed, with runners (infrastructure) as an essential component of CI/CD.

DevOps properly conceptualized is a culture unifying development and operations. How, then, can we incorporate configuring and managing our operational infrastructure into the GitLab flow already used and understood by developers? The answer lies in implementing **GitOps**. GitOps is a development practice that falls under DevOps, which encourages using a similar iterative change management model already used by development teams. As the term suggests, Git is an essential part of the workflow. Infrastructure should be under version control, just like application source code. Changes to infrastructure are then made by contributing changes to the code base, which in turn triggers CI/CD pipelines updating our environments with the committed changes.

> **GitOps Means Generally Putting Infrastructure Under Software Version Control**
>
> The GitOps described in this chapter is broader than the specific GitOps workflow for Kubernetes clusters that we previously discussed. Here, GitOps simply means applying Git development workflows to any manner of infrastructure management. This chapter uses Terraform and Ansible as reference examples that can be cross-applied to many different configuration management tools.

Recall *Figure 3.10* from *Chapter 3* (shown again here), when we introduced GitLab flow as an iterative branching model for developers to make changes in a structured yet efficient way:

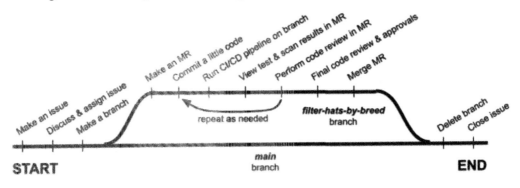

Figure 12.7 – Major steps in GitLab flow

A core motivation of this workflow is removing friction from the development process. Textual changes to files in a Git-versioned code base trigger automated pipeline building, testing, and deploying to appropriate environments. Reviews and approvals are baked into the merge request feature, ensuring all our changes are intentional, and version control ensures we can roll back as required.

How, then, do we apply this model to infrastructure management? Just as developers use programming languages to engineer applications, the industry now has a plethora of text-based tools that can be used to describe, provision, and configure an operational environment. These tools are described as infrastructure as code because they are designed to put infrastructure (servers, networking, storage, databases, identity, and access) under a similar programmatic model as traditional software applications.

IaC is a quickly evolving field, where new tools are constantly being supplanted by newer tools. It can be difficult to decide which software to introduce in this kind of book due to rapid innovation threatening to render today's common tooling obsolete. However, as of this writing, we've seen a couple of IaC tools widely used for GitOps with GitLab. We present them here with the understanding that in infrastructure tooling, the state of the art is rapidly changing. That said, the tools we see frequently used are **Terraform** for infrastructure provisioning and **Ansible** for configuration management.

Using Terraform to deploy and update infrastructure state

Terraform is an IaC tool used to describe how your infrastructure should look. The core project is open source, with enterprise versions developed and sold by HashiCorp. Terraform includes a language and syntax for describing infrastructure state, as well as a set of command-line tooling for validating and updating the said infrastructure. The configuration model used is *declarative*. We describe how our compute, networking, storage, and so on should look, and the software performs the minimum necessary changes so that our infrastructure reflects the configuration.

Let's look at a very basic example where we use Terraform to provision an object storage resource in AWS. Terraform has you describe your configuration in state files that end with the extension .tf. The details of Terraform syntax are well outside the scope of this book, but the following syntax shows how an S3 bucket might be configured in AWS. This "code" might be stored in a file called bucket.tf:

```
resource "aws_s3_bucket" "coreSite" {
    bucket = "travelBlog"
    acl = "private"
}
```

This simple state file specifies an S3 bucket resource in AWS with a name and access permissions. It is then up to Terraform to "make it happen." In the context of GitOps with GitLab, the "making it happen" takes place via a CI/CD pipeline. The pipeline will run the necessary Terraform commands to initialize, validate, and apply the configuration to your AWS account.

Installing and configuring Terraform can take a bit of work. Thankfully, GitLab packages Terraform's tooling in a Docker image that can be launched using the image keyword in .gitlab-ci.yml.

GitLab maintains a public example project with a sample `.gitlab-ci.yml` file (https://gitlab.com/gitlab-org/configure/examples/gitlab-terraform-aws/-/blob/master/.gitlab-ci.yml) containing the relevant jobs and commands for applying or updating a Terraform configuration in AWS. We recommend exploring this page and testing the examples in your own AWS account. Notice how the `prepare`, `validate`, `build`, and `deploy` stages and accompanying jobs are conceptually similar to the `build`, `test`, and `deploy` stages in typical application development.

Terraform is a tool primarily used to deploy or provision infrastructure. The second tool we will discuss is primarily used to configure the resources that have been provisioned.

Using Ansible to manage resource configurations

Ansible is also an open source IaC tool, with paid versions offered by Red Hat. Like Terraform, Ansible is used by declaring resource configurations in files, whose contents are then translated into configuration changes by running commands. These Ansible resource configuration files are called **playbooks** and are written in YAML format. The content of an extremely basic playbook that installs and starts Apache might look like the following:

```yaml
---

- hosts: web
  become: yes
  tasks:

    - name: ensure Apache is installed
      yum:
        name: apache2
        state: latest

    - name: ensure Apache is enabled and started
      service:
        name: apache2
        enabled: yes
        state: started
```

Like Terraform, we use a declarative syntax to describe how our environment should look, and rely on the tool (in this case Ansible) to make it so. Here, we specify that a collection of hosts called `web` should have the `apache2` package installed, and the corresponding service should be enabled and started. Ansible would then connect to the hosts in question, and once connected, install and start `apache2`.

Also like Terraform, we would define CI/CD jobs that run the tool's commands to apply the configuration change. In the case of Ansible, GitLab does not have an official Docker image with Ansible tooling. So we might instead tell GitLab to use a runner that we know is an Ansible host to run our playbook:

```
ansible-run:
    stage: run
    tags:
        - ansible
    script:
        - ansible-playbook apache-playbook.yml --key-file $REMOTE_HOST_CREDENTIALS
```

The preceding job is assigned to a runner with the `ansible` tag (which we may assume is a runner with Ansible installed and configured). The job script then runs the playbook and might also pass in credentials using CI/CD variables so that Ansible can authenticate to the servers it is configuring.

For more details about using Ansible with GitLab, including interpreting and parsing CI/CD job output when Ansible commands are run, we refer you to this article (https://about.gitlab.com/blog/2019/07/01/using-ansible-and-gitlab-as-infrastructure-for-code/) published by GitLab as a more in-depth reference. Please also refer to the official Terraform and Ansible docs sites for further details on setup and system requirements. Ultimately, the goal of this section has been to introduce you to GitOps concepts as a paradigm for incorporating IaC tools into the CI/CD workflows we have learned so far.

Future industry trends

It goes without saying that learning anything new comes with the expectation that the knowledge will remain relevant in the future. Looking forward, continuous integration and delivery are well positioned to persist as critical practices in the software landscape, while continuing to undergo evolutionary changes. We can identify three likely ways the software development life cycle will change in the coming years. Those trends are increased automation, increased abstraction, and reduced development cycle time. We can also expect that GitLab as a platform will continue to play an important role. The concepts, examples, and tools presented in the previous chapters will serve as a good foundation to be a more productive developer right now while providing the confidence needed to adapt as the industry inevitably shifts.

Automation will create more software at a larger scale

Ask any organization today what is the most expensive part of operating, and they will likely respond that it's the humans. Skilled human workers, which includes technologists, are particularly pricey. Talented engineers are hard to find, harder to replace, and expensive to keep. Moreover, those same engineers have designed software and tooling to make their own jobs easier and more productive.

Organizations are now leveraging that tooling so that they can create and deploy more software using fewer people.

Think about the teams of manual quality assurance testers that companies employed 20 or even 10 years ago. Now consider the role that tools like GitLab play in allowing a single developer to automate the process of releasing software, from conceptualization to deployment. Moreover, cloud service providers now offer almost limitless amounts of infrastructure to any developer with a credit card—dedicated teams for racking and stacking servers are no longer required.

Yet, predictions of the singularity aside, humans aren't going anywhere anytime soon. The prevalence of automation requires people who can understand and maintain that tooling. The more you can speak the language of automation and the platforms such as GitLab powering the trend, the more equipped you will be to contribute to the automation revolution.

Abstraction will lead to everything-as-code business models

In 2011, Marc Andreessen wrote his now-famous article titled *Why Software Is Eating the World* (`https://a16z.com/2011/08/20/why-software-is-eating-the-world/`). Andreessen predicted that the next generation of internet companies was leading a broad economic shift in which software becomes the language and engine of most, if not all, industries. Ten years later, in 2021, Jon Eckhardt wrote a follow-up article called *Software Is Eating the Software That's Eating the World* (`https://eiexchange.com/content/software-is-eating-the-software-thats-eating-the-world`). Eckhardt recognized that not only have traditional industries been disrupted by software, but there is a whole generation of new tooling disrupting existing software models. This tooling can be thought of as powerful, easier-to-use programs that allow developers to work at a higher layer of abstraction. That is, developers can focus on the business logic while the tool handles the finer details.

A good example of increased abstraction is how infrastructure has changed over the past 30 years. The industry has moved from mainframes to the server model. It then moved to virtual machines, so we can start to view operating systems as flexible, software-defined resources on a shared host. Then, configuration management helped take care of maintaining our IT resources so that we could focus more on the "what" and less on the "how." Then, cloud services took off so that no one needed to set foot in a data center. And now, additional tools, such as containers and functions, allow developers to focus solely on their code without even needing to think about the computers and networks it may be running on.

We expect this abstraction trend to continue. Like automation, we by no means anticipate that humans will be rendered irrelevant. Rather, we expect increased consolidation and specialization. Code will always be running on someone's computer, somewhere, and we'll need infrastructure experts to build and maintain those environments. But we also expect tools like GitLab to continue to proliferate, offering self-documenting, programmatic models that offer observability into all layers of the business.

Reduced cycle time will help teams release better software faster

The DevOps philosophy is primarily cultural, but it also represents a system of work inspired by the lean manufacturing revolution. Building on the trends of automation and abstraction, combined with project management methodologies such as Agile and Scrum, teams are now developing software in such a way that they release early and often, incorporating small improvements, and rolling back as needed.

Books such as *The Lean Startup* by Eric Ries have introduced the language for this development model, and tooling has proliferated that allows developers to build, test, and release software in a very fast but controlled way. GitLab is one of these core platforms. Source code management and version control ensure continuous integration into a shared code base, and pipelines allow for a common set of build, test, and deploy tasks after every small commit. This allows for rapid, iterative development that can constantly adapt to meet business needs.

The combination of automation, abstraction, and smaller release cycles will require developers to be comfortable with iterative approaches to project management and design. Don't be afraid of failure, as rapid small changes will inevitably cause some broken or buggy code. Adopt a mindset of continuous improvement, focusing on developing better software rather than perfect software.

Conclusion and next steps

This book has guided you through using GitLab as a platform to manage your software development life cycle. After discussing the state of the industry before DevOps emerged as a culture and methodology, you were then guided through the basics of Git version control and GitLab's project management components. Then, GitLab CI/CD pipelines were introduced as the central feature for organizing, designing, and automating your development workflow.

You learned that GitLab CI/CD comprises three components: the text-based pipeline configuration file, the runners that execute pipeline tasks, and the main GitLab application that coordinates between the configuration and the runner agents. We then walked through how to leverage pipelines to verify, secure, package, and deploy your code. You learned that you can use GitLab CI/CD as a unified tool to perform these often-disparate steps in the software life cycle.

After covering the supported CI/CD features and workflows, we moved to some advanced topics and best practices. You learned how to improve pipeline speed and maintainability, and how you can leverage GitLab CI/CD in other workflows that might not be immediately obvious.

Finally, *Chapter 11* introduced you to an end-to-end example using all the concepts and features previously covered. That chapter's objective is to show a basic but real use case of GitLab supporting all steps in the workflow of planning, building, and deploying an application. We then concluded with this chapter, offering some final troubleshooting tips, guidelines for next-gen infrastructure management with GitLab, and a look at where the industry is likely to go in the coming years.

We hope your journey with GitLab, CI/CD, and DevOps doesn't end with the conclusion of this book. GitLab itself is open core, and GitLab the company is transparent in how it intends to steward and evolve the software over time. We encourage you to continue following GitLab's evolution and product roadmap by keeping tabs on the core product's issue-tracking system and referring to the product's online handbook pages, which document the category directions for each of GitLab's features.

Ultimately, as technologists, we know that learning never stops. We hope this book was helpful in familiarizing you with GitLab as a software platform, the problems it's designed to solve, and how you can use it to meet the challenges faced in your own organization. We wish you the best as you continue your DevOps journey.

Index

Symbols

.gitlab-ci.yml
   GitLab Runner, running CI/CD jobs specified 112, 113
.gitlab-ci.yml file 104

A

alphabetize function 7
Amazon Web Services (AWS) 223
amigos 79
analyzers 168
anchors 240, 241
Ansible
   used, for managing resource configurations 308, 309
approval rules 191
architecture and workflow, fuzz testing
   CI/CD job 154, 155
   code under test 153, 154
   fuzz engine 155
   fuzz target 156
artifacts
   characteristics 236
   leveraging 235
   leveraging, as job dependencies 238, 239
   using 237, 238

automated functional tests, CI/CD pipeline
   enabling 149, 150
   results, viewing 150, 151, 152
   running 149

B

Bandit 169
Brakeman 168
branch 78
   adding 70, 71, 72
   creating 70
branches 40, 41, 42, 43
   managing, with Git commands 43
branch pipelines 98, 99
browser performance testing 163
   integrating 254

C

caching
   characteristics 235
   leveraging 234
   using 236, 237
C, compiling with GCC 143
   application, adding 144
   application, configuring 144, 145

Index

child pipeline 248
CI/CD job 154, 155
CI/CD pipeline
  accessibility, checking 160
  accessibility testing, enabling 161
  accessibility testing results, viewing 161, 162
  automated functional tests, running 149
  built code, storing as artifacts 145, 146
  C, compiling with GCC 143
  code, building 138
  code quality, checking 146
  fuzz testing 153
  Java, compiling with javac 138
  Java, compiling with Maven 141
  third-party tools, integrating into 259
CI/CD pipelines 23
  commands 97
  defining 86
  fitting 98
  jobs 96
  list, viewing 87, 88
  project, defining 87
  stages 94
  usage 87
  using, for developing mobile apps 262
  using, to spot performance problems 253, 254
CI/CD pipelines, using for mobile app development 263
  Fastlane 263, 264
  Fastlane, automated testing 265
  Fastlane, deploying 264
  requisites 263
CI/CD syntax and logic
  configuration logic and job order 302, 303, 304
  errors in .gitlab-ci.yml 298, 299, 300, 301
  troubleshooting 298
code
  building manually 4
  committing and pushing 272, 273
  deploying 293, 294
  deploying manually 16
  manual security testing 12
  packaging manually 16
Code Climate 146
code deployment
  license compliance scanning 17
code quality, CI/CD pipeline
  checking 146
  enabling 146, 147
  results, viewing 147, 148
Code Quality scanning
  adding, to pipeline 280, 281
code security
  Dependency Scanning, adding to pipeline 287
  License Compliance, adding to pipeline 288
  SAST, adding 284
  Secret Detection, adding to pipeline 285, 286
  third-party security scanner, integrating to pipeline 289
code smells 170
code under test 153, 154, 282
code verification
  Code Quality scanning, adding to pipeline 280, 281
  functional tests, adding to pipeline 277, 278, 279, 280
  fuzz test, adding to pipeline 281, 282, 283, 284
code verification, Hats for Cats
  functional tests 6
  fuzz tests 10
  load tests 9
  performance tests 9

Index   315

performing, manually 5
soak tests 10
static code analysis 10
code verification, ways
browser performance testing 163
code coverage 163
load performance testing 163
code, writing 271
Git branch, creating 271, 272
MR, creating 272
commands 97
commits
history 73
tagging, to identify versions of code 39, 40
container registry
packages, building and pushing to 212, 213, 215, 216, 217
Container Registry 186
container's build
automating 261
container scanning 15
Container Scanning 262
configuring 187
enabling 186, 187
findings, viewing 187, 188
using, to find Docker image vulnerabilities 185, 186
continuous delivery (CD) 85, 90, 91
benefits 92
code deployment 92
code packaging 92
review environment 91
continuous deployment (CD) 90, 92
continuous integration (CI) 85, 89
benefits 89, 90
code quality scans 89
functional tests 89
fuzz testing 89

license scanning 89
performance tests 89
security scans 89
copyleft 189
corner-case testing 6
corpus
used, for fuzz testing 160

D

DAG
used, for speeding up pipeline 290, 291
Dangit Git
reference link 53
DAST
configuring 180, 181
enabling 180, 181
findings, viewing 182
using, to find web application vulnerabilities 179, 180
default branch 42
Dependency Proxy 131
dependency scanning 14
Dependency Scanning
adding, to pipeline 287
configuring 184
enabling 184
findings, viewing 184
using, to find vulnerabilities in dependencies 182, 183
DevOps 21
automate feature 21
collaboration 21
fast feedback 21
features 21
implementing by GitLab 22
iterative improvement 22

DevOps practices
   enabling, with GitLab flow 80, 81, 82
directed acyclic graph (DAG)
   creating, in GitLab CI 232, 233
Docker executor 119
Docker images 15
docker-in-docker 280
Docker Machine executor 121
dynamic analysis 14
dynamic environments 221

E

edge case testing 6
environment setup 267
   GitLab project, making 268
   local Git repository, setting up 271
   work, planning with GitLab issues 269, 270
errors 161
executors
   selecting, considerations 129
extends* keyword 241, 242

F

Fastlane 263, 264
   automated testing 265
   deployment 264
feature flags
   application, configuring for 258, 259
   used, for allowing business-driven release decisions 256, 257, 258
first-in, first-out (FIFO) 117
functional tests
   adding, to pipeline 277, 278, 279, 280
functional tests
   corner-case testing 6
   edge case testing 6

happy path testing 6
   unhappy path testing 6
future industry trends
   increased abstraction 310
   increased automation 309, 310
   reduced cycle time 311
fuzz engine 155
fuzz target 156
fuzz test
   adding, to pipeline 281, 282, 283, 284
fuzz testing 10
   architecture and workflow 153
   considerations 159
   coverage-guided fuzz testing 153
   in CI/CD pipeline 153
   results, viewing 158, 159
   web API fuzz testing 153
   with corpus 159
   workflow 157

G

Gemnasium 167
General Public License (GPL) 17
Git
   blame feature 29
   code, committing 33, 34, 35, 36
   drawbacks 32, 33
   features 30, 31, 32
   files, excluding from repository 37, 38, 39
   references 53
   using 27
Git branch
   merging, into another 74
Git commands
   used, for managing branches 43
git fetch command 51, 52

Index   317

GitLab 22, 57
  benefits 22
  container and package registries, locating 202, 203, 205
  deployments 220
  DevOps implementation 22
  environments 220
  problems, solving 57, 58, 59
  projects 60, 61, 62
  reference link 49
  release stage 59
  secure stage 59
  stages 57, 58
  used, for registering runner 123, 124, 125, 126, 127, 128, 129
  verify stage 59
GitLab Agent for Kubernetes 120
GitLab CI
  code, building for multiple architectures 233, 234
  directed acyclic graph (DAG), creating 232, 233
GitLab CI/CD pipelines
  branch pipelines 98, 99
  configuring 103, 104, 105, 106
  Git tag pipelines 100
  merged result pipelines 100
  merge request pipelines 100
  merge trains 101
  operation and runner assignment, troubleshooting 304
  running 98
  skipping pipelines 101
  status, reading 102, 103
  troubleshooting and best practices 298
  types 100, 101
GitLab flow
  DevOps practices, enabling with 80, 81, 82

GitLab Flow
  deploying, to different environments with 220, 221
GitLab group 61
GitLab GUI
  stages, viewing 95
GitLab issue
  structure 65, 66
  tasks, tracking with 67
GitLab issues
  work, planning with 269, 270
GitLab Operator 120
GitLab package registry
  packages, building and pushing to 210, 211
GitLab project
  making 268
GitLab Runner
  architecture 113, 114, 115
  CI/CD jobs specified, running in .gitlab-ci.yml 112, 113
  executor 118
  group runners 115, 117
  shared runners 115, 117
  specific runners 115, 116
  supported platforms 113, 114, 115
  written, in Go 112
GitLab Runner agent
  installing 122, 123
GitLab Runner, executor
  Docker executor 119
  Docker Machine executor 121
  Kubernetes executor 120
  Parallels executor 120
  Shell executor 119, 120
  SSH executor 121
  VirtualBox executor 120

GitLab Runner, installing with
    GitLab repositories
  reference link 123
GitLab runners
  defining 112
  relationship to CI/CD 112
GitLab Runners 93, 94
GitLab's container registry
  code, storing 217
  images, using 217
GitLab's package registry
  authenticating 206, 207, 208, 209
  code, storing 202, 217, 218
  packages, using 218, 219
  supported formats 206
  using 205
GitOps
  operational infrastructure,
    managing with 306, 307
GitOps workflow 225, 226, 227
git pull command 52, 53
git push command 51
Git tag pipelines 100
Gnu Compiler Collection (GCC)
  C, compiling with 143
Go
  GitLab Runner, writing 112
golden repository 47
group runners 117
groups 62

H

happy path testing 6
Hats for Cats
  organizing 63, 64
Hats for Cats software 85

Hats for Cats web app 4
  code, building manually 4, 5
  code verification, challenges 11
  code, verifying manually 5
Helm chart 120

I

includes
  from remote areas 247
  leveraging, for maintainability 244, 245
  leveraging, for reusability 246, 247
Infrastructure as Code (IaC) 193
Infrastructure as Code (IaC) Scanning
  configuring 193, 194
  enabling 194
  findings, viewing 194, 195
  using, to find infrastructure
    configuration files problem 193
integration tests 7
issue 78
issues
  versus merge requests 79, 80
  workflow 68, 69
  work, tracking with 64

J

Java
  compiling, with javac 138
javac
  Java, compiling with 138
Java, compiling with javac 138
  application, adding 139
  pipeline, configuring 139, 140, 141
Java, compiling with Maven
  Java application, adding 142
  pipeline, configuring 142, 143

jobs 96

K

k6
    performance testing, integrating with 255, 256
kaniko 213
Keeping Infrastructure as Code Secure (KICS) 167
Kubernetes cluster
    CI/CD workflow 225
    deploying to 225
    GitOps workflow 226, 227
Kubernetes executor 120

L

labels 67
License-Check 191
License Compliance
    adding, to pipeline 288
    configuring 192
    enabling 192
    findings, viewing 192
    GitLab rulesets, used for unblocking MR 191
    using, to manage dependency licenses 188, 189, 190
license compliance scanning 17
load performance testing 163
load tests 9
local Git repository
    setting up 271
login-feature branch 43

M

main branch 42
manual software development life cycle practices
    challenges 18, 19, 20, 21
Maven
    configuring 141
    Java, compiling with 141
merge conflicts
    handling 44, 45, 46
merge request 148, 195
merge request (MR) 69, 74, 75, 78
    code reviews, enabling 75, 76
    creating, before code commit 76
    source branch 75
    target branch 75
    used, for improving collaboration 77, 78
    using, as dashboard for code 77
    versus issues 79, 80
Merge Requests (MRs) 269
    creating 272
metadata fields, issues
    assignee 65
    due date 65
    labels 65
    weight 65
minimum viable product (MVP) 269
monitoring considerations 132
    GitLab Runner, logging 134
    GitLab Runner Prometheus metrics 134, 135
    GitLab UI analytics 133, 134

O

operation and runner assignment, troubleshooting
  containerized CI/CD pipelines, managing 305
  runner tags, managing 304, 305
outside security scanners
  integrating 198, 199

P

Parallels executor 120
parent-child pipelines
  leveraging 247, 248
parent pipeline 248
performance considerations 129
  caching dependencies 131
  repository size 130
  runner availability 130
performance testing
  integrating, with k6 255, 256
performance tests 9
permissive licenses 189
pipeline
  Code Quality scanning, adding 280, 281
  creating 273, 274
  Dependency Scanning, adding 287
  functional tests, adding 277, 278, 280
  fuzz test, adding 281, 282, 283, 284
  improving 290
  infrastructure, establishing 273
  License Compliance, adding 288
  runner, creating 274, 275, 276, 277
  SAST, ading 284
  Secret Detection, ading 285, 286
  speeding up, with DAG 290, 291
  splitting, into several files 292, 293
  third-party security scanner, integrating into 289
pipeline details page 195
Pipeline Editor 300
pipelines, with directed acyclic graph (DAG)
  accelerating 231, 232
pipelines, with parent-child architecture
  accelerating 231, 232
playbooks 308
pre-production environment 17, 91
production environment 17
projects 60
protective licenses 189
pull-based approach 227
pull requests 76
purpose-built container
  example 250
  used, for securing and accelerating jobs 248, 249
push-based workflow 226

Q

Quality Assurance (QA) 89
Quality Assurance (QA) team 11

R

real-world production environments
  deploying to 223
rebasing 53
reference tags 243, 244
regular expressions (regexes) 176
remote repositories
  configuring 48, 49, 50

repeated configuration code
  reducing 239
  reducing, with anchors 240, 241
  reducing, with extends* keyword 241, 242
  reducing, with reference tags 243, 244
repository 33
  golden repository 47, 48
  local and remote copies, syncing 47
review app
  deploying, for testing 221, 222, 223
review environment 91
runner
  registering, with GitLab 123, 124, 125, 126, 127, 128, 129
Runner tags 122
runner types
  selecting, considerations 129

S

scanner profile
  setting up 180
scoped labels 68
secret detection 13, 14
Secret Detection
  adding, to pipeline 285, 286
  configuring 178
  enabling 177
  findings, viewing 178
  historic mode 177
  using, to find private information in repository 175, 176
Secure Hash Algorithm (SHA) 36, 73
security considerations 131
  runner executor, options 131, 132
  secrets, managing 132

security reports
  merge request 195, 196
  pipeline details page 195, 196
  types 195
  vulnerability report 195, 196
security scanning strategy, GitLab
  different analyzers, using 168, 169
  findings 170
  GitLab-provided scanners, used by pipelines 170
  languages, selecting 167
  open-source scanners, using 167
  principles 166
  scanners, packing as Docker images 167, 168
  vulnerabilities 169
security testing 12
  container scanning 15
  dependency scanning 14
  dynamic analysis 14
  secret detect 13, 14
  static code analysis 12, 13
  summarizing 15
security vulnerabilities
  managing 196, 197
Semgrep 168, 169
shared runners 117
  configuring, on self-managed GitLab instances 118
Shell executor 119
  challenges 119, 120
site profile
  creating 180
skipping pipelines 101
soak tests 10
Software-as-a-Service (SaaS) 16, 49, 86
software-as-a-service (SaaS) runners 118
software deployment 17, 18

software development life cycle (SDLC) 4, 85
source branch 44
Sourcetree 272
specific runners 116
Splunk 133
SSH executor 121
stages 94, 95
  build 94
  deploy 94
  test 94
  viewing, in GitLab GUI 95
staging environment 17
Static Application Security Testing (SAST)
  adding, to pipeline 284, 285
  configuration, by overriding
    job definition 174
  configuring 173
  configuring, with global variable 173
  configuring, with GUI 174
  enabling 171
  enabling, manually 171, 172
  enabling, with GitLab GUI 172, 173
  findings, viewing 175
  using, to scan vulnerability
    source code 170, 171
static code analysis 10, 12, 13

T

target branch 44
Terraform
  used, for deploying and updating
    infrastructure state 307
test environments 17
third-party security scanner
  integrating, to pipeline 289

third-party tools
  integrating, into CI/CD pipeline 259
  invoking 262
three amigos 79
tool container
  Dockerfile, creating 260
Tower 272
trigger files 168

U

unhappy path testing 6
unit test 7
user tests 8

V

version control system (VCS) 27
  features 28
  issue scenarios 29, 30
  issues, solving 28
versions of code
  identification, by tagging commits 39, 40
VirtualBox executor 120
vulnerability report 170, 195

W

warnings 161
Web Content Accessibility
  Guidelines (WCAG) 160
white box scanning 170

packtpub.com

Subscribe to our online digital library for full access to over 7,000 books and videos, as well as industry leading tools to help you plan your personal development and advance your career. For more information, please visit our website.

Why subscribe?

- Spend less time learning and more time coding with practical eBooks and Videos from over 4,000 industry professionals
- Improve your learning with Skill Plans built especially for you
- Get a free eBook or video every month
- Fully searchable for easy access to vital information
- Copy and paste, print, and bookmark content

Did you know that Packt offers eBook versions of every book published, with PDF and ePub files available? You can upgrade to the eBook version at packtpub.com and as a print book customer, you are entitled to a discount on the eBook copy. Get in touch with us at customercare@packtpub.com for more details.

At www.packtpub.com, you can also read a collection of free technical articles, sign up for a range of free newsletters, and receive exclusive discounts and offers on Packt books and eBooks.

Other Books You May Enjoy

If you enjoyed this book, you may be interested in these other books by Packt:

Learning DevOps - Second Edition

Mikael Krief

ISBN: 978-1-80181-896-4

- Understand the basics of infrastructure as code patterns and practices
- Get an overview of Git command and Git flow
- Install and write Packer, Terraform, and Ansible code for provisioning and configuring cloud infrastructure based on Azure examples
- Use Vagrant to create a local development environment
- Containerize applications with Docker and Kubernetes
- Apply DevSecOps for testing compliance and securing DevOps infrastructure
- Build DevOps CI/CD pipelines with Jenkins, Azure Pipelines, and GitLab CI
- Explore blue-green deployment and DevOps practices for open sources projects

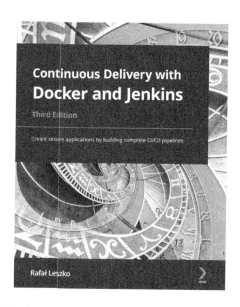

Continuous Delivery with Docker and Jenkins - Third Edition

Rafał Leszko

ISBN: 978-1-80323-748-0

- Grasp Docker fundamentals and dockerize applications for the CD process
- Understand how to use Jenkins on-premises and in the cloud
- Scale a pool of Docker servers using Kubernetes
- Write acceptance tests using Cucumber
- Run tests in the Docker ecosystem using Jenkins
- Provision your servers and infrastructure using Ansible and Terraform
- Publish a built Docker image to a Docker registry
- Deploy cycles of Jenkins pipelines using community best practices

Packt is searching for authors like you

If you're interested in becoming an author for Packt, please visit `authors.packtpub.com` and apply today. We have worked with thousands of developers and tech professionals, just like you, to help them share their insight with the global tech community. You can make a general application, apply for a specific hot topic that we are recruiting an author for, or submit your own idea.

Share Your Thoughts

Now you've finished *Automating DevOps with GitLab CI/CD Pipelines*, we'd love to hear your thoughts! Scan the QR code below to go straight to the Amazon review page for this book and share your feedback or leave a review on the site that you purchased it from.

`https://packt.link/r/1803233001`

Your review is important to us and the tech community and will help us make sure we're delivering excellent quality content.

Download a free PDF copy of this book

Thanks for purchasing this book!

Do you like to read on the go but are unable to carry your print books everywhere? Is your eBook purchase not compatible with the device of your choice?

Don't worry, now with every Packt book you get a DRM-free PDF version of that book at no cost.

Read anywhere, any place, on any device. Search, copy, and paste code from your favorite technical books directly into your application.

The perks don't stop there, you can get exclusive access to discounts, newsletters, and great free content in your inbox daily

Follow these simple steps to get the benefits:

1. Scan the QR code or visit the link below

https://packt.link/free-ebook/9781803233000

2. Submit your proof of purchase
3. That's it! We'll send your free PDF and other benefits to your email directly

Printed in Great Britain
by Amazon